Oct. 13, 1968

SAN FRANCISCO BAY
FERRYBOATS

SAN FRANCISCO BAY
FERRYBOATS

By GEORGE H. HARLAN

Howell-North Books • Berkeley, California • 1967

SAN FRANCISCO BAY FERRYBOATS

Printed and bound in the United States of America

Library of Congress Catalog Card No. 67-20998

ENDPAPERS

San Francisco's waterfront in 1908, photographed from a "Captive Air Ship 2000 Feet Over San Francisco Bay." *(Marion Gorrill collection)*

FRONTISPIECE

The *Sacramento* steams alone under the bridge that brought an end to the busy lanes of ferry traffic that once criss-crossed San Francisco Bay. *(Mike Roberts photo)*

Published by

HOWELL-NORTH BOOKS

1050 Parker Street, Berkeley, California 94710

To
KATHLEEN

(Southern Pacific)

Foreword

~~~~~~~~~~~~~~~~

As the shadows have lengthened in the twilight of the ferryboat and time has slowly ebbed away for that glorious period of steamboats on the Bay, the occasion of their passing cannot be ignored, for a record of it is most justly deserved. It would be folly indeed to assume that the story of these trim vessels could be told by virtue of the efforts of one person alone, for such is not the case.

No pictorial history of San Francisco, whether on the subject of the ferries, or any other historical adventure, could be produced without the able assistance of Roy D. Graves, whose fabulous collection of pictures was made available to the author. Roy was not only a pictorial chronicler of the ferries; he was also an engineer on two of the lines, the Key System and the Rodeo-Vallejo Ferry, and his personal recollections are invaluable.

To Stanley Moore and George Kraus of the Southern Pacific Co. goes credit for a pictorial record of the Central Pacific and the Southern Pacific, and also for collateral pictorial material on other lines which the Southern Pacific has so meticulously retained.

The San Francisco Maritime Museum, with its wealth of information on all subjects marine, and the nearby Maritime State Historical Monument, with its display of vessels including the ferry *Eureka*, have both come into being since Clement Fisher, Jr. and I wrote the first comprehensive book on the subject of ferries. To Karl Kortum, Director, and to Harlan L. Soeten, Matilda Dring and Al Harmon of the Museum, and to Harry Dring and Jack Hesemeyer of the Monument I wish to express appreciation for most valued assistance and encouragement.

Pictures and information on San Francisco Bay ferryboats at the present have been made available through the courtesy of Luther Conover of Sausalito, Admiral Sydney B. Dodds of San Diego, Dick Fitzgerald and Stephen T. Weidinger of Redondo Beach, W. C. Helman of San Francisco, R. Ken Jordan of San Pedro and Ralph E. White of Seattle.

Historical and pictorial material on the Key System have been provided through the kindness of Mrs. Virginia Dennison of the Alameda-Contra Costa Transit District.

To Stephen DeBenedetti, of Benicia, and Appellate Court Justice Bray, of Martinez, I am indebted for the information on the Martinez-Benicia Ferry.

From the files of the Society of California Pioneers came much valuable pictorial and historical data.

Pictorial information received from Edward Zelinsky filled in many of the gaps in the graphic story of the days of the ferries on the Bay.

My sincerest thanks to my former writing associate, Clement Fisher, Jr., who is still a great contributor even though not actually engaged in preparation of this manuscript.

To Marshall Silverthorn, who, as always, vigorously supported me in my writing project, I wish to extend again my sincerest thanks.

To Jack E. Shekell, who helped with all photographic operations at innumerable times, I am greatly indebted.

To my daughter, Kadeane Harlan, my darkroom helper when I desperately needed assistance, goes my loving appreciation.

This was the "team" that made this volume possible, and it, together with the stenography of the manuscript that my dearest wife Kathleen so ably produced in record time, has brought into being a work, that will, I sincerely hope, fill a void in the voluminous and imposing maritime history of San Francisco Bay.

GEORGE H. HARLAN

San Rafael, California

March, 1967

Table of Contents

Foreword 7

Chapter I   Ferry Lines and Lanes 11

Chapter II   Passengers and Crew 29

Chapter III   The Anatomy of the Ferryboat 66

Chapter IV   Fires, Fogs and Fractures 87

Chapter V   History of the Ferry Companies 97

SECTION ONE: North Bay Lines 97
Martinez-Benicia Ferry . . . Mare Island Ferry . . . California
Pacific Railroad . . . Aden Brothers Ferry Co. . . . Monticello
Steamship Co. . . . Sacramento Northern Railway

SECTION TWO: The Southern Pacific and Its Antecedents . . 107
Contra Costa Steam Navigation Co. . . . San Francisco &
Oakland Railroad . . . San Francisco & Alameda Railroad . . .
Central Pacific Railroad . . . South Pacific Coast Railroad . . .
Southern Pacific Co.

SECTION THREE: San Francisco-East Bay Competition . . . 121
Nickel Ferry . . . Atchison, Topeka & Santa Fe Railway . . .
Key System . . . Western Pacific Railroad

SECTION FOUR: Across the Golden Gate 131
Sausalito Land & Ferry Co. . . . North Pacific Coast Railroad
. . . North Shore Railroad . . . San Francisco & North Pacific
Railway . . . California Northwestern Railway . . . North-
western Pacific Railroad

SECTION FIVE: Ferries for Automobiles 143
Richmond-San Rafael Ferry . . . Rodeo-Vallejo Ferry . . . Six
Minute Ferry . . . Golden Gate Ferry . . . Southern Pacific-
Golden Gate Ferries, Ltd.

Chapter VI   Ferryboats Today 155

Glossary of Ferryboat Terms 166

Illustrated Roster 168

Bibliography 188

Index 189

This was how San Francisco appeared to the transcontinental traveler approaching the City by ferry in about 1895. Five vessels are docked at the ferry terminal built twenty years earlier by the Central Pacific; its diminutive tower can be seen between the second and third boats. From left to right are the Southern Pacific's *Newark* from Alameda, the Nickel Ferry's stern-wheel *Alvira* from downtown Oakland, the SP's *Piedmont* from Oakland Mole, the San Francisco & North Pacific's *Tiburon* from its namesake port and the North Pacific Coast's *San Rafael* from Sausalito. *(Bancroft Library)*

I

Ferry Lines and Lanes

～～～～～～～～～～～～～

FERRYBOATS WERE ONCE the hallmark of one of the finest and most beautiful harbors of the world, San Francisco Bay. Rimmed with hills, tawny or emerald acording to the season, the grey-green waters of the Bay were dotted with great ships from the seven seas, usually black-hulled, to which the ferries offered vivid contrast. Most were white, some orange, others yellow, a few red or even olive green. Life and movement they brought, as well as color, for they were always on the go, converging on San Francisco from various points to the north and east, followed by sea gulls whose white markings matched the broad mile-long wakes behind the moving boats.

The presence of the ferryboat was born of necessity and maintained by utility. It profoundly influenced the settlement of the Bay Area and affected the daily life of the people who lived and worked in the communities dotting the shore. Inevitably it found a secure place in the affections of those whose lives it touched, more so in its day than even the cable cars, a few of which survive and are cherished links with San Francisco's romantic past when the city was steeped in excitement born of the gold fields.

The ferryboat bowed to an age of speed and was succeeded by great bridges which served the needs of commerce, industry, and a rapidly growing population in a manner which the ferryboat could not match. With its passing came the end of an era and a more leisurely way of life which began when the majestic clipper ships sailed the seas.

San Francisco Bay was discovered, it is said, by José de Ortega, a member and pathfinder of Gaspar de Portolá's expedition of 1769, but it was not until 1775 that Manuel de Ayala sailed his ship *San Carlos* into the harbor, the first vessel to enter the Golden Gate within recorded history. The Spanish community was slow to develop as was all of Alta California and in 1822, the country came under Mexican rule and brief settlement began. During the 24-year rule of Mexico, land was parceled into huge grants, many of which were given to persons of foreign birth who obtained Mexican citizenship. Many of these individuals were sailors from foreign vessels who were impressed with the charm and vastness of the country, its mild climate and its leisurely pace of living, a Mexican importation which enjoyed immense popularity.

One of the Mexican grantees, John Reed by name, was reported as using his British seagoing background to operate a sailboat on the Bay as early as 1826, eight years before receiving his grant to Rancho Corte de Madera del Presidio. After 1841, William Richardson, another British sailor grantee, operated a boat between his Rancho Saucelito* and San Francisco. All of these operations were informal, boats being operated at the whim of the owners who obligingly pleaded that their crews could not be found at the moment, should some suspicious-looking passengers desire a trip to the distant shore too quickly to suit the ferryman's recently-acquired Mexican habits.

All of this changed overnight. In 1848, following the war of 1846-48, Mexico ceded California to the United States. Almost immediately came word of the discovery by James Marshall of gold in California's American River. This news spread rapidly in the East of the United States and

---

*"Saucelito" was the common English spelling of the name during early years of American occupation. The local post office was opened and given that name in 1870. The original, and correct Spanish, "Sausalito" was restored by the Post Office Department in 1887. The city was incorporated in 1893, but it was well into the 1900s before the older spelling disappeared from use.

Captain Thomas Gray's *Kangaroo*, first ferryboat on San Francisco Bay, is shown abandoned with smokestack lowered in the 1851 view above. Of all vessels that served as Bay ferries, none traveled more widely than the *New World*, pictured at San Francisco in the 1856 view below, moored to the right of her colleague in river service, the *Senator*, at Cunningham's Wharf near the foot of Battery Street. The 1851 photograph at the bottom shows "gold ships" moored in the Bay, abandoned by crews that went to the mines. (*Three photos, courtesy San Francisco Maritime Museum; top and bottom: Society of California Pioneers collection*)

abroad. Soon thousands of gold seekers were on their way to California. As the overland route was, at best, uncertain and these people had no time to waste along the trail, most of the prospective amateur miners came in the sailing ship, arriving in countless droves in the harbor by the Golden Gate.

The arrivals of wooden sailing vessels in 1850 and 1851 were so numerous that the conglomeration of ships in San Francisco Bay at the time defied a census. More likely than not, the ships were completely abandoned by crew and passengers alike, all of whom headed for the foothill regions where gold could be conveniently picked up without effort—or so the stories went. Most of these ships were of deep-water draft and could not venture up the rivers and sloughs to shorten the distance to the mining districts, but some vessels which came to San Francisco were built for navigation in shallow water. Many of these enjoyed years of service on the California rivers.

One of these craft was the *New World*, launched in New York in 1849 and immediately attached by creditors as soon as the master carpenter's certificate was signed to signify the builder's completion. Captain Ned Wakeman, the vessel's master, eager to get to the gold fields of California, pursuaded the lienholders that a trial trip was necessary, and they agreed providing two sheriff's deputies made the day-long voyage. When the captain was satisfied with his ship, he placed the deputies in a lifeboat, sent them ashore and disappeared into an Atlantic storm which furnished him with adequate protection from all pursuers. On January 19, 1850, just 150 days after leaving New York, the captain landed his vessel on the San Francisco waterfront and promptly set about the more productive livelihood of seeking gold. The *New World* spent many a satisfactory year in the river and ferry trade following her spectacular cruise to California.

From 1849 on, navigation on the San Joaquin and Sacramento Rivers was undertaken extensively on both a formal and informal basis. Recognized landings were not only established on the rivers, but also at critical Bay points where passengers and freight were congregated during the early settlement of the counties which border on the Bay. Point San Quentin, Point San Pablo,

Point Richmond, Point Pinole, Dumbarton Point and other promontories were convenient stopping places, and served as an adequate substitute for ferry landings prior to the advent of the ferry lines as such. But this type of service was not reliable, and with the growth of Oakland, the first of the larger communities of the Bay other than San Francisco itself, a need for regular ferry service was recognized.

The first recorded Bay ferry operation to San Francisco was established in 1850, when Captain Thomas Gray placed his small ship, the *Kangaroo*, in service between San Francisco and the east shore of the Bay in San Antonio Creek, now Oakland Estuary. The following year, Oakland was formally chartered as a town and the Council gave serious thoughts to the establishment of a public ferry, recognizing the uncertain and unreliable service which had existed up to that time. The so-called "Creek Route" presented many hazards that made it a disturbing voyage for the passengers, particularly the sand bar which built up at the mouth of the estuary every spring, sometimes leaving a suitable opening for the small steamers, but more likely than not leaving such a small passage that groundings were too frequent to assure any measure of certainty about the trip. The sand bar was particularly dangerous when combined with other common hazards to Bay navigation. In heavy fog the opening could not be located. In the strong westerly winds which arise on the Bay in the afternoons, boats became unmanageable for this "thread-the-needle" type of navigation.

In 1852, Charles Minturn, who had a background of experience on the rivers of three years' standing, (and who in California could claim more than that?) received the backing of the steamboat men and applied to the town of Oakland for the right to operate the public ferry. He had a reliable reputation, and the route he chose avoided the creek. After some deliberations, Minturn received the first ferry franchise which had any intimation of municipal sanction and approval. And so the beginning came for the ferryboat, without much fanfare and with little distinction as to the differences between river and Bay craft which were to become so apparent in the years to come.

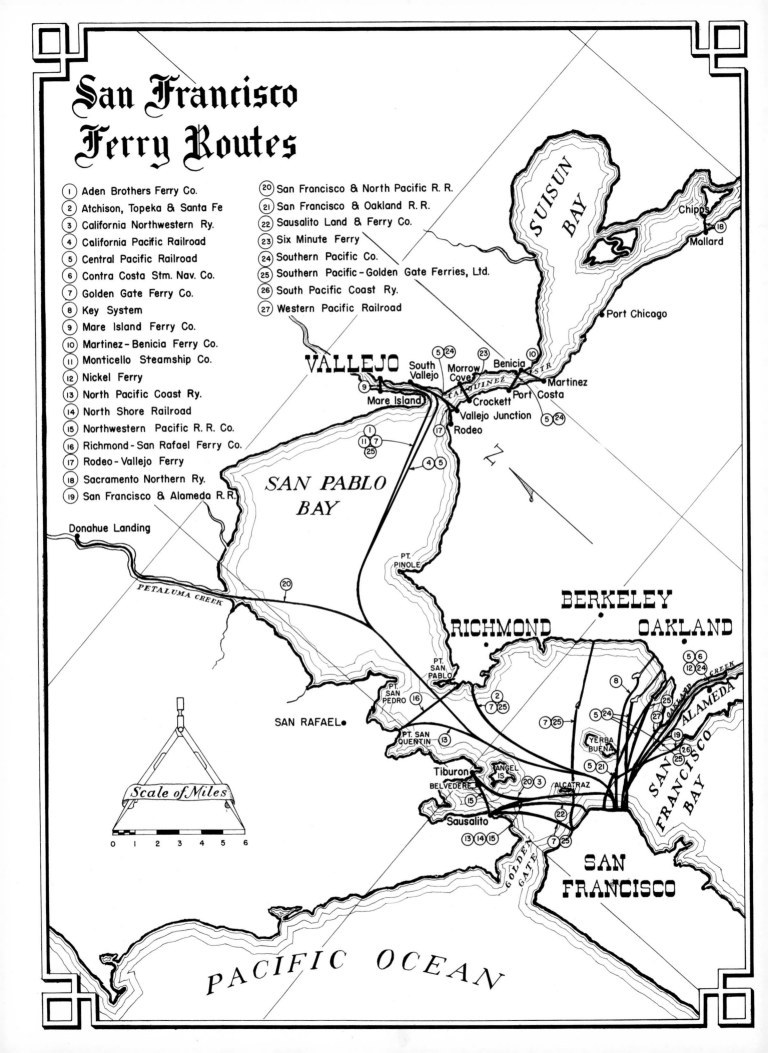

San Francisco Ferry Routes

1. Aden Brothers Ferry Co.
2. Atchison, Topeka & Santa Fe
3. California Northwestern Ry.
4. California Pacific Railroad
5. Central Pacific Railroad
6. Contra Costa Stm. Nav. Co.
7. Golden Gate Ferry Co.
8. Key System
9. Mare Island Ferry Co.
10. Martinez–Benicia Ferry Co.
11. Monticello Steamship Co.
12. Nickel Ferry
13. North Pacific Coast Ry.
14. North Shore Railroad
15. Northwestern Pacific R. R. Co.
16. Richmond–San Rafael Ferry Co.
17. Rodeo–Vallejo Ferry
18. Sacramento Northern Ry.
19. San Francisco & Alameda R. R.
20. San Francisco & North Pacific R. R.
21. San Francisco & Oakland R. R.
22. Sausalito Land & Ferry Co.
23. Six Minute Ferry
24. Southern Pacific Co.
25. Southern Pacific–Golden Gate Ferries, Ltd.
26. South Pacific Coast Ry.
27. Western Pacific Railroad

SUISUN BAY

Chipps

Mallard

Port Chicago

VALLEJO

South Vallejo

Morrow Cove

Benicia

Martinez

Mare Island

CARQUINEZ STR.

Crockett

Port Costa

Vallejo Junction

Rodeo

SAN PABLO BAY

PT. PINOLE

Donahue Landing

PETALUMA CREEK

BERKELEY

RICHMOND

OAKLAND

PT. SAN PABLO

PT. SAN PEDRO

SAN RAFAEL

PT. SAN QUENTIN

ALAMEDA CREEK

Scale of Miles

0 1 2 3 4 5 6

Tiburon

BELVEDERE

ANGEL IS.

ALCATRAZ

YERBA BUENA

SAN FRANCISCO BAY

Sausalito

GOLDEN GATE

SAN FRANCISCO

PACIFIC OCEAN

Many of the early lines commenced operation with river craft without any appreciable refitting to adapt them to the new service. Charles Minturn's Contra Costa Steam Navigation Co., Oakland's new municipally-franchised ferry, placed the river craft *Erastus Corning* and *Kate Hayes* in service. The California Pacific, a new railroad from Sacramento to Vallejo, commenced operation with two former river vessels, the *New World* and the *Capital*. The San Francisco & North Pacific, a railroad running north from Tiburon in Marin County, made quick use of the former river boat, *Antelope*, whose ferry history was short of being distinguished, but whose immortality was assured when it befell her to carry the first pouch of Pony Express mail to terminate the western leg of the initial pony run from Sacramento to San Francisco on April 15, 1860. So it was with many other lines; the river craft were the pioneers of the run, and the development of the more utilitarian double-ended Bay ferryboat was retarded in this manner.

When arguing the advantages of the single-end versus the double-end boat for ferry service, much can, of course, be said on both sides. A ship which is designed for service that lends itself to single-end operation has the advantage over all comers in speed under way, but the involved operation of turning a vessel for a return trip may be so time consuming as to negate this advantage. So it was with the ferryboats; whereas there were no double-ended boats at the beginning, they had all but taken over exclusive rights to the service when the end approached for the ferryboat on San Francisco Bay.

The ferry lines and lanes saw many types and many combinations of types of boats in service. The topography of the Bay and the river delta area was such that two railroad lines chose to ferry entire trains on the ferryboats. Some ferry lines catered only to the foot passenger, some to automobiles and foot passengers, some were maintained for the purpose of providing the necessary train connections while others were operated to carry railroad cars, principally freight, to the various landings on the shore.

There were times when from fifty to sixty boats operated simultaneously on the Bay, through fair weather and foul, their busy whistles resounding with timely regularity—a symphony with overtones from the paddles churning their frothy wake behind. And what a sight they were, their white hulls bright in the morning sun, their plumes of rich smoke billowing into an atmosphere cleaned with the breezes from the sea!

After the first twenty years or so of operation, it can be said without too great a fear of contradiction that the ferries of San Francisco were owned, lock, stock and barrel, by the railroad companies whose lines they served. Initially they were a necessary adjunct of railroad operation, for without the ferries, service into San Francisco was out of the question. But as the communities built up around the Bay, local trade produced a demand for ever more frequent ferry schedules and for interurban lines which grew to feed the ferry terminals. In later years, the automobile's climb to vehicular supremacy sounded the death knell of the short-line railroad and molded the future of the ferryboat. Boats were either reconfigured or specially built to accommodate the automobile. Thus the auto's challenge to the railroads was not only on shore, but also on the inland waters where railroad-owned boats had once been as dominant as the trains had ever been in the mighty inland empire. It was the auto ferries which were the last to go, defeated in turn by the ingenuity of man in the construction of great bridges to span stretches of water considered but a few years before, impossible to cross.

There were nearly thirty major ferry routes operating on the Bay at one time or another. In making this count, there is some overlapping, of course, for certain companies fade from the picture, discontinue service, and years later service would be re-instituted by other companies because the economy once more required it. A brief description of these routes will be given on the pages that follow to acquaint the reader with the magnitude of the ferry operation during its rise, its heyday and its declining years.

Way up in the Sacramento-San Joaquin Delta region, the electric Oakland & Antioch Railroad had the distinction of establishing the most northerly and easterly ferry service on the inland waters of San Francisco Bay. This company later became dear to the juice fans as the Northern Electric or the Sacramento Northern. In the magnificence of

In Mare Island Strait was the South Vallejo terminal of the California Pacific. The *Capital*, in the slip, was still a single-ender when the picture above was taken, about 1872, as she had been during her days as a river boat. A few miles east on Carquinez Strait was the Port Costa terminal of the train ferry *Solano*, from which, below, is seen emerging a passenger train hauled by a diamond-stacked Central Pacific eight-wheeler. Benicia and the northern terminal of the train ferry are visible across the Strait. *(Above: Roy D. Graves collection; below: Southern Pacific)*

a David slaughtering Goliath, the railroad ferried entire trains between Mallard and Chipps Island, near Pittsburg, with no more than a 500 horsepower gasoline engine to do the job. With the heavy tides of winter and the spring freshets of the rivers as a major pair of obstacles, the ferry often disrupted the schedule of the trains by many an hour when the captain was unable to make a landing with a full load of electric coaches on the boat.

Proceeding down the delta region towards tidewater, one passes Suisun Bay and enters Carquinez Strait, the site of the crossing between Martinez and Benicia. In 1847, Robert Semple, founder of Benicia, commenced boat service between the two communities, which was intermittently maintained for over a century until the opening of the Martinez-Benicia Bridge in 1962 put an end to the last vestige of ferry service in Bay navigation.

Deeper in Carquinez Strait was an outstanding ferry line on which plied colossal steamers, much the largest of the ferryboats to operate inside the Golden Gate. This was the train ferry inaugurated in 1879 by the Central Pacific after its purchase of the faltering California Pacific enabled it to use that line's rails between Sacramento and the Bay. The train ferry made it possible for the Central Pacific and its successor, the Southern Pacific, to shorten the rail distance between Sacramento and Oakland by more than fifty miles.

Although the crossing from Benicia to Port Costa was short, the boats used in the service were of such tremendous size as to accept an entire passenger train, including the locomotive, on the deck of the ferry in four parallel tracks. These boats were also used to haul freight trains, although the larger freights were routed via Stockton, Tracy and Niles Canyon into Oakland and in later years to San Jose and San Francisco. The tremendous ferryboats *Solano* and *Contra Costa* used on this unique service were the largest ferryboats anywhere in the world, being in excess of four hundred feet long and capable of transporting gigantic tonnage.

This service continued until 1930 when the Southern Pacific replaced the ferryboats with a steel lift-span bridge. It is interesting to note that the Southern Pacific restricted the size of the pas-senger locomotives in mainline California passenger service over the Overland Route to an engine weight no greater than that of a heavy Pacific, which was the largest engine that could be carried on the two ferry behemoths.

Almost under the shadow of the present-day west span of the Carquinez Bridge lay the route of an auto ferry from Morrow Cove on the Vallejo shore to Crockett, called the Six Minute Ferry, for the length of time a boat took to make the crossing. After three years of successful business, which appeared well on the way to skyrocketing proportions, the Morrow Cove terminal was demolished by an earthslide and the Six Minute Ferry passed into oblivion in 1922.

West of the Carquinez Bridge, Mare Island Strait enters the Bay. Just inside this strait is South Vallejo, where the California Pacific Railroad transferred passengers between trains for Sacramento and ferryboats for San Francisco. This direct ferry service to the City was also a convenience to the residents of Vallejo; a similar service was provided by river boats of the California Transportation Co. In the 1870s, after the Central Pacific absorbed the California Pacific, direct service to San Francisco was discontinued and the ferries operated from South Vallejo across Carquinez Strait to Vallejo Junction, a station stop on the Central Pacific main line between Crockett and Rodeo.

The terminal of the California Pacific in South Vallejo continued in use for many years by the Central Pacific and by the Southern Pacific which succeeded it. Southern Pacific ferries plied the waters of Carquinez Strait until the mid-1920s. This ferry service was used heavily during World War I, when thousands of shipyard workers at the Mare Island Navy Yard were recruited in the San Francisco-Oakland metropolitan area and commuted from home to the Navy Yard on the Southern Pacific.

The Navy Yard was opened on Mare Island in 1854 and since the days of its first Commandant, David Glasgow (later Admiral) Farragut, ferry service was required to transport workers from mainland Vallejo to the Island. This ferry was in various hands over its century and more of service. Ferry transportation is still provided by launch during commuting hours.

Mare Island Strait's narrow waters bore surprisingly heavy ferry traffic, of which a remnant survives to this day. Below, soon after World War I, at the Vallejo water front are four steamers of three different ferry lines. At the left is the big *Napa Valley* and beside it the smaller *General Frisbie* of the Monticello Steamship Co. These swift boats were met by the graceful electric Niles cars of the Napa Valley Line. Southern Pacific's *Bay City* must have had special business at Vallejo, for her regular terminal was a mile south at South Vallejo from which she crossed Carquinez Strait to Vallejo Junction. At the right is the Mare Island Ferry's *Vallejo* which made the short run to her Navy Yard terminal which appears just to the right of the *Napa Valley's* stack and, much more clearly in the picture above, with the *Vallejo* in the slip. This neat columned Georgian structure was one of the most picturesque ferry landings on the Bay. On the opposite page is Donahue Landing on Petaluma Creek, southern rail terminus of the San Francisco & North Pacific Railway until 1884. At the landings are the *Antelope* and the *James M. Donahue*. (Above: Official U. S. Navy photo; below: C. F. Hatch collection; opposite: Roy D. Graves collection)

One of the earliest ferries primarily for use by automobiles was the Rodeo-Vallejo Co. which operated between the towns named in its corporate title. This company began service with a tiny steamer, the *Issaquah,* and was soon all but wiped out by competition from the Six Minute Ferry, with its much shorter route. After the demise of the latter company, the Rodeo-Vallejo ferry enjoyed a few prosperous years until completion of the Carquinez Bridge in 1927 ended for all time the need for ferry service across the Strait.

Ferry service between South Vallejo and San Francisco has already been mentioned; the first service to the City from Vallejo proper was opened in 1890 by the Aden brothers, Martin, John and Joseph. Their stern-wheelers had scarcely begun to show a profit before the enterprise succumbed to the competition of the swift steamers of the Monticello Steamship Co. During World War I the Monticello company was confronted by a heavy influx of workers for the Navy Yard. Larger steamers were obtained which could carry several thousand passengers each trip. These boats were later converted into auto ferries and enjoyed a brief period of popularity and prosperity prior to the construction of the San Francisco-Oakland Bay Bridge. The Monticello Steamship Co. run was the longest on the Bay, approximately thirty miles in length, which was accomplished in a schedule of an hour and 45 minutes between terminals.

The second longest run on San Francisco Bay was that of the San Francisco & North Pacific from Donahue Landing on Petaluma Creek to the San Francisco Ferry Building, which operated between 1871 and 1884. This service was provided as a continuance of the railroad line from Cloverdale to Donahue and was discontinued after the railroad was extended from Petaluma to Tiburon.

The next locality touched by ferries was Point San Quentin on the Marin shore, which was joined with the county seat, San Rafael, by the standard gauge San Rafael & San Quentin Railroad in 1869. Since Point San Quentin had been a stopping place for the river steamers on both the up-river and down-river journeys, the operation of the railroad was keyed to the arrival times of the various vessels which touched at the Point. Regular ferry service did not commence until 1877, following purchase of the San Rafael & San Quentin Railroad by the North Pacific Coast Railroad. A railway-owned ferry then made regular trips from San Francisco connecting with the rail service at Point San Quentin. This arrangement continued until 1884 when the San Quentin wharf was demolished by fire and the service never resumed.

In 1916 Point San Quentin once more became a ferry terminal with the establishment of the Richmond-San Rafael Ferry to carry automobiles between the Marin and Contra Costa communities mentioned in its title. For over four decades ferryboats operated on this beautiful route until com-

Tiburon was a pastoral village in 1907, with a picturesque harbor. That year, as shown above, the newly-organized Northwestern Pacific was operating two former North Pacific Coast steamers, the *Tamalpais* and the stern wheel car float *Lagunitas*. The activity in the 1924 view of Sausalito's water front, below, reflects the prosperity of the time and the growth of the automobile ferrying business.

At the left is the Northwestern Pacific terminal with the steamers *Cazadero*, *Sausalito* and *Eureka* and, behind the live oak tree, the motor vessel *Marin*. The shiny new motor vessel *Golden West* is in the Golden Gate Ferry terminal at the right. Richardson Bay was famous for the old sailing ships anchored in it. *(Above: Marshall F. Silverthorn collection; below: William Knorp collection)*

pletion of the Richmond-San Rafael Bridge in 1957.*

The city of Richmond was the terminus for two ferry lines to San Francisco, the first of which formed the last leg in the transcontinental journey of the only railroad to run from Chicago to San Francisco Bay entirely on its own tracks, the Atchison, Topeka & Santa Fe. In 1901 the line opened for combined rail-ferry service and continued until 1933.

A second Richmond-San Francisco ferry was operated by the Golden Gate Ferry and its successor, the Southern Pacific-Golden Gate Ferries, Ltd. during the heyday of the automobile boat enterprise on San Francisco Bay.

Another ferry route which enjoyed great popularity on the Bay for many years was the San Francisco & North Pacific Railway's ferry from Tiburon to San Francisco, which carried foot passengers and freight from the San Francisco & North Pacific main line following its completion to Tiburon in 1884. The Tiburon-San Francisco ferry operation ceased in 1909, although the successor corporation, the Northwestern Pacific Railroad Co. provided service from Tiburon to Sausalito via Belvedere to connect with the trains and ferries of the N.W.P. on a regular basis until 1933.

Only exceeded by the ferry service to Oakland in the length of time of operation of ferryboats on San Francisco Bay was the ferry service between San Francisco and Sausalito. This operation commenced as a promotion scheme of the Sausalito Land & Ferry Co. in order to sell lots in the residential development carved out of Captain William A. Richardson's Rancho Saucelito. Ferry service began in 1868 between a landing at the foot of Princess Street in Sausalito and Meiggs Wharf at the foot of Powell Street in San Fran-

---

*The bridge almost precisely spans the route of the boats from Point San Quentin on the west to Castro Point on the east, according to the Coast & Geodetic Survey chart for the Bay. Ferry timetables called the eastern terminus "Point Richmond," probably because it is near the section of Richmond known by that name. The actual geographical Point Richmond is a promontory nearly two miles to the south of the ferry landing. Old-timers often refer to the pier as being at "Point Molate," which is the name of a promontory about a mile to the north, in the old days the site of a resort known as Winehaven and since World War II the name of a Navy station which extends almost to the ferry wharf.

cisco. In 1875 the land company relinquished operation to the narrow gauge North Pacific Coast Railroad which operated boats between Sausalito and the Ferry Building in San Francisco until 1902, when the road was purchased by the North Shore Railroad, a company which electrified the Marin County interurban rail lines. Following construction of the electric line and its successful operation, the North Shore was purchased by the Southern Pacific and the Santa Fe and the ferry was operated by the new jointly-owned Northwestern Pacific until 1941.

In 1922 a parallel line for auto service was begun by the Golden Gate Ferry Co. from Sausalito to the foot of Hyde Street, San Francisco. The golden-yellow boats of this line were painted white when the company was absorbed by the Southern Pacific-Golden Gate Ferries, Ltd. in 1929 and operated until the year following the opening of the Golden Gate Bridge in 1937.

Although the city of Berkeley is one of the more prominent metropolitan areas on the shore of the Bay, direct ferry service to the university town was of short duration. In 1883, a land development scheme in West Berkeley employed a former Mare Island ferryboat to give service to its properties, although such service was of little benefit to Berkeley proper. This service was discontinued about 1890 and it was not until 1927 that ferry service to San Francisco was re-established from this community. A wide and shallow shoal extended from Berkeley's water front out into the Bay for a distance of approximately three miles, and it was the Golden Gate Ferry Co. which conquered this shoal with a three-mile long wooden trestle on concrete piling to a terminal which appeared to exist virtually in the middle of the harbor waters. Following completion of the Bay Bridge in 1936, service was discontinued as part of the Southern Pacific-Golden Gate Ferries' orderly retrenchment of facilities. The magnificent three-mile wharf, a tribute to perseverance, engineering skill and successful financing, stood intact for over twenty years. A rehabilitated remnant of the wharf is now in use as a fishing pier in Berkeley's Aquatic Park.

Ever since Charles Minturn consummated his pact with the town of Oakland in 1852, the Alameda County metropolis had ferry service to San

This magnificent view from Yerba Buena Island, Goat Island as it was then known, shows the Oakland Long Wharf and the Southern Pacific's Oakland Mole in relation to each other, as they appeared before the turn of the century. Meiggs Wharf, San Francisco, in the 1865 pic-ture below, one of the early docking places for seagoing ships, was built by Henry Meiggs, who went bankrupt and fled to Chile to begin a new and spectacular career building railroads in the Andes. *(Above: San Francisco Maritime Museum; below: Ed Zelinsky collection)*

Francisco which continued until 1957. Between Oakland, Alameda and San Francisco there operated such a multitude of boats and routes that the channel toward the estuary resembled a "freeway of the ferries." In 1865, the San Francisco & Alameda Railroad Co., a subsidiary of the Central Pacific, commenced operation from the island city to the Broadway Street Wharf in San Francisco as the first ferry to connect, in the East Bay, with transcontinental trains. Later in the same year, the Central Pacific completed its own passenger terminal, or Mole as it was called, on the Oakland shore, and this route remained in existence for 88 years. In 1871, a ferry was established by the railroad to transfer freight cars across the Bay from the Oakland Long Wharf (Oakland's first seaport terminal) to the Second Street Wharf in San Francisco.

Ferry service by the Central Pacific to Alameda was discontinued in 1873, but on March 20, 1878, another company took over the facilities and re-established the line. This was the narrow gauge South Pacific Coast Railroad which functioned for nine years before being bought by the Southern Pacific. The S.P. had succeeded the Central Pacific as an operating entity in 1884-5, and so the Alameda Ferry reverted to its original owners. In 1875 the Central Pacific began to use the first "Ferry Building" which it built at the foot of Market Street in San Francisco, and thereafter this location became the central terminal for all the major ferry lines.

The Creek Route, up what is now the Oakland Estuary, had been hazardous in 1850 when Captain Thomas Gray and his *Kangaroo* offered the first ferry service between San Francisco and Oakland. By 1876 the channel was better and the Central Pacific was operating a ferry from the foot of Broadway in Oakland, down the Creek and across the Bay to the Ferry Building. Business on this route was enlivened in 1893 when John L. Davie challenged the Southern Pacific ferry with his parallel and competing Nickel Ferry. While the Nickel Ferry was a short-lived business, it forced the S.P. to adopt the five-cent passenger fare on this route which lasted over forty years and was a great boon to unemployed job-seekers during the Great Depression of the 1930s. The Creek Route was the site of the pioneer auto ferry on the

Bay, accepting the horseless carriage on a published tariff basis as early as 1908.

In 1903, the San Francisco, Oakland & San Jose Railway commenced ferry operation of San Francisco Bay from a pier which closely paralleled the present East Bay approach to the San Francisco-Oakland Bay Bridge, ending with a finger pier a mile northeast of Goat—now Yerba Buena—Island. This company adopted the key as an emblem from the shape of its track system and finger pier, and hence the name "Key Route" or "Key System" supplanted the more formal corporate name with which the company started life. The San Francisco terminal was, of course, the Ferry Building and the company operated its orange ferries through most of 1940. The last two years of operation were from San Francisco and Oakland to the Golden Gate International Exposition on Treasure Island, with two terminals located one each side of the fairgrounds. This was the first regular ferry service to a fair, for although the Panama Pacific International Exposition of 1915 sported a ferry slip, it was used only on special occasions when direct service was on an excursion basis.

In 1909 the Western Pacific completed construction of its railroad line from Oakland to Salt Lake City with transcontinental connections, and commenced ferry service from a terminal on the Oakland side of the Estuary's mouth into the Bay. The route was maintained until 1933, when its single boat was sold to the Southern Pacific in exchange for trackage rights for passenger trains into Oakland Pier.

Automobiles were accepted on the Southern Pacific ferries both at the Oakland Mole and Alameda, and in the 1920s, specially constructed auto ferryboats were placed on both of these runs. The Oakland Pier auto ferry to the Ferry Building in San Francisco continued until 1939, and it was the last Southern Pacific-Golden Gate Ferry line to disappear from Bay operation.

Ferryboating south of Alameda is all but unheard-of, for wide shoals were not conducive to cross-bay navigation. The only line to operate in the South Bay was from San Francisco to Alviso, beginning in 1865. The boats stopped at many landing places along the route, hauling freight and a few passengers. Captains A. Nelson and N. E. Anderson, the owners, formed the California

When the Central Pacific rebuilt the famous river queen *Chrysopolis* as the fine double-end ferryboat *Oakland*, sail still predominated on seagoing ships and the clippers were the talk of the world. The "forest of masts" on the San Francisco water front was beginning to sprout some smokestacks and a steam tugboat was nearby. The *Garden City* is seen, below, entering the Estuary beside the new Western Pacific terminal. The old Oakland Long Wharf is dimly visible in the mist astern of the vessel. The Key Route pier and the steamer *Yerba Buena* were both new in 1903 and the post card view, opposite, was made not much later than that. Steamer and terminal were both painted orange, but the white trim on the train shed did much to moderate the gaudiness of the color. *(This page: Southern Pacific; opposite: Alameda-Contra Costa Transit District)*

Transportation Co. in May, 1875, and took their steamers up the rivers for a long and successful venture in tule navigation.

Not to be classed as ferry service, but still a regular route on the Bay were the government steamers serving Angel and Alcatraz Islands. These boats charged no fares, ran on a schedule, but were not for public use. The Lighthouse Board served Alcatraz beginning in 1854 when the first lighthouse in the State was built there. With the establishment of the military prison on the Island in later years, the Army commenced regular ferry service to "The Rock." The first Army vessel was the *General Mifflin*, and following the establishment of the Transport Service in 1896, the Quartermaster Corps operated steamers to both islands, the one which will be most recently remembered by San Franciscans being the *General Frank M. Coxe*. For the duration of the time that the U. S. Immigration Service was on Angel Island it operated a steamer called the *Angel Island*, eventually surrendering this vessel, when the immigration station was closed, to the Quartermaster Corps. Also operated to the two islands were two water tankers, the *El Aguador* and the *El Aquario*, since neither island had a self-sustaining water supply. The last vessel to serve either island regularly was the *Warden Johnston*, a launch belonging to the Bureau of Prisons.

In the sunset years of the ferries, a few older boats, destined to ignominious gravesites, were kept alive for a four-year reprieve before the scrapper's torch spelled their finish. The War Shipping Administration operated ferries from the Transport Building at the foot of Mission Street, San Francisco, to the Maritime Commission Shipyards in Richmond and Sausalito. Boats operated were the *Sierra Nevada, Alameda, Santa Clara, City of Sacramento, Hayward, San Leandro* and *Yerba Buena.* The latter two were transferred to the Army Transportation Corps in 1944. These shipyard ferries were not for the public but were maintained as a commuting means for shipyard workers. They provided convenient employment for veteran ferrymen who were not yet ready for retirement, and gave ferryboat and ferryman alike a useful purpose and a chance for a proud exodus from an honorable profession.

These are the routes which built San Francisco and its environs, an undertaking which was monumental, a never-ending ceaseless task, through rain, storm and fair weather alike. The ferryboat was the San Francisco Bay Area resident's means of getting to his work, his home, to the hospital, to the theater, to the Sunday picnic and any other outing he might undertake. It was a way of life in leisurely manner which set the pace of the cities by the Bay.

On the San Francisco-Oakland Bay Bridge workmen in the picture, opposite, are making finishing touches on the track that will early in 1939 make the twin-stacked *Santa Clara*, in the distance, surplus. The nearly-empty Diesel *Mendocino*, in the foreground demonstrates the futility of the early attempt to operate the automobile ferries in competition with the bridge. By the time the picture on this page was made, ferries only operated between San Francisco and Oakland to meet transcontinental trains, while traffic hummed on the bridge. *(Southern Pacific)*

The ferries were kept shipshape and Bristol fashion, as demonstrated by this lifeboat—boat fall flemished down and oars neatly stowed. Here all was in readiness for the passengers who would never have need for the lifeboat, for the ferries' days were nearly over on the Bay this brilliant day of the 1950s. *(Southern Pacific photo)*

II

Passengers and Crew

FROM THE overland traveler, whose transcontinental train trip was climaxed by a magnificent ferry voyage, to the commuter who spent the better part of his traveling years on the ferries of San Francisco Bay, the crossing on the paddle steamers was always a thrilling experience. To see the City from the ferry decks, its white buildings freshly bathed in the gentle sea fog, was convincing evidence that no city in the country enjoyed a more fabulous approach. The blue waters of the Bay, the sharp outlines of the structures which towered skyward from their nesting places close to the water's edge, and more often than not, the wisps of fog which clung to the hilltops of the surrounding areas: all led one to speculate as to whether he was approaching a city of reality or some Brigadoon from the fantasies of ages past.

The approaches to the City were innumerable; each presented its own particular advantages and each could be seen best at particular times of the day. From Oakland or Alameda, the early morning approach, with the sun struggling through the filmy fog was the reward of more travelers and commuters than the view from any other vantage point. From the Marin shore and from Vallejo, the approach to the City in the evening was the most preferred. Then the waning light of day tinged in the glow of sunset, reflected from the channel fogbank upon the whiteness of the City's skyline. The view of the City in the springtime, when intermittent rains had cleared the air so that visibility was virtually unlimited, presented a seasonal vista of singular magnificence. As the boat passed the open waters through the Golden Gate, Mile Rock loomed up with its white-tipped lighthouse, and 18 miles beyond, the Farallon Islands could be distinctly seen where shipping disappeared over the horizon.

The approach to San Francisco was not the only view from the ferryboat which captured the eye and caught the breath. The return to Oakland, with the Berkeley and Piedmont hills beyond and the peak of Mount Diablo as backdrop was a splendid sight of an afternoon. The northward voyage to Marin, with hills green in the springtime or bleached gold in the months that followed, was ever rewarding with the spectacular views of Mount Tamalpais. On clear days, the wisp of smoke from the locomotive of the Mount Tamalpais & Muir Woods Railway, the "Crookedest Railroad in the World," could be seen on the face of the mountain slopes as the train wound its tortuous way to the summit.

The islands of the Bay always fascinated the riders of the ferries, especially the three nearest the ferry lanes to San Francisco, which were dotted with federal installations. Alcatraz, of course, was a big conversation piece of Bay travel, particularly in the last years of the ferryboats, for in 1933 its military disciplinary barracks became a federal prison for dangerous criminals. Considered "escape-proof," it became the detention place of America's most legendary gangster, Al Capone. On Goat Island, now called Yerba Buena, were fine government residences and the Coast Guard lighthouse tending station. Fort McDowell, the Army's overseas staging area, shared Angel Island, north of Alcatraz, with the U. S. Immigration Service detention station and the U. S. Public Health Service Hospital. Bay travelers always examined these installations intently when the boats passed within hailing distance of the islands.

The Marin islands, Red Rock and Point San Pedro were scenic points of interest to travelers on the Richmond-San Rafael Ferry and the fast Monticello boats. Point San Pedro was one of the few wooded promontories of the Bay, and when

Alcatraz Island's modern lighthouse had not yet been built and the Army had yet to construct the big cell block for the disciplinary barracks that was later used as a famous federal prison, when the picture above was taken from the deck of the steamer *Sausalito*, with the *Tamalpais* heading for San Francisco in the distance. The view below was taken during the 1890s; Goat Island's trees were not yet in evidence, the *Newark* still had her big paddle wheels and the now double-end *Capital's* wheels had been reduced in size. The Golden Gate International Exposition on Treasure Island, dominated by the Tower of the Sun, was a favorite sight from the ferries. In the upper picture, opposite, the *Tamalpais* steams past this man-made island. The Ferry Building clock says high noon, and high noon it is in the era of the ferryboat, as the *Alameda,* and just behind her the *Peralta,* leave their slips simultaneously for Oakland. Soon to depart for Alameda is the *Piedmont* in the slip to the left. *(Two photos this page: Roy D. Graves collection; opposite above: Zan Stark photo; below: Southern Pacific)*

From Sausalito's wooded hillside slopes, the view of Angel Island at the left, taken in the late afternoon of a clear winter day in 1940, shows the *Eureka* steaming out from behind a graceful eucalyptus tree. On this page are views of the pleasant experiences of children and tourists on a ferryboat after the Bay Bridge had claimed the commuter traffic. The *Berkeley's* passengers enjoy the morning sun on the afterdeck as the boat pulls away from the Ferry Building; a little side photography is in progress, but nobody, at the moment, was using the dime telescope to examine the San Francisco skyline. Youngsters on the lower deck watch the twin-stack *Alameda* prepare to dock at Oakland Pier in the bottom picture below. The East Bay cantilever span of the San Francisco-Oakland Bay Bridge is in the background. A tunnel through Yerba Buena Island, at the left, connects this span with the more famous pair of suspension spans connecting the island with San Francisco. Servicemen in and out of uniform look over the Bay from the rail, their gear on the deck behind them. Children are intrigued by the approach to the City; relaxed adults take their pleasant trip on the Bay more casually. (*This page: Southern Pacific*)

When the Ferry Building was completed, hoofs and drays clattered over the cobblestones of East Street. The building's main tower dwarfs the picturesque white bell tower on the piling between slips, in the 1928 view below taken from the general office building of Southern Pacific at 65 Market Street. One of the famous Bay scow schooners has just crossed the bows of the twin-stacked *Santa Clara,* steaming in from Oakland, and the *Yosemite,* arriving from some unusual errand to the north.   *(Above: Ed Zelinsky collection; below: Southern Pacific)*

approached from Carquinez Strait or Petaluma Creek, it formed a particularly lovely foreground to Mount Tamalpais. These views could be enjoyed both from the spacious open decks of the boats or from the heavily windowed interiors where one was protected from the wind.

✓   ✓   ✓

Ferry travelers came from all walks of life and from all corners of the globe. By some the journey was thoroughly enjoyed, for if it was not the scenic beauty of the trip itself, a visit with an old friend, a chance to observe fellow passengers or an opportunity for relaxation and reading added to the pleasure of the voyage.

On the other hand, although this seems somewhat difficult to comprehend, there were ferry riders who were obviously disgusted with this mode of travel, whose sense of appreciation certainly was not trained on the views of San Francisco Bay, and whose sighs of relief at the conclusion of the trip were unmistakable. There were people who rode the ferries who were actually fearful, particularly when the weather was rough or the fog was thick. Their thoughts obviously turned to the legends of the ferry sinkings which were startlingly few in the hundred-year history of Bay navigation, and loss of life on Bay travel was less than one millionth of a percent. Statistics proved there was no safer place to be than on a ferryboat.

Aboard the ferryboats life proceeded for humanity as it does on shore, this brief interlude in the traveler's existence was not without its pleasures, its surprises and its heartaches. Since women of the outlying communities had to go to San Francisco for hospitalization, many births occurred aboard the ferries with the cabin matron and the astonished husband the only medical assistants. Captain John Leale in his "Recollections of a Tule Sailor" recounts that a minister performed a marriage in the pilothouse of the *Newark* due to the fact that the couple had obtained a marriage license in the wrong county. By completing the ceremony on the ferry while docked in the proper county, everything was legal. Captain Leale said his only stipulation was that he got to kiss the bride, and he further attested to the fact that he was well repaid. Death, too, occurred on the fer-

Captain John Leale, master mariner on the Bay of San Francisco for over forty years, models the 1908 uniform of the Southern Pacific Co. This Guernsey-born skipper had his first master's berth on the *Newark* for the South Pacific Coast Railroad in 1877 and retired in 1914. *(San Francisco Maritime Museum)*

ries, and many an old timer breathed his last from his ferry seat in those tranquil surroundings.

✓   ✓   ✓

The San Franciscan of today might well ask what people bent on suicide did before there was a Golden Gate Bridge to provide an economical and effective place from which to jump. The answer is, of course, that they jumped from the ferryboats and bestowed no particular favoritism on any line, as all routes had their share of jumpers.

Apparently the jumpers put very little thought into this method of eliminating themselves from the face of the earth. In the first place the decks of the ferryboats were not high enough above the water to insure death by impact, and most jumpers had no stomach for jumping forward of the paddles so that crushing in these huge wheels would be the immediate cause of death.

The deck hand is hooking the mooring line at the ferry slip. At the right is a slip at San Francisco's old ferry terminal. By 1928 the busy streetcar loops and steel overpass were established parts of San Francisco's "front door."

The stern wheeler at the left is the *Delta King*. Northwestern Pacific's fine new auto ferry *Mendocino* is about to arrive from Sausalito. *(Above right: Society of California Pioneers; two photos: Southern Pacific)*

Deck hands were pretty well trained to watch for jumpers and anyone acting peculiarly was closely watched for the duration of the voyage. Through experience the ferrymen were often able to recognize a prospective jumper as he walked aboard the boat, and thus was many a suicide attempt averted. Ferry captains interviewed by the author agree that, in their experience, if someone jumped off the bow, the boat would pass over the body which would surface immediately astern and be quickly retrieved. Those who jumped from the afterdeck were less likely to be missed or picked up, since they were not within the surveillance of the navigator.

Actual death by this bizarre means might have been much more common, were it not for the chill of San Francisco Bay water, which averages between 48 and 55 degrees, Fahrenheit. One who, in the warmth of the cabin, had contemplated suicide in the Bay was quite likely to have a sudden change of heart on hitting the frigid water, and to be glad when picked up. Some sort of record may have been set by the passenger who leaped unobserved from the *Cazadero* five minutes before she docked at the Ferry Building at 11:15 one cold January night in 1941. After an hour and a half layover the vessel began her return trip to Sausalito. A few minutes on the way, Captain August Palmer, noting an object in the water, turned his searchlight on the hapless shivering ex-passenger, and then proceeded with his last rescue before retirement from a long career on the Bay. Within little more than a month the *Cazadero* herself was to retire with the termination of Northwestern Pacific ferry operations. For nearly three years the Golden Gate Bridge had been open to traffic and had already begun its career as a launching place for suicides.

On another occasion a Southern Pacific ferry captain, after coming off watch, decided to visit a jumper he had delivered to the emergency hospital after fishing him out of the water the day before. He asked his former passenger how he felt when he struck the water. "Not so good," replied the would-be suicide, "but when the steamer went away, I felt so lonesome. . . . Say, Captain, is it in the paper? I sure want *her* to see it."

All of the ferry berths at the Ferry Building in San Francisco, which was constructed and opened to traffic in 1898, were fitted with upper and lower landings as were the terminals in Oakland and Sausalito. The ferryboat's second officer was in charge of hoisting the gangplank assisted by shore personnel who manned the booth for hydraulic operation of the apron. These aprons were adjusted during the course of the day to suit tidal conditions and in the majority of cases physical connection was made with the ferryboat through mere operation of the counterbalanced gangplank. Following the raising of the gangplank at both deck levels the deck hands would loosen and untie the two bowlines which were secured to giant hooks attached to the innermost piling of the slip, with the bitter ends of the rope belayed around a cleat on the ferryboat's deck. The second officer would then signal to the first officer who waited in the after pilothouse to receive the hand signal indicating readiness to get under way. The first officer would then pull an inter-pilothouse bell cord which permitted the Captain to know that the boat was clear to go. He would sound the whistle and ring down "Full Speed Ahead" to the engine room below. The engineer was always ready, for the inter-pilothouse bell cord passed through the engine control platform and the clanking of its chains alerted the engine room that things were about to happen. As the paddles slowly turned, gradually picking up speed until the maximum revolutions could be reached, the deck hands completed securing for sea.

Most double-end passenger and automobile ferries on San Francisco Bay were fitted with independently operated rudders fore and aft. When the boat was under way, the forward rudder had to be locked in place by a huge steel pin inserted through a guide hole in the deck. At each end of the run, the forward rudder, which was to be the after rudder on the ensuing voyage, had to be unlocked, and the after rudder, which was to be stationary on the following trip, had to be locked in position. If this could not be successfully accomplished on the inbound voyage, it was one of the most mandatory tasks to be performed upon departure from the slip. This act, which was performed simultaneously at each end of the boat,

First Assistant Engineer Manuel Silviera works the bar to start the Southern Pacific's steamer *Sacramento* out of the slips while Assistant Chief Engineer Robert Williams looks on. The large metallic wheel in the right foreground is the injection valve for the jet condenser which was used to maintain vacuum. The engine crew of the steamer *Tamalpais* included, left to right, First Assistant Engineer "Babe" Malone, Fireman Tony Simas, Chief Engineer Harry C. Smith, Fireman Otto Jacobi and Oiler "Baldy" Hughes. (*Above: Southern Pacific*)

required great coordination between the men in the pilothouses and the deck hands who inserted the locking pin or removed it. This was one of the most exacting tasks of steamboat operation.

Following the removal of the after rudder pin, a large chain was secured in place on the lower deck, closing the opening between the rails to prevent vehicles from accidentally rolling off the boat, should they be improperly secured during the voyage. As a further precaution, a smaller hand rope was placed inboard of the chain to detain passengers from debarking while the boat was being tied up. The gangplank opening in the upper deck was closed by means of a sliding gate and a hand line was stretched inboard of the gate to prevent passengers from encroaching upon the gangplank landing area when the boat again should reach the terminal.

One of the ferry captains tells this story and swears that the circumstances are true: A large Swede made a run for the ferryboat after the gangplank had been raised. He took great strides, since the boat was about ten feet beyond the end of the gangplank. Then he made a magnificent leap which he completed by ungracefully tripping over the sill of the boat. He landed on his head and was unconscious for a period of about ten minutes. When he awoke from his temporary black-out, the ferry was abreast of Alcatraz Island, and the terminal appeared as a mere white dot in the distance. With incredulous surprise he looked at all those around him and exclaimed, "Yee, what a yump!"

Docking a ferryboat was a complicated procedure always performed in full view of interested passengers preparing to disembark. A traveler boarding the ferry might or might not choose to witness the operations of casting off, but in his haste to leave the boat as soon as it was tied up, he joined those who strained against the hand lines as they impatiently observed the tying up procedure. Tying up was always heralded with a multiplicity of jingles from the bridge and engine order telegraphs, which indicated numerous changes in direction of the paddle wheels. "Slow Astern," "Half Ahead," "Full Astern" and "Stop" would indicate on the telegraph in the engine room and the engineer had to be quick and alert

to every command from the pilothouse for a rapid and successful docking.

On the foredeck more things were happening. The big chain was released from the opening between the rails and cast aside. The deck hands fixed the loops of the bowlines onto the huge iron mooring hooks of the pier, and when the loops were properly secured the slack in the line was taken up on the cleats on the deck to complete the mooring. The second officer then stepped aboard the gangplank, his weight tipping the counterbalance so that as contact was made with the deck, a slight hand signal was given to the deck hand who held the hand line which restrained the passengers. The line was dropped and the passengers surged forward into the terminal.

The entire departure and tying-up operations took only a minute or two each since the workers were so well trained in all of its various facets. Tying-up at the storage slips was an entirely different proposition. The mooring lines were made fast to dolphins, or clusters of piling, which were spaced in such a manner as to require long hawsers for the tying-up operation. The slack line of the hawsers was taken up by hand capstans which were impressive accessories common to the sailing ships of years gone-by. The capstan had a vertically mounted drum and above the drum was located the drive hub, equipped with large holes for the insertion of poles. In order to turn the capstan the deck hands walked round and round the capstan hub, gingerly stepping over the hawser they were taking in, while the friction dogs clanked noisily into place, in true windjammer fashion.

✓ ✓ ✓

At night the ferryboat under way was a beautiful sight. The rows of illuminated windows on the sides reflected mellowly on the surface of the water. Above decks, only the navigation lights were visible. The pilothouses were completely dark, for navigation had to be accomplished with such light as was furnished by moon, stars, and city lights reflected on clouds. Lighthouses on islands and points along the shore and buoys on the Bay pointed out particular hazards. If a steersman detected an unidentified object on the surface of the water, he had a powerful searchlight on the roof of the pilothouse available.

On these pages and several more to follow are seen the routines of docking a ferryboat. Pulling the rudder pin was a necessary ritual. The *Alameda* hugs one side of the slip so that contact can be used for braking the speed of the boat if the engine response is not sufficient. The *Santa Clara* is arriving at Oakland Pier and this trip will connect with a main line train; the cart with hand baggage will clear the foredeck before the passengers leave the boat. Second Officer Grande watches the deck hands prepare the hawsers for tying up as the *Cazadero* docks in San Francisco. *(This page and lower opposite: Southern Pacific)*

As the *Berkeley* enters the slip at Oakland Mole, the second officer stands in the center of the foredeck to direct mooring operations. The deck hands on either side will each handle a hawser. Another deck hand stands at the right of the lower deck with the passenger restraining line, while one on the upper deck is manipulating the gate to permit the apron to lower onto the deck. Below, he is sliding the gate open. The chafing strips on the deck are to accommodate the sliding of the apron. On the opposite page are two views of passengers debarking from the *Alameda* at Oakland Pier. The apron off the bow of the boat leads to the main line trains, the upper and lower aprons to the side lead to the electric interurban trains.   (*Southern Pacific*)

Baggage carts and their tenders stand at the bow of the ferryboat approaching its landing after a trip with passengers from the main line trains at Oakland Pier, so that the carts may be rushed ashore at the very moment the apron is lowered. The baggage then will be ready for the passengers to pick up on their arrival ashore. Passengers in wheelchairs were taken ashore ahead of the passengers afoot. *(Southern Pacific)*

The derby hats and styles of dress date the pictures on this page to the turn of the century, when the *Bay City* still came to the new Ferry Building and the *Tiburon* of the California Northwestern still went to the terminal in the town of its name. The passengers in the pictures opposite, boarding and debarking from the ferryboat at Oakland Pier, are dressed in the fashions of the late 1930s. The large ramp in the picture above was operated hydraulically in accordance with tidal conditions, but the apron was operated by hand. *(Above: Roy D. Graves collection; below: Society of California Pioneers; opposite: Southern Pacific)*

(Southern Pacific)

To keep the navigator's vision from being distracted by unnecessary glare from the cabin lights on to the vessel's outer deck, the cabin boy was always dispatched to close all the blinds on the windows and doors of the forward cabin in order to assure a dark foredeck.

✓ ✓ ✓

Since many of the ferries were incidental to the operation of a mainline railroad business, mail, baggage and express were handled on all of their regular runs. At times the volume of these commodities was such that extra trips of the ferryboats were required to handle the express and mail. This was true particularly at Christmas time. All of this traffic was handled in unwieldy-appearing carts, each equipped with four wheels, the front pair of which was attached to a swivel tongue. On the rear of each cart was a Raymond hook, and the eye of the following cart's tongue could be attached to this hook, forming trains of express carts, often a dozen in a group. In later years they were pulled on and off the boats by the use of small, noisy, gas-propelled runabouts at speeds which terrified onlookers who felt sure that the high-wheeled, top-heavy, flimsy, iron-tired vehicles would come to disaster long before they would be safely aboard the deck of the ferry. The runabouts, which were necessary evils of all ferry terminals, were driven by rather skilled individuals who, in spite of their apparent reckless speed, artfully whipped their queue of express carts through the terminal, around stanchions and around right-angle turns with a deftness to be admired.

The one exception to this mad, snap-of-the-whip operation, was the movement of the remains of a deceased, in the standard-appearing four-handled redwood shipping cases, one to an express cart. The cart in this case was handled individually about the boat by a quartet of deck hands who gently rolled their sacred cargo aboard and doffed their hats reverently before going about their other duties.

Before the days of the slam-bang gasoline jitney, the express carts on many of the ferryboats were pulled by horses which were quartered on board the boat. The most memorable of these faithful animals was "Old Dick," who was well known to the commuter as the horse who refused

to leave the North Pacific Coast's ferry steamer, the *San Rafael*, when this vessel was sinking in 1901 under dramatic circumstances. This inspired Jack London's novel, "The Sea Wolf."

✓ ✓ ✓

In the early days of San Francisco one would not have to go far either on the Peninsula itself or into the bordering counties of the Bay before encountering dairy ranches, beef cattle ranches, sheep ranches, and all the other activities of rural life in a sparsely populated area. It was not uncommon for a cattleman to deliver his stock to the San Francisco market by driving them to the nearest ferry terminal after having made previous arrangements with the ferry company to accommodate the cargo. A certain portion of the main, or lower deck of the boat would be roped off for the livestock. One might assume that it was a great hardship for the ferry deck hands suddenly to be required to punch cows. However, most of the local dairymen came from Portugal or the Portuguese-owned Azores Islands and the Portuguese who did not choose the life of ranch and farm, quite frequently became ferry mariners in the maritime tradition of their native land. Handling cattle was second nature to deck hands whose last names were Silva, DeBorba, Vierra, Pacheco and Taxiera.

Although the ferry *Eureka* did not appear on the waters of the Bay until 1922, not long after she was built a load of cattle was driven on board at Sausalito, destined to the stockyards of San Francisco. The deck crew had forgotten the precautions required to contain the bovine passengers and the single rope intended for this purpose was no match for the animals. When the boat got out into the middle of the Bay, the cattle got loose, ventured onto the upper deck where they scattered the female passengers, stylishly dressed for San Francisco shopping and theater going. There were many anxious moments before the cattle drovers and the cow punchers dressed in mariner's blue, restored the beasts to order.

✓ ✓ ✓

As the ferries plied their routine and regular courses on the waters of the Bay, they were followed by flocks of sea gulls who looked upon the ferryboats as an institution designed solely for the perpetuation of their multitudinous hordes. Since

The hull dining room of this Southern Pacific ferryboat was arranged for the prompt service necessary on a twenty-minute crossing, rather than for elegance of accommodations. Within the limitations imposed by this necessity for speed, the quality of the food was excellent. The other pictures on this page are of commuters during the 1930s, except for the one at the right immediately below. This night view is in the rather cramped atmosphere of the *San Leandro's* cabin and the sparse number and festive manner of the passengers would never be confused with the assured nonchalance of daily commuters on their accustomed boats. *(All except game: Southern Pacific)*

all of the garbage and refuse from the boats was unceremoniously dumped into the Bay, the ferryboats were prime attractions for these scavenger birds. Scarcely would a morsel of refuse hit the water than the sea gulls would gulp it down, should it be at all edible. Since time immemorial on the ferries, certain passengers either came equipped with tidbits to feed the gulls or purchased food at the restaurant or newsstand, which they would throw into the air and watch the raucous recipients "dive bomb" and catch them on the fly.

Some of the sea gulls were injured and by their deformities both the ferrymen and the commuters could easily identify them. Every boat on the Bay was trailed by "Peg Leg Pete," the sea gull who had lost a leg in an altercation with another bird. "Peg Leg Pete" was seen so often and remembered so well by young and old alike through all the commuting days, that there were probably many birds that filled this description and helped to make "Peg Leg Pete" a legend in his own time.

Earle Ennis, the fabled writer of the column "Ferry Tales" in the San Francisco *Chronicle*, continued writing for some weeks after the ferries had ceased to operate and he speculated at length as to where the sea gull would get his food once the ferries had departed. His question remains unanswered, but there is no indication that there was a mass starvation among these scavengers once their benefactors on the ferries were no longer their providers.

✓　　✓　　✓

The commuter was an institution on the ferryboats and so many of the working citizens of the Bay Area relied on ferry transportation to get them to work that the term "commuter" was a title of honor bestowed upon the high castes of the employed in San Francisco. That one could work in one locality and afford to live in an exclusively residential area was a status symbol and the object of many Bay Area toilers who were charged with ambition.

The word "commuter" is used only in larger metropolitan areas and is unknown in many parts of the country. The story is told of a professor from Indiana who taught at the University of California and who obtained a home close to the campus. Shortly after his arrival, he attended a party in Berkeley and heard the word being bandied about. He was entirely unfamiliar with it but when asked as to whether he was a commuter or not, he replied in the affirmative, since it would appear from the tenor of the conversation that his social life in California depended upon his attaining this rank within the community.

The commuter was not an individual, but he was a member of a closely knit group which had traveled to and fro on the ferryboats for many years. He doggedly remained with his group, and it was beneath him to contemplate joining another commuter clique composed of his juniors in length of Bay travel. For the newcomer and the uninitiated into Bay commuting, it was hopeless to join the old established clans; and it was not until his acquaintance with contemporaries permitted the neophyte to form his own clique, that his status would increase in dignity and prestige.

The die-hard not only had his own group with which to ride but he also had his own seat aboard the boat. A newcomer dared not sit in that seat for it was as valuable to the veteran as a seat on the stock exchange. There might be times when it was necessary to substitute another ferry on the run for some reason and if the commuter's regular seat was on the *Newark*, and he was forced to ride the *Oakland*, his day was so disrupted that he let the company know about it.

Many of the cliques played cards aboard the boats and continuing card games lasted for years without any indication that it was necessary to have a winner. The ferry companies provided large boards which were kept in wooden racks on both decks, with the inscription stencilled thereon, "Please return to rack when you are through." The commuters themselves supplied the cards; there were cards for sale at the newsstands with the insignia of the Southern Pacific, the Key Route and other lines with the company's advertising on each pack.

Close to the paddle box was a particular area where the noise of the paddles drowned out the voices of the groups that met there. These distinctive assemblages were the "Paddle Wheel Masons," lodge members who were learning Masonic ritual as they were taking the various degrees of Freemasonry. The learners were passengers on the ferry, but the instructors often had to refer diffi-

The *Eureka's* deep and mysterious-sounding triad was the sweetest voice on the Bay. *(Southern Pacific)*

cult points to more proficient brethren in the ferry crew, for the preponderance of ferrymen were entitled to wear the square and compass.

The nearest thing to a rugged individualist type of passenger was the walker, or pacer as he was known, who found his own particular area aboard the boat where he might take his constitutional. The favorite haunt of the walker was the lower foredeck or afterdeck, either of which was usually clear of passengers and permitted a brief space the breadth of the boat, for this to-and-fro pacing. The more rugged of these exercisers accepted the biting cold of the forward section of the main deck, and often obtained their walking pleasure in spite of gales, fogs and rain. A portion of this deck was covered over by the upper deck overhang, although in inclement weather this protection was scant indeed. The semi-hardy souls took the protection of the lee of the afterdeck where the main cabin broke the gales and rain to which the passenger might otherwise be subjected. The walker was usually uncommunicative with passenger and crew alike, and upon arrival at his destination would charge up Market Street in reckless defiance of the city streetcar system.

↑   ↑   ↑

Indoors on the ferries there were all kinds of diversions for the convenience and amusement of the passengers. The most frequently patronized of these enterprises was the restaurant, often a concession not under the management of the ferry company. The most famous of these were the eating facilities operated by the National Service Company on the Key Route boats. The chefs were as well trained in the culinary art as any on the Bay and their menus featured three dishes in particular: "Key Route Corn Beef Hash," a very succulent rendition of this all-time favorite dish; "Key Route Apple Pie," which knew no peer when served with a scoop of vanilla ice cream, and "Key Route Coffee," a blend which was apparently specially packed for the National Service Company, for the flavor was one that couldn't be matched elsewhere.

Restaurants on the Northwestern Pacific and Southern Pacific boats permitted the commuter, if pressed for time, not only to have an in-between snack on his way to and from work, but, if need be, he could enjoy a substantial and satisfying meal which was served with great rapidity, assuring him time for a second cup of coffee if he was so inclined. The Southern Pacific, in addition to the restaurant facilities, often in the hold, also operated a buffet counter on the lower deck providing stand-up coffee and doughnuts in the morning, sandwiches and milk at noon and hot dogs and various beverages in the early evening.

Captain Raymond Clarke, reminiscing about his forty years of service on San Francisco Bay, said this of the restaurant on the Richmond-San Rafael Ferry; "I've dined with the most desperate criminals, men manacled to the accompanying sheriff's deputies, men who had their last meal outside of the prison walls on the restaurant of my boat." The Richmond-San Rafael line was a direct route to San Quentin prison, the State's largest penal institution.

Prior to Prohibition days, the more palatial boats were outfitted with bars which served wines, beer and hard liquors. On one occasion a passenger forced his way up to the captain, busy with navigation in the shipping lanes, and stated that a gentleman in the bar wished to report that he had sighted the "Loch Ness Monster," off the starboard bow!

Jim McCue of Corte Madera, a passenger on the steamer *San Rafael*, on her ill-fated journey of November 30th, 1901, was in the restaurant on the boat when the collision occurred. A timber unseated by the blow struck by the steamer *Sausalito* fell so close to Jim's head that it took off one of his ears. During the course of litigation which ensued, McCue was heard to say that had he been in the bar where he belonged, the incident would never have happened.

In the early days of the Monticello Steamship Co., operating between Vallejo and San Francisco, the hour and 45 minute ride provided ample opportunity for the ferry riders to imbibe. Since many of the passengers on the Monticello boats were shipyard workers or crewmen from Navy ships undergoing repairs at the Mare Island Navy Yard, business was brisk, to say the least. Years later, C. Ferry Hatch, one of the owners of the Monticello Steamship Co., stated that the bar had been a top money-maker for years and as a matter of fact it was from the profit of this facility that the Monticello Steamship Co. weathered the early

At the wheel of the *San Leandro* on its final day of operation was Capt. Richard Thomas, last skipper of a ferryboat for the Southern Pacific. *(Southern Pacific)*

financial storms which plagued their operation. To attest to the popularity of this institution it was not Prohibition which closed the bars on the Monticello boats, but rather the commandant of the Navy Yard who considered that this facility was too great a temptation for the servicemen.

The radio-telephone was in its infancy when the ferries ceased to ply the waters of the Bay, and no attempt was made to place this facility on board the boats as long as ferry service was maintained. Such an instrument would have been out of keeping with the leisurely pace which the ferries induced but, in later years on many boats, a hardwood writing desk of the stand-up variety was placed at either end of the engine casing on the upper deck, with telephone directories for the passengers' convenience. These facilities were maintained by the Pacific Telephone & Telegraph Co., and the desks were backed up with a hardwood sign lettered in gold-leaf which explained that although there were no telephones on board, the books were maintained so that numbers could be conveniently researched while under way for the convenience of the caller when he could reach a phone at the terminal. The passenger who paid no particular attention to this sign might easily be convinced that there actually were telephones on the ferries. And on occasion, some wag would go through the crowded lower deck yelling, "Telephone for Mr. Smith on the Upper Deck." This ruse found a taker in more than one instance.

The large, spacious steamers of the Monticello company boasted a barbershop on board, but this is the only line which had such a convenience. A bootblack stand adapted itself well to the boats, and served to accommodate the frustrated passenger whose boat had commenced loading before his turn had come at the Ferry Building bootblack parlors. These were manned by one or two bootblacks on two shifts, who became more proficient at putting a gloss on a pair of shoes than their landlubber brothers who were blessed with more time to pursue their customers' desires. The polish was applied deftly with the hand, seams and sole tops were the only parts touched by applicators, and an over-all brushing followed by the lambskin finish shine, all with vigorous strokes, topped the performance. These men were tipped well, had their regular customers, and many of them plied their trade successfully ashore many years after the ferries ceased.

Concessionaires maintained newsstands on board the ferries with every magazine imaginable, comic books, crossword puzzle books, and a host of other commodities to distribute. The shelves were filled with candy bars and peanuts, cigars, cigarettes and pipes, and a delicacy repeated over and over again in the raucous voice of the news-butcher "Popcorn-a-nickel-five-cents." There were souvenirs such as could be found anywhere in the novelty stores of the City, guide maps, film and a featured volume on "Interesting Places to See." It was evident that this enterprise was profitable, for no boat was without this concession, even if it boasted no other, and to the memory of the writer, the stands were always manned except at extremely late hours when travel had fallen off to nothing. Then portable cage structures were erected and locked around the stand, for there was quite an investment in inventory on the shelves of the ferryman's "slop-chest."

In later years, a new evil was added to the newsstand, the electric crane which was fed by nickels to commence its operation. The crane was encased in glass, and the lower portion of the glass case was filled to a depth of a foot or more with peanuts and small candies and fifty or so prizes of questionable value which tempted the prospective customer to hope he might be so fortunate as to hook a prize on his first try. The nickel prompted the crane to open its clam-shell bucket, the passenger could then direct its boom toward the object of his desire by means of a manual wheel. Then the clamshell would drop, partially seize the "prize," but slip off at the crucial moment and perhaps reward the player with a peanut or a candy. In the endless hours of either viewing or playing by the author, no prize was ever witnessed coming out of this machine, and those on the Golden Gate Ferries often bore the sign "out of order," attesting to the violence of some disgruntled player.

To the author, the mechanical baseball game was the most interesting—three outs for five cents. This machine was designed to be operated on rigid foundations ashore; on the boat it had its problems. A mechanical pitcher fired a steel ball at home plate, the person who had squandered his

The *Sausalito* was returning from San Francisco when her walking beam sheared at the crank end; here is what happened. The accident was partly blamed on the fact the black paint on the beam obscured flaws in the forging. Thereafter, to facilitate inspection, all beams were painted white. *(Mike Barnes collection)*

nickel was then to operate a lever which swung the bat at the ball. The machine was cleverly designed for put-outs, walks, and base-hits. Once in the heavy ground-swells crossing the Golden Gate, the author remained at bat for the entire voyage with 87 consecutive doubles and only one out as the boat drew in to Hyde Street Pier. How he was tempted to stay aboard and make the return trip!

Pin-ball machines had their heyday on the ferries, even to those exasperating signs which read "Please do not tilt." This was a superfluous instruction on a ferry, for there was often tilting without any prompting from the passenger-player. Needless to say, there was an element of chance in a marine pin-ball game which gave it a charm not shared by its counterpart uptown.

On some of the boats, an old blind man used to sell lavender, by going through the upper deck cabin at the beginning of the journey and passing out his wares, recovering either the lavender or the price in a collection just before the boat docked.

✓   ✓   ✓

The earlier ferries boasted a glass enclosure of wonders which was a boon to mothers traveling with children of the curious age. With noses pressed close to the glass panes on which every breath was graphically recorded, the young fry were often entertained for the entire voyage. From the lower deck, these panes gave a good view of the engine face and its mysterious cams and levers. From the upper deck could be seen the cylinder rod extending from the cylinder head to the crosshead, and then the linkage to the walking beam. Further along in the glass enclosure, was the main rod, connecting the opposite end of the walking beam with the crank. These tremendous pieces of steel and iron, moving at a rate of 20 to 24 times a minute, were fascinating to observe, and many an oldster found himself watching the workings of the giant engine for more than a fleeting minute. If one were fortunate, an oiler might be spotted climbing around the machinery, lubricating it while in motion to add to the extensive show in the glass enclosure.

Some passengers were alarmed by the sight of such massive machinery in motion close at hand and in a 1922 incident demonstrated a real danger.

Fortunately few passengers were on board when the *Sausalito's* walking beam and main rod clattered down into the upper deck cabin. Prudently the Northwestern Pacific replaced the glass windows with solid steel on the engine casing bulkhead. Apparently the Southern Pacific found other ways to protect passengers from the lurking danger, for the *Sacramento* appeared a couple of years later with gleaming windows through which the machinery could be seen in action.

✓   ✓   ✓

Christmas was always a joyous time for ferrymen, commuters and shoppers alike who found the Yuletide spirit present in every nook and cranny of the ferryboat. The South Pacific Coast ferries were decorated in greens and Christmas trees from the Santa Cruz mountains. The Southern Pacific boats received their decorative material from the timber forests of Cisco Grove, high in the Sierra Nevada, and the Northwestern Pacific boats were decked out in distinctive attire appropriate to the "Redwood Empire Route," with greens from the coast redwoods of the Eel River Canyon. All hands turned to making garlands, wreaths and other items of décor to enhance the appearance of each boat, and in the spirit of competition each crew tried to outdo the others in festooning the edge of the hurricane deck, the paddle boxes, the upper deck rails and posts, and the stanchions on the main deck. On the older boats which were still equipped with masts, a small fir tree was lashed to the foremast head, to sweep the seas at Christmas time. In later years volunteer committees would get together and trim a Christmas tree in the upper deck cabin, in readiness for the morning of Christmas Eve. The ferry companies themselves generally had a token gift to present to the commuters on the morning boats, such as commutation book cases or holders for coins. During these festivities would appear Santa Claus, often a robust deck hand who had been a favorite with the commuters throughout the year, selected by a volunteer commuters' group. Among Santa's more pleasant chores was kissing giggly, short-skirted stenographers for the benefit of press photographers who were inevitably on hand to report the occasion.

✓   ✓   ✓

While the teamwork among the crew may appear dubious in this lifeboat drill on the *Newark* in 1882, the lifesaving record of this ferryboat under the command of Captain John Leale was outstanding. He may well be the moustached figure in the pilothouse of the *Bay City*, in the Christmas scene below which is from his personal collection. *(Both: Southern Pacific)*

To the fortunate commuter or occasional traveler, who might be returning from the theater late at night, an aria from the "Caruso of Ferries" might be his reward. Since Key Route, Southern Pacific and Northwestern Pacific commuters all claimed at one time or another to have heard this magnificent voice coming from a stocky man standing fire watch on the lower deck with an extinguisher in a canvas bag over his shoulder; it may be assumed that more than one ferry deck hand earned this legendary title when the ferries still crossed the Bay. The author can attest to having heard a marvelous operatic voice booming out over the noise of the engine and the thump of the paddles on the steamer *Tamalpais*. Its owner, Dick Hunter, was probably the last of a long line of "Carusos of the Ferries," but his contribution was among the finest of them all.

✓   ✓   ✓

Steamboat regulations required a fire and boat drill, once a week on the ferryboats. This gave the second officer and his deck hands an opportunity to launch a boat, more for the purpose of practicing to save a jumper than to prepare for that unthinkable occurrence, the sinking of a ferryboat. The skill of the boat commander and his crew who launched and retrieved the lifeboat by hand falls, was a sight to behold, and each man knew his job, both in the launching crew and the boat crew. Although these drills were held during the course of a regular ferry trip, a delay of not more than four to ten minutes could be anticipated in the entire voyage. The testing of the fire hoses was always a great sight for the children who enjoyed the huge streams of water, which issued from the great nozzles. No fire and boat drill would be complete without some waggish young one warning the deck hands that if they kept up the play of the hoses that they would soon fill up the Bay.

No season can be designated the "fog season" on San Francisco Bay. Certain weather conditions induce the fogs that drift in from the sea. These are usually heralded by a cloud barrier across the channel from the Golden Gate to Alcatraz. In the winter months, the "tule fogs" from the inland lowlands venture down upon the Bay, often so thick that navigation seemed out of the question. It was at these times that the ferryman showed his true mettle as a navigator, for he not only had all the ocean traffic to avoid, but he had the Bay and river trade, plus the pleasure craft that swarmed like locusts of the sea on the ferry routes of the Bay. There were horns, bells and whistles maintained at critical points by the Lighthouse Service, and to obtain an inland pilot's license, the ferryman had to memorize these sounds and the locations from which he might expect them to originate. It was also to his advantage to be familiar with the distinctive whistles of the ferries themselves, as well as the ocean steamers and other craft commonly encountered on the Bay.

Due to dredging operations and the constant changes which took place in the contour and depth of the Bay, additions were made to the navigational aids for the mariner, both afloat and ashore. The story is told of the Chinese owner of an artichoke farm on a point in the Bay who was called upon by agents of the government to condemn his land for a station. He told them how this had happened to him at a previous farm, and protested the futility of the warning device. As he explained it, "Fog horn go 'Whoo-oo, Whoo-oo,' but fog come in just the same!"

Captain John Leale wrote in his *Recollections of a Tule Sailor*, "I prefer in fog to have my first officer steer, then I may give all of my attention to the sounds of the whistles and bells, having compass in view all the while." It was common practice to station a deck hand or an officer on the forward sector of the main deck to listen for all sounds, and point them out to the navigator in the wheelhouse above, giving direction as near as possible. The navigator would then verify the direction. If it coincided with his own appraisal of the sound source, he would satisfy himself that this was correct, otherwise a check was hastily made when the sound was again repeated. The compass was the ferryman's only true navigational aid. Radar came to the last of the Southern Pacific ferries, but only after 98 percent of the ferry and river traffic had vanished from the ferry lanes and after coastwise shipping was a mere token of its former glory.

In spite of the hindrance which the fog was to the Bay navigator, the accidents resulting from it were few, considering the risk involved. The ferry captain was entrusted with thousands of lives on

The *Mary Garrett* and the North Pacific Coast's first *Tamalpais*, originally the *Petaluma*, appear to be racing in the picture below, but neither vessel could lay much claim to speed. Excursions such as that of the California Camera Club on the *James M. Donahue* provided many of the fine marine scenes which have been left to document the colorful history of the Bay. (*Above: Roy D. Graves collection; below: Archie J. Treat photo*)

a single vessel; he had to use every bit of common sense, instinct, intuition and skill at his command. The low incidence of accidents on the Bay is a tribute to the care and devotion which won him immortality in the annals of Bay navigation.

The care and the pride of the ferry captain after a century of ferry operation is in marked contrast with the reckless practices which characterized the early days of steamboating. Just as the Mississippi enjoyed its races to Natchez in the infancy of river travel, so did San Francisco see steamboat racing between rival lines back in the days when the river boat conquered the Bay. Such queens as the *Chrysopolis* and the *Capital* could put on the speed when the spirit moved them, and bets were placed in the cabin among the gentlemen present. One company expressed its views on racing by issuing an edict that all ferry captains caught indulging therein would be fined five demerits, and all captains losing to the boat of the rival concern would be fined ten! The North Pacific Coast steamer *San Rafael* not only risked taking on the *Tiburon* of the San Francisco & North Pacific Railway, but also enjoyed a few encounters with William Randolph Hearst's *Aquilla*, a speedboat which burned a distillate known as naphtha, which was quite popular in the Gay Nineties. After three or four losses, the Hearst boat made one final effort, won the race, burned out her engine and never raced again!

One engineer on the boats told a harrowing story, after the manner of Mark Twain, concerning a race between the North Shore's car ferry *Lagunitas* and Alcatraz Island, embellishing the recounting with breath-taking heroics on the part of the noble crew, but concluding that, as the tide was running out, the victory belonged to the immovable island.

No ferryman would ever admit to racing, but there were some remarkable times clocked on San Francisco Bay. The engineers would give the piston a boost on every stroke with a slight advance of the admission of steam by using the hand lever meant for starting the engine. The newer Diesel electric boats made the mistake of challenging the steamers, but this was strictly "no contest." The steam jobs had a tremendous reserve of power when occasion demanded it.

✓   ✓   ✓

On one beautiful Easter Sunday morning, the *Tamalpais* was steaming across the Golden Gate on its ten o'clock trip. Enjoying the bright sun and the breeze on the upper afterdeck was a happy holiday crowd with the ladies attired in their finest new hats and bright spring dresses. Suddenly a black cloud of soot and cinders issued from the stack and was tossed by a down wind on top of the resplendent crowd.

This was the unfortunate result of one of the necessary evils of steamboat operation, the periodic requirement to clean the boiler tubes while under way. In the fire tube boilers used on the ferryboats this was normally accomplished by throwing a scoop of sand into the firebox. If this practice was accomplished regularly, reasonably clean boilers could be expected, so chief engineers posted instructions requiring tube cleaning at stated intervals. The incident on the *Tamalpais* was a necessary operation at the wrong time. Needless to say, tubes were blown at night thereafter and the Northwestern Pacific bought 73 new Easter outfits.

A boiler flare-back on the *Eureka* deposited nearly a hundred red-hot bricks on the passenger deck. Luckily no one was in the vicinity at the time and the company was not subject to claims by passengers this time.

✓   ✓   ✓

No treatise on the ferryboats of San Francisco Bay would be complete without mention of the excursions operated on special occasions, often by the company itself, to foster business along the rail line. The South Pacific Coast ran Sunday excursions to Felton and Big Trees in the Santa Cruz Mountains, and the North Pacific Coast took holiday crowds to Camp Taylor in Lagunitas Canyon. These excursions by train and ferry started out quietly enough, but after a day of merriment and heroic consumption of beer, windows would be broken out of the coaches on the train and a fist fight or two on the boat would round off the day. Said Captain John Leale, "A German picnic was safe and orderly. I will leave unsaid what nationality indulged in the most scrapping."

The California Camera Club often chartered a boat for the day so that aspiring photographers could take pictures at interesting localities on the Bay. There is no doubt that many of the fine old

Captain John Leale is the third seated man from the left in this picture of the *Newark's* 100% hirsute crew as of June 10, 1899. To the captain's right is Chief Engineer George Scott. By the door in the background and slightly separated from the crew is the bartender. The brass pendulum-type clinometer in the background was commonly found on the center line of old ferryboats. The crew of the *Tamalpais,* photographed on deck at Sausalito in 1927 was only one-third hirsute. From left to right are Assistant Engineer A. Leslie Smith, Deckhand A. Simas, Chief Engineer Richard S. Wosser, Deckhand Nels Nelsson, First Officer A. Costa, Deckhand John Johnson, Captain M. J. Homburg, Deckhand J. Martignoni, Second Officer John Sawdon, Deckhand A. Silviera, Cabin Watchman W. Tobias, Deckhand M. V. Silva. *(Above: Southern Pacific; below: Northwestern Pacific)*

photographs which decorate this volume originally came as a result of the Bay outings of the Club. From the early 1890s until the late 1920s, a marvelous marine display known as the "Nights in Venice" was held in that beautiful cove between Corinthian and Belvedere Islands. Houses would be decorated with lanterns and colored lights, presenting a fantasy of loveliness on the gentle Marin shore. Special evening ferry excursions from San Francisco would bring boatloads of viewers to delight in observing this gorgeous spectacle from the water.

⁂

The ferryboat's whistle had an important place in the routine of a crossing, particularly on the congested routes converging on the Ferry Building. First came the long blast to warn all nearby craft that the vessel was about to leave the slip. Under way there were more soundings to inform other vessels of the pilot's intentions. He could notify the pilot of an approaching craft that he intended to pass port-to-port or starboard-to-starboard, by sounding one or two blasts. A similar signal in response from the other vessel acknowledged the notice. In fog, the whistle would be sounded at regular intervals.

There was one clear day when the *Tiburon* found herself sounding a salute every few seconds. The whistle cord had fouled in the walking beam and was pulled with every stroke. The cord could not be extricated while the wheels were turning and an unscheduled stop crossing the Golden Gate could be hazardous, so the *Tiburon* whistled her way clear to the terminal, where the cord was cleared easily.

On ferry steamers the whistle was mounted on the forward face of the smokestack, one facing either direction on the double-enders. Its impressiveness of appearance and tone was usually in proportion to the distinction of the vessel itself. Thus the *Alameda*, the *Santa Clara* and the five original Key Route boats all had big, beautiful polished brass whistles with deep throaty roars. The *Edward T. Jeffrey*, matching the Key boats in many respects, went them one better with her whistle, for it emitted a deep, hoarse, two-tone chord. Apparently the style in steam whistles changed from deepness to mellowness after the first World War, for the steamers built in the

1920s, with aspirations to distinction, all had pleasant chime tones. In the later Key System boats, two nicely-harmonized tones came from what appeared to be a single brass whistle. The Southern Pacific Shipyard's last two products were equipped with brass triads. The *Sacramento* had a cheerful calliope chord in middle range and major mode; the most musical sound on the Bay came from the low, mournful, minor chord of the *Eureka.*

Mass-produced auto ferries and the less pretentious boats of the more remote routes were generally equipped with unspectacular iron whistles that produced routine toots. The *City of San Rafael* was exceptional in that her two whistles did not match. Going toward San Quentin her voice was a toot from a thin whistle; Richmond-bound she had an undistinguished double tone from a stubby one.

The *Berkeley* was a boat of great beauty, one of the most distinguished on the Bay for sixty years. Her voice was certainly in a class by itself. To hear it was a memorable experience, evoking emotions akin to those aroused by the sight of a child on roller skates for the first time, or the sound of a 14-year-old boy trying to sing. The whistle started bravely with an earnest hiss of escaping steam; the sound progressed tentatively, hovering between a wheeze and a snore, until it finally reached its triumphant climax in a breathy and uncertain toot!

The Diesels arrived on the Bay in the 1920s with efficient air horns mounted on their pilot-houses. Their deep-toned, lingering blat was effective, dependable and standardized; it carried well and far, but did nothing whatever to lend character to the boat.

Commuters, except for the more musically inclined, came to take the whistle for granted, but to children it provided one of the big thrills of a trip, every aspect of which was an adventure. Small children were often frightened by the sudden blast of a loud whistle. Not unusual was the child waiting, with fingers in his ears, for it to sound at the beginning of a trip. After repeated ferry rides children became accustomed to the whistle, but it continued to lend a thrill of conquered terror to the experience of a trip on the Bay. Children were usually fascinated to discover

Captain Axel Lindstrom, commander of the Northwestern Pacific's relief ferry crew, had the heavy-lined face typical of Scandinavian veteran mariners and wore his modern uniform with a dignity befitting the responsibility of his chosen profession. His enviable record of several thousand trips without accident won him the admiration of his fellow sailors. By the pilothouse of the *Tamalpais* Captain Andrew Arntzen stands with First Officer Anders J. Gustafson in 1941, nearly at the end of N.W.P. ferry operations. Of the crew of the *San Leandro* on the very last day of Southern Pacific ferry service, in 1958, only Captain Richard Thomas and the officer to his left would be considered in uniform by the 1927 standards evident in the picture on a previous page. The *Eureka* made her run to San Francisco against the backdrop of the Golden Gate Bridge, as depicted opposite, just two days before the end of the Northwestern Pacific's ferry service. *(Opposite: Southern Pacific)*

the fact that a considerable amount of time elapsed between the visible puff of steam on the stack of a distant vessel and the sound of its whistle. The Diesels lacked the visible steam, but some of them had a light that went on while the air horn sounded.

✓ ✓ ✓

The ferryboat officers on the passenger boats were always decked out in neat blue serge uniforms trimmed in gold, which closely resembled the current naval officers' uniform. One ferry captain stated that in a marine emergency there is nothing which helps an officer more than his uniform when the need for asserting authority arises. The officers' uniform stands out in a crowd so that there is no question who is in charge and who is to give orders. Until 1908 the captain was the only officer with the insignia of his office on the cap, but thereafter the railroad company adopted standard uniforms for all officers which varied seasonally in but one respect: From November first to May first the crowns of the officers' caps were blue serge to match the uniform; from May first to November first the crowns of the caps were pure white. The officer's position was designated by the lettering on his cap and his years of service were indicated by the number of stars worn on the left sleeve, about six inches above the cuff, one gold star for every five years of service. In later

years, even the cabin attendants were uniformed and only in a work detail would blue dungarees be noted.

Retirement of ferry employees was always a sad day, for it was not uncommon for the retiring person to have as much as 45 years of service with the same company. When a captain retired, his brother master mariners on the Bay were fully cognizant of the occasion and frequently the boats would be decorated in gala international signal flags, house flags and pennants. As the boats passed, the exchange of whistles in a salute of tribute to the captain who had so justly earned retirement, brought many a tear to the commuters who had learned to admire and respect these first citizens of the Bay of San Francisco. The most spectacular of these occasions took place on March 1, 1941, when six ferry skippers handled the steamer *Eureka*, on a farewell tour of the Bay as captains, and ferry steamers bid "Good-bye" to the Marin trade that had flourished since 1868. As the *Eureka* passed the company's shops at Tiburon, the *Cazadero* and the *Tamalpais* stood silently in the slips, not yet cooled down from the previous day's operation. Whistles were blown by shopmen in a resounding salute, answered by the *Eureka's* mellow chime blown by Captains Veredellet, Arntzen, Palmer, Wahrgren, Jaeckel and Lindstrom. The end had really come, and no one was ready for it.

III

The Anatomy of the Ferryboat

THE MATERIAL used for the construction of the first San Francisco Bay ferries was wood, fine fir from the greatest of the forests of Oregon, shaped by master craftsmen, shipwrights who, for the most part, had learned their magnificent trade in European shipyards long before they made the journey to California. Many had been lured to the land of promise by the news of gold, and after fruitless pursuit of this precious metal, one by one they deserted the mines and found ready employment in their former trades, where their excellent training and experience brought them a ready livelihood again. The early shipwrights were artisans of the highest order, whose education not only included the ability to loft and lay out frames and planking and all the rough work of the shipyards, but also resulted in their being able to do the most exquisite paneling, graced with carvings from their skillful knives.

The stanchions, deck beams, knees, braces, balustrades and framing of the saloon deck cabins were masterpieces in joinery. Elaborate moldings were carefully fashioned into decorative trim, often in graceful curved lines approximating the shape of the vessel which they artistically adorned. In the cabins was exceedingly intricate glasswork, stained, colored or etched, set in beautiful hardwood framing which enhanced its beauty.

The old shipwright could hew out the planking from the tree, if necessary, but he carefully selected his timber, assuring that it was of proper grain for steaming and bending into shape without loss of strength. A most prized asset to the shipbuilder was the steam box, for timbers could be shaped into the most graceful of lines after they had been prepared in it.

Principal members were secured with huge driftbolts, and the balance of the timbering and planking was attached with ship spikes which, in the olden days, were made of copper alloy. Most of the ferryboats had a double hull below the water line, with planking applied to the frames both on the exterior and interior of the vessel. These hulls were caulked to keep the seams tight, using oakum and various favorite caulking compounds from pitch to white lead.

Steel hulls were constructed for many of the later ferryboats beginning in 1898, but wooden-hulled boats were still being built as late as 1928. With a few exceptions, the superstructures continued to be made of wood, but on most of the later boats they were much plainer in finish than the elegant boats built before World War I. The *Peralta* and second *Yerba Buena* were in a class by themselves for latter-day elegance.

On San Francisco Bay were many builders of boats and ships, busy constructing a great variety of vessels for ocean and inland waters. Many of them in the old days were noted for their sailing ships, coastal schooners and river boats. Production of ferries was not their most significant output, but it was due to the extensive marine activity on the Pacific Coast that the shipyards were available for ferryboat building. Most of the ferries on the Bay were locally built; some were built elsewhere, but of these only five are known to have been built specifically for service on San Francisco Bay. From the ideas of local builders emerged the special characteristics that became the hallmark of the San Francisco Bay ferryboat.

Although plans for these steamers often came from the naval architect's drawing board, many of the builders maintained an in-house capability of boat design, and plans were actually at a minimum. This accounts for the fact that very few drawings exist today, for those which were prepared have been lost or destroyed. As one boatbuilder said to his crew after he had been com-

and slightly to the left is the main and cabin deck superstructure in process of prefabrication for a ferryboat. The *Alameda* is high in the dry dock at the right, still bearing her old square pilothouses. Perhaps this visit to the yard was the time they were to be replaced with the more graceful rounded "New York" style wheelhouses. In the foreground of this picture is the west yard of the Moore Shipbuilding Co. At the bottom of the page is the Monticello Steamship Co.'s *Asbury Park* undergoing routine drydocking in 1920 at the Barnes & Tibbets yard in Oakland. On the top of the opposite page is John W. Dickie's Alameda shipyard with the *San Jose* and the first *Yerba Buena* under construction for Key Route. The big scissors rig at the end of the outfitting pier is for hoisting machinery into the boats. The Santa Fe steamer *San Pablo* is on the marine railway of the Moore & Scott Iron Works, Oakland. The big *Sausalito* of Northwestern Pacific looms high in the S.P. drydock in Oakland for repair of rudder damage. The peculiar configuration of the underwater body was to permit acceptance of a freight apron for transfer of narrow gauge cars. (*Above and top right: Roy D. Graves collection; below: Gabriel Moulin photo, William Knorp collection; bottom, this page: Monticello Steamship Co.; bottom, opposite: Northwestern Pacific*)

Here are two views of the Southern Pacific shipyard at the foot of Peralta Street in Oakland. The closeup view, above, shows the end of the steamer *Newark*, at the left, entering the marine railway slip. Below that is a 1919 view showing the yard at a time of great activity with at least three boats on hand and a fourth under construction, and with the *Garden City* steaming down the Estuary toward the Bay. The boat in the yard nearest the Estuary, with the tall thin stack, is the *Melrose*. Just this side of her with the shorter, thicker stack is the Northwestern Pacific car ferry *Ukiah*, about to be dismantled for her subsequent rebuilding as the *Eureka*. In front of her

The fine Western Pacific ferry *Edward T. Jeffery* was launched at the Moore & Scott Iron Works yard in Oakland on July 19, 1913. Below, the workmen are putting finishing touches on the Southern Pacific's auto ferry, *Klamath*, at the Bethlehem Steel Co.'s Union Yard in San Francisco, and the stand is being constructed for the launching ceremony that was held December 27, 1924. *(Above: Gabriel Moulin; below: Bethlehem Steel Co.)*

missioned to build a vessel, "Now, boys, we're going to build a steamboat, about this—long!"

While the older builders were less prolific than some of the later firms, they deserve mention in this history. John G. North in San Francisco built the ferries *Clinton*, 1853, and *Contra Costa*, 1857, first of the name, as well as the river queens *Chrysopolis*, 1860, and *Capital*, 1866, both of which were later converted to double-end ferry operation.

The *Amelia*, 1863, was built by the Owens Shipyard in San Francisco, the only known ferry steamer produced by this early yard. Patrick Tiernan, a fine naval architect, built the *Amador* in 1869 as a single-ender, although she was later rebuilt by the Central Pacific into a double-ended ferry. He also designed the *Tiburon*, 1884, and the *Ukiah*, 1890, which were built in Tiburon by the San Francisco & North Pacific Railway.

William E. Collyer, a brilliant designer of inland vessels, was one of the famous family of New York shipbuilders, including George (*Rip Van Winkle*, 1845; *Niagara*, 1845; *Francis Skiddy*, 1852), Thomas (*Armenia*, 1848; *Reindeer*, 1850; *El Dorado*, 1850; *Daniel Drew*, 1860) and William (*Black Warrior*, 1852). At his Potrero yard at the foot of Humboldt Street in San Francisco he built the *James M. Donahue*, 1875, that saw nearly sixty years of service on the Bay despite being a single-ender. He probably also built the *Newark*, 1877, *Bay City*, 1878, and *Garden City*, 1879, there. His associate Austin Hills, is said to have designed and built the *Encinal* in 1888. The Potrero yard must have gone out of business, as it disappeared from the city directory in 1879.

The Central Pacific Railroad went into the boatbuilding business in 1868 at Oakland Point, that year producing the passenger ferry *El Capitan*. There followed three car ferries, the *Thoroughfare* in 1871, first of the name, *Transit*, 1876, and the capacious *Solano*, 1879. Finally in 1883 came the passenger boat, *Piedmont*. These boats were built to the Central Pacific's own requirements; in addition to them the yard also modified and repaired vessels already in the service of the company, notably the river speedster *Chrysopolis* which was converted to the double-ended *Oakland* in 1875.

The Southern Pacific took over Central Pacific operations on February 17, 1885, including the shipyard, which it soon moved from Oakland Point to the foot of Peralta Street in Oakland. Here boats were repaired and remodeled for 23 years; then the yard built 7 big ferries in 15 years: the *Melrose*, 1908, the second *Thoroughfare*, 1912, assembled the second *Alameda*, which had been prefabricated in the East in 1913, as was the *Santa Clara* in 1915; the train ferry *Contra Costa*, 1914; the Northwestern Pacific's *Eureka*, 1922, from the remains of the *Ukiah*, and the second *Sacramento*, 1923, from the bones of the old *Newark*. The last two were the largest double-end passenger ferries to be built anywhere in the world; the *Solano* and *Contra Costa* were the largest ferries built anywhere, for they were made to haul entire transcontinental trains. These records stood for many decades, so the Southern Pacific yard's output compared favorably with that of any shipbuilder.

Barnes & Tibbets maintained a shipyard in Oakland where a large marine railway was used to drydock the boats, but there is no record of any ferries being constructed in that yard.

The Dickie Brothers gained fame as designers of ferryboats on San Francisco Bay, and constructed many of the boats they designed, but they are primarily noted in maritime history for the development of the Pacific Coast steam schooner. These men were alert to the requirements of coastal shipowners and able to produce vessels which met their needs and produced long service. John W. Dickie was the firm's naval architect and, with his brothers James, William and George, had offices at 642 Second Street in San Francisco and a shipyard at Hunter's Point. In 1882 they suffered reverses that forced them into bankruptcy, but soon opened shop again at 7 Spear Street. In the 1890s John W. Dickie bought the old Hay & Wright yard in Alameda which had constructed the Nickel Ferry's *Rosalie* in 1893. Here he built the *Sausalito* in 1894 for the North Pacific Coast and for the same railroad the *Cazadero* and the narrow gauge car ferry *Lagunitas* in 1903. That same year he built the first *Yerba Buena* and *San Jose* for the Key Route; these were followed by three sister boats, the *San Francisco*, 1905, *Claremont*, 1907 and *Fernwood*, 1908.

Both of James Robertson's yards appear in these three pictures. The *Charles Van Damme*, left, was built at Benicia. Robertson himself appears in the left foreground. Five years later, at the same yard, occurred the problem shown in the bottom picture when the *Aven J. Hanford* stuck halfway down the ways and needed the assistance of two tugs to tow her into the water. The well-dressed spectators for the launching of the Rodeo-Vallejo Ferry's fine new boat had more of a show than they expected. Mr. Hanford stands directly behind Miss Marileah Speas, the girl with the flowers in the center picture, taken at Alameda in 1923. She was the nine-year-old daughter of Harry E. Speas, general manager of the Golden Gate Ferry Co., second from the right in the picture; Oscar H. Klatt stands between father and daughter. The boat being launched this time is the *Golden Gate*. (*Top: Captain Thomas Newsome collection; bottom: San Francisco Maritime Museum*)

The most prolific of the boatbuilders was the Union Iron Works in San Francisco, a firm founded by the enterprising Peter Donahue, who also owned the San Francisco & North Pacific Railway. Peter might have started the Iron Works, but he apparently did not believe in patronizing it for his S.F.&N.P.'s wooden ferryboats were all constructed elsewhere. The Union Iron Works built no ferryboats until 1898, but once in the field, this yard produced more boats than all the others during the ensuing years. No wooden hulls were built here; all were of steel, but the skill of Union's master shipwrights was demonstrated in the fine wooden superstructures they produced. This firm built the first steel-hulled ferryboat on the Bay, the *Berkeley* in 1898, and followed her with the *San Pablo*, 1900, and the *Tamalpais*, 1901. In 1905 the Union Iron Works was purchased by Bethlehem Steel Corporation and has since operated as Bethlehem's Union Yard. Since this change in ownership, the yard produced the *Napa Valley* in 1910, *San Pedro*, 1911, *San Mateo* and *Shasta* in 1922, *Yosemite*, 1923, *El Paso* and *New Orleans* in 1924, *Klamath*, 1925, and *Fresno, Stockton* and *Mendocino* in 1927.

The brothers Boole were shipwrights. In the 1870s George W. did business as Boole & Webster, Shipwrights, Calkers & Sparmakers. In the 1880s William A. opened a yard in Oakland which built many sailing vessels. Later the Boole name appears in the maritime history of San Francisco Bay as Middlemas & Boole, which sold out to Moore & Scott in 1909. This partnership built the car ferry *Bridgit* for the Oakland & Antioch and the Western Pacific's *Edward T. Jeffrey* in 1913 before it became involved in World War I shipbuilding. After the firm changed its name to Moore Dry Dock Co. it produced four fine ferryboats in 1927, the *Redwood Empire*, the *Lake Tahoe*, the ill-fated *Peralta* and the second *Yerba Buena*. It then went on to build three ferries for the San Diego & Coronado Ferry Co.: the *Coronado* in 1929, the *San Diego*, 1931, and in 1954 the *Crown City*. This most honored and skillful shipbuilding institution survived until 1960 and at this writing the ferries it produced are still active on the waters of San Diego Bay and Puget Sound.

James Robertson was the builder of many of the later wooden ferryboats, first at his yard in Benicia and later in newer quarters in Alameda. His boats included the *Charles Van Damme* in 1916 and the *City of Richmond*, 1921. The next year he brought out the *Aven J. Hanford* and the first Diesel-electric ferry on the Bay, the *Golden Gate* and followed her with another the next year, the *Golden West*. After these pioneering efforts he produced in 1924 the *City of San Rafael*, last of the many side-wheelers built on San Francisco Bay. This fine shipbuilder was killed in an accident while moving a lathe in his own plant and the Bay lost a master craftsman in his passing.

George Arms' General Engineering & Drydock Co. built the last of the wooden boats for Bay ferry service, and also rebuilt the *Yerba Buena, San Francisco, Claremont* and *Fernwood* from passenger ferries to automobile configuration for the Golden Gate Ferry Co. General's yard was in Alameda during its ferryboat building years, and its artisans produced fine sturdy vessels which withstood the ravages of time and sailed for many years after the companies for which they were built had long disappeared. Several were still operating well into the 1960s. All the new boats were built for automobile service: the all-steel *Santa Rosa*, 1927, for the Northwestern Pacific and, for the Golden Gate Ferry, the wooden *Golden State*, 1926, *Golden Bear, Golden Poppy* and *Golden Shore* in 1927 and the *Golden Age*, 1928.

The Pacific Coast Engineering Co. of Alameda in 1956 built the last ferryboat to be constructed on San Francisco Bay, the *Carquinez*, for the State of California which was then operating the Martinez-Benicia Ferry. This steel Diesel vessel was designed by Philip H. Thearle, a San Diego naval architect, on lines markedly different from those of any other boats seen on the Bay.

On only three occasions were ferryboats made specifically for service on San Francisco Bay by builders elsewhere. In 1877 John Englis of New York built the *San Rafael* and the *Saucelito* for the North Pacific Coast Railroad. The Los Angeles Shipbuilding & Drydock Co. of San Pedro was the successful bidder in 1923 for construction of the *Hayward* and the *San Leandro* for the Key System. Finally, in 1957, long after most of the ferries had disappeared from the Bay, the Western Pacific had its new car ferry, the *Las Plumas*, built by

Governor Goodwin J. Knight looks on approvingly as his wife cracks the champagne bottle over the bow of the State of California ferryboat *Carquinez* in September 1956 at the Pacific Coast Engineering Co.'s Alameda shipyard. Thirty years earlier, when the Key System's last word in ferries, the *Yerba Buena*, was to be launched on a cold November day at the Oakland yard of the Moore Dry Dock Co., Mrs. Lester S. Ready, wife of the Key's president, was ready with a bottle of prohibition champagne to christen it. Among her guests were the Mesdames Tirzah Jones, Edward L. Soulé, L. H. Bullock, Harold Johnson and Iva Sutter. The completed *Yerba Buena* appears in the bottom picture. (*Left: Pacific Coast Engineering Co.; middle: Gabriel Moulin photo*)

the Albina Engine & Machine Works of Portland, Oregon.

The Risdon Iron Works, which adjoined—and was later absorbed by—the Union Iron Works in San Francisco, built ferryboat engines, as did the Fulton Iron Works which was located at Gashouse Cove in San Francisco's Marina district.

The boatbuilders, the engine builders, all artisans who took great pride in their work, fashioned the ferryboats of San Francisco Bay. They built into them a reliability which withstood the ravages of time, and gave the ferryman the tools with which to perform his valiant service.

✁   ✁   ✁

Arrangements of the passenger ferries followed a familiar pattern which was pretty much standardized. The boats had a long hold, terminated by a collision bulkhead at either end, which was a subdivision requirement of both the Steamboat Inspection Service of the Department of Commerce and the Classification Society. The portion of the vessel's hull from the collision bulkhead to the bow (or stern, as case might be) was usually devoted to tanks or steering apparatus. The long hold between the collision bulkheads contained the machinery spaces, boiler rooms, crew locker space and, on some vessels, the restaurant.

The main deck was the largest deck on the vessel and was sponsoned out over the side of the hull to provide adequate deck space for carrying both mail carts and passengers. This overhang was cantilevered to a point amidships which, on paddle wheel boats, extended twenty feet beyond the hull on either side, to accommodate the paddles. The deck was supported on the hull by means of struts which jutted from the main body of the ship. Athwartship, a truss of steel stanchions and tie rods supported the midship structure in way of the paddles, and from the outboard extremities of the truss, an outboard girder supported the outboard bearing of the paddle wheels. This construction was unique with ferryboats, and is not to be found on any other type of vessel.

The hulls were usually copper-sheathed to protect the wood, and this sheathing added to the life of the planking to such a degree that its high cost was offset by reducing the interval between planking renewals. The extreme edge of the main deck was protected with a guardrail of ironbark, since

this was the point of contact between the boat and the piling of the slip. The guardrail took a terrific beating, for the progress of the boat as it entered the slip was broken by veering the vessel from side to side as well as reversing the engines. In stormy weather a boat would frequently receive so violent a jar in landing as to tear off sections of the guardrail.

The arrangement of the main deck was relatively uniform on the double-ended boats. The entire center section, or fidley (sometimes spelled fiddley), was taken up with the engine casing which housed the engine control platform, the uptakes and breeching from the boilers, the escape pipes and whistle pipe. It also housed the A-frame which supported the walking beam, and the cylinder as well as the main rod and main crank occupied this compartment. The fidley was constructed of steel, usually the only part of the superstructure made of this material.

Two long alleyways ran longitudinally on either side of the fidley, with huge sliding doors at either end. These were used for the express and baggage carts and, in the early days of motoring, for the horseless carriages which the railroad companies reluctantly chose to accept. Outboard of the alleyways were large spaces devoted to thwartship seats or benches, divided amidships by the paddle boxes which were massive enclosures with watertight doors at either end to enable ready servicing of the paddle wheels. Rest rooms were generally located at ends of the paddle box housing. A newsstand was common on the main deck, since the prospective customers could stand in the freight alleyways while pawing over the merchandise without encroaching on the areas devoted to seats. The bootblack stand was usually nearby. The interior appointments of the main deck were austere, raw planking covering the deck and tongue-and-groove lumber constituting the finish work.

The upper, or cabin deck was a different story. Here the joinerwork of the shipwrights basked in the glory of its magnificence, for this was the ladies' deck, complete with cabin attendant, cabin matron, ladies' lounges, and outdoor seats shielded from the raw Bay winds by glassed partitions of elegance which rivaled the cabin. On the upper deck, in the older boats, luscious red velvet coverings on the seats and potted palms gave color

Captain Alfred Wahrgren stands at the steam tiller in the wheelhouse of the *Cazadero*. The wooden steering wheel, no longer in use at the time the picture at the left was taken, was detached from the steering gear so that the spinning handles would not endanger someone in the pilothouse. The small wheel in the *San Leandro*, below, controls a steering engine. Captain Richard Thomas's hand is on the engine room telegraph. *(Below: Southern Pacific)*

and dignity to the cabin that could scarcely be matched on any other conveyance available to the public. The view from the upper deck was normally unobstructed, even when the boat was tied up in the slip and hence this was the favorite seating locality of most of the ferry travelers. But if the commuter wore dungarees or other clothes which would normally not be seen in the parlor, he avoided the upper deck, for he was not in harmony with its décor.

The uppermost deck on the ferries was called the hurricane deck, or texas deck, after the grand manner of the river boats which were the proud antecedents of the ferryboats. This deck was clear save for the pilothouse and adjoining officers' quarters at either end, the ventilators, stack and walking beam. Passengers were not welcome on this deck which was strictly for the boat's officers and crew. The sanctity of the pilothouse was enforced by law and was not to be encroached upon by any persons who did not have to do with the navigation of the vessel. Said Captain John Leale of the *Newark*, "One rule of the company I must plead guilty of having broken, and that is having guests in my pilothouse. Many of the old Oakland and Alameda commuters can testify to that. Nevertheless my mind was always on the job. Many children now grown to manhood and womanhood have told me of the thrill that came to them with the privilege of blowing the whistle. The responsibility of the act was first impressed upon all these young guests by the Captain. I would even pick up an interesting stranger and show him Bay points."

Captain Leale was not alone among Bay ferry captains who enjoyed company in the pilothouse. The author has enjoyed many a trip even the more as a guest of one of the venerable masters of San Francisco Bay. Invitations to the pilothouse were, however, extended infrequently and carefully, and never at a time of fog, storm or when steering might otherwise be difficult.

The steering wheel in the pilothouse of the ferryboats was a massive thing to behold, particularly in the older vessels which were built before the days of the steering engine. These wheels were made of the finest hardwoods, doweled together and polished with great care. On some boats, a wheel large enough to provide the neces-

sary steering power would have had to be so huge that, as an alternative, two wheels were mounted on one shaft. This arrangement enabled four sailors to man the wheel at once, when navigating under difficult conditions. Even then, when tides were running hard, the men had to strain at their labors to hold the vessel on her course.

The pilothouses were generally elevated a few feet above the hurricane deck so that there would be room, below the level of the wheelhouse floor, for the wheels of large diameter to be recessed into the space below and permit the sailors to stand close to the horizontal diameter of the ponderous wheels which they were obliged to manhandle. Activity in the pilothouse in the days of "Scowegian Steam" steering was lively and marked with a display of brawn seldom encountered in the machine age. A deck sailor on the ferryboats needed all his health and strength to operate the helm of those inland giants.

Pilothouse activity changed greatly in later years with the coming of the steering engine. Steering was easier with the little throttle lever of the steam steering engine, or the miniature wheel of the more modern electric steering engine. Nevertheless, this took some of the dignity out of the art of steering by command, at which four powerful sailors strained at the double wheel in the magnificent tradition of the sea.

The work horse of the San Francisco Bay ferry, until the turn of the century, was the famous walking beam engine. Nearly all major boats built before 1898 had it; the only new one built since then appeared on the *Cazadero* in 1903. Many walking beams were still noticeable on the Bay in the 1920s; by the end of the 1930s most were gone, although two were still in operation in the 1950s.

The walking beam was the most conspicuous part of the vertical beam engine, a low-pressure, single-cylinder steam engine which had progressed but little from the Cornish pumping engines in England in the days of James Watt. The principle of these engines was based upon a large volume of steam working on a huge single piston area; pistons and cylinders five or six feet in diameter were not uncommon. Steam pressures ranged from 50 to 65 pounds per square inch, steam being supplied in enormous quantities by two or more fire tube boilers. All of these engines exhausted into

Pictures of two different walking beams illustrate the difference between the crosshead and crank ends. The black beam of the *James M. Donahue* is tilted in a position to display the massive rod that turns the crank of the vessel's paddle wheel. The figure of Northwestern Pacific's Port Engineer Joseph Wosser suggests the size of the huge apparatus. The white walking beam of the *Cazadero*, built 28 years later, is tilted to show the massive linkage, U-straps and keys that held these gigantic assemblies together as it was pushed and pulled by the great piston rod, here shown at the upper end of its 12-foot stroke. The structure, usually hidden, of the engine, A-frame and paddle wheel, is well shown in the two pictures opposite, taken in 1920, of the dismantled *Ukiah* before she was rebuilt as the *Eureka*. They show the immense wooden gallows A-frame, the paddle detail, the transverse tie bars to support the outboard beam and the Howe truss to hold the outboard bearing of the paddle shaft. The lower view clearly shows the single cylinder and the immense steam chest. The large white cylinder at the left of the upper picture is the vessel's donkey boiler. *(Above: Roy D. Graves photo; opposite, two pictures: Marshall Silverthorn collection)*

Assistant Chief Engineer Charles A. Kircher bars over the engine of the Northwestern Pacific's *Cazadero* to bring up vacuum. The stars on his sleeve represent over 35 years of service, as of November, 1940, when the picture was taken. At the left is the crank end of the *Eureka's* walking beam, showing the inside of the hatch opening and the tremendous connecting rod. Below is the corresponding view of the crosshead end of the beam, showing the keys of the linkage bars connecting crosshead and beam. *(Left and below: William Knorp photo)*

a vacuum produced either by a surface or jet condenser, and this pressure differential from 50 pounds or more per square inch of steam to 27 inches of vacuum was adequate to develop the required horsepower.

The charm of the engine rested in the fact that almost every moving part was large and impressive, exposed to the view of the passenger if he desired to watch the ponderous engine in its working. The power was transmitted from the single cylinder to the enormous crank which drove the paddles by means of a gigantic linkage bar or beam, known as the walking beam, which rocked in its cradle atop an A-frame in the open air of the hurricane deck. The beams were usually 24 feet from the center of the crosshead link bearings at their one extremity to the main rod bearing at the other. The bearing shaft upon which it operated was at least 12 inches in diameter and the crosshead and main rod pins were at least 8 inches. All the beams were of the same construction, a center casting with six strut arms at strategic localities which formed a diamond pattern entirely surrounded by a forged steel rim. These beams rocked with a rhythmic stroke of from 20 to 24 times a minute, and their graceful operation lent both dignity and fascination to the ferry craft which they so ably propelled.

All of the connections at the bearing points on the beam engines were made with U-straps and keys, which were tapered in such a fashion that when driven home the bearing could be tightened, when driven in the opposite direction, the assembly could be taken apart. The A-frames which supported the walking beam bearings were huge wooden structures in the early boats, made of massive timbers which toed on the bedplate stringers at the vessel's keel. The timbering was held together with huge driftbolts, with hardwood knee braces to arrest any motion. In spite of this massive construction, the wooden A-frames gradually worked loose through the years and had to be replaced, either with new wooden structures or with new A-frames of steel.

The main shaft for the paddles was continuous, being broken only at the point of location of the crank. The bearings of this shaft were located on the A-frame, at the point of the hull where the shaft left the vessel, and on an outboard steel beam at the outer extremity of the paddle box. The shaft was about 15 inches in diameter, and the paddle wheel hub was keyed to the shaft in way of the paddle wheel. These wheels were over 20 feet in diameter, and the largest on the Bay were the original 42-foot monsters on the *Newark*. The hub, spokes and rims of the wheels were made of steel; the buckets, or driving members of the paddles, were huge wooden timbers 2 feet wide and 6 inches thick. These were expendable members which, if damaged, could be replaced by carpenters without drydocking the ship. The buckets were held in place by bolted U-straps and could be adjusted as to position on the spokes if the draft of the vessel changed for any reason.

The *San Pablo* and the second *Tamalpais* had steel buckets which feathered, presenting a thin edge to slice into the water, straightening to present a flat surface for the power pull, then slicing out again. This was accomplished by an eccentric which changed the angle of the buckets as the wheel turned. On neither of these vessels was the new design particularly successful, and horses could never be transported on either boat due to a peculiar rocking motion attributed to the wheels. It had a tendency to make the animals dizzy. Since the cost of upkeep of this type of wheel was not commensurate with the advantages gained, if any, its design was not repeated on Bay ferryboats.

The majority of the walking beam boats were equipped with jet condensers in which the exhaust steam was mixed with a continuous spray of salt water, causing a vacuum at the exhaust side of the cylinder. The mixture thus produced was pumped over the side, and as one can readily see, a tremendous amount of feedwater was required for the engine. Later beam engines and all other types of steam engines used in the boats were equipped with shell and tube condensers wherein the condensed exhaust steam was recovered for boiler feed.

The face of the beam engine at the engine control platform was a virtual masterpiece of machine-work, magnificently polished and glistening with fresh applications of lubricant. The steam chest console was adjacent to the cylinder and housed the valves, four in number, two for admission of steam and two for exhaust. The valve gear which

Many of the screw-propelled ferryboats were powered by marine compound engines like the one, left, which was used by the U.S. harbor boat *General Mifflin*. At the bottom of the page is the engine room of the Monticello steamer *General Frisbie,* showing the momentarily halted high-speed triple expansion engine of the type affectionately known to marine engineers as "knee action turbines." The engraved likeness of a marine engine of the same type appeared for years on chief engineers' licenses issued by the Department of Commerce. *(Below: U.S. Department of Commerce)*

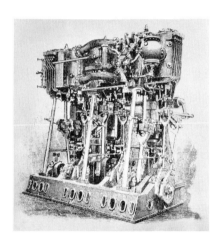

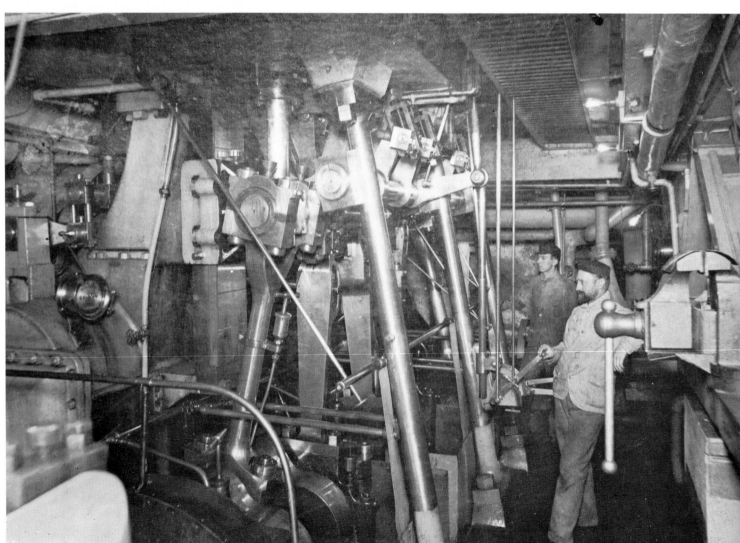

was attached to the steam chests was resplendent with polished guide strips secured by acorn-headed bolts, and intricate stems and cams, spring-actuated for closing, working within the guides. A thwartship camshaft operated the valve stems once the engine was started, but the starting was accomplished by hand. A smaller camshaft also could operate the valves when manually pried with a long, steel bar. A spare bar was always carried for emergencies, but who would expect a bar of steel almost two inches in diameter to break when operated by a mere man?

To start the engine, the engineer would bar the desired valves into the open position, turning the engine over slowly. The ends of the eccentric shafts on the main crank were marked to permit the engineer to know in what position the crank was at any given time, for the crank could not be seen by the operator. After the engine gained momentum, the engineer would throw the reverse lever which dropped the eccentric arms down on the camshaft, and the engine would continue automatically. Reversing, or docking by reversing, was accomplished all by hand and took great skill and dexterity.

On the main deck of each beam-engined boat, there was an enormous pole carried in a holder on or near the paddle box. Should the single-cylinder engine become stuck on dead center, the pole was used to pry the shaft by means of the paddles so that the engine could be started once more. When the pole was required, all engine hands were called to man it, and a watertight door to the paddlebox would be opened and the wheel would be thus pried, using a spoke as the point of contact.

Boilers for these beam engines were large, and all of them were fire-tube, the Freeman Dryback being the most frequently used. This boiler derived its name from the fact that the back wall was made of dry brick as opposed to the type of boilers which had water legs. The fire was created in burners at the front of the boiler, would progress through the lower portion of the boiler to the rear combustion chamber, and then pass through the tubes to heat the water. All early-day ferries burned coal, but in 1901, William J. Thomas, genius master mechanic of the North Pacific Coast Railroad, installed the first oil burners for the successful oil firing of ferry boilers on the Bay in the

second *Tamalpais*. Since then crude oil was used as a fuel for all steam vessels on the Bay.

In 1898 the Southern Pacific went to higher pressure steam engines in ferry service with the *Berkeley*, which had a triple expansion engine; in the next five years the Key Route followed suit with triples and twin two-cylinder compounds. The *Berkeley*, first double-end ferryboat on the Bay to be propelled by a screw, was not particularly successful at first and much experimentation with propellers was needed to make the boat manageable. She knocked down more piling than any other boat on the bay until the trouble was eventually corrected. Although the *Berkeley's* life span in service was nearly sixty years, her owners never built another propeller driven passenger ferry. Paddle wheels had a fine record with the S.P., and back to paddles they went.

The *Berkeley* was equipped with dynamos at the builder's yard and one by one they appeared on the other boats. Electric lights replaced the oil and gaslights on the ferries. With departure of the gas lamps, the Victorian era of ferryboat appointments drew to a close, and the flicker of the gas flame was superseded by the flicker of the Mazda lamp which derived its power from the single-cylinder steam-driven generator. The first use of electric lights on the ferries had been an experimental installation on the *Piedmont* in 1888, and soon proved safe and dependable.

In 1922, the Key System went to turbo-electric drive for ferries, and its first vessels for this purpose were the smoothest riding ships on the Bay. In spite of this advance in boat design, records kept by the Southern Pacific and the Key System showed that no significant economies could be demonstrated, either in use of fuel or in repairs, to justify the newer design, and the old walking beam engine rocked in its cradle for many a year alongside the modern turbo-electric boats of the Key System. An engineer on the Key is supposed to have been the author of the following instruction on turbine operation, written after long years of service on the reciprocating engines:

"De firs ting is for commence hoil pump. When preshur hits Ho-K, den commence de turbeen. Hopen de trottel valve pretty slow so de steam what has turn to water come out de lille hole on bottom. When de water hain't no more, plug de

The turbo-electric *San Leandro's* engine controls have none of the romance of the hand-operated bar of walking beam boats. A modern electric rheostat controls the speed with a small handwheel and a few well-placed switches. The detail of the paddle wheel on the opposite page clearly shows the huge beam supporting the outboard paddle shaft bearing. The paddles or buckets, bolted to the wheel frame, can be adjusted to suit the vessel's water line. *(Above: Southern Pacific)*

---

lille hole by shut de valve, dan hopen de trottle some more when de turbeen has start to turn over (not whole mashine, just de rotor). Hif you hain't done it by now, get some vacuum!

"Now's de time for look for see hif you hear someting, when you look good she is Ho-K for mak go more fast.

"Look de hoil.

"Look de water.

"Look de steam.

"Look hefry ting. Hif she Ho-K, take hime to top speed.

"Now if she hain't blow up, she is Ho-K for put de load. Try firs de hexiter, see if she work. Put your han' hon de wire, de hodder han' hon de turbeen. Hif your harm feel like your foot's asleep, she Ho-K, so switch de load and let her go!"

When the Key System brought out its last two boats, the *Peralta* and the *Yerba Buena* in 1926 and 1927, these boats were intended to be the finest ferryboats known. Steel hulls, decks and superstructure were set off by gleaming plate glass windows, mahogany pilothouses and fine murals on interior bulkheads. The power, of course, was turbo-electric.

Naval architects of the Moore Dry Dock Co. cleverly designed these vessels with a good deal of reserve buoyancy and two other singular features. All other propeller-driven double-ended boats had the disadvantage that the forward, non-driving screw rotated at full speed. The new Key System boats were designed so that the forward propeller rotated at one-third full speed to minimize the friction which would be caused if the wheel were allowed to "windmill."

The other unusual feature of these boats was a pair of counterbalance ballast tanks, one at either end of the vessel. Whichever direction the double-ended ferry was moving, the after ballast tank was kept full of salt water to control the trim of the ship when passengers surged forward as she approached the slip at the end of the trip. While passengers were boarding the boat for the next trip a huge centrifugal pump transferred the liquid ballast to the opposite tank which soon would be the stern. We will presently see an unexpected result of this feature on the *Peralta*.

When the *Golden Gate* appeared in 1923, the Golden Gate Ferry Co. brought an important innovation, San Francisco Bay's first Diesel-electric ferryboat. One of the first Diesel engineers to be hired by this line was Christian B. Nielsen who, as a young man, had been second assistant engineer on the maiden voyage of the first seagoing craft to be powered by Diesel, the Danish ship *Selandia*, which appeared on the Atlantic in 1912. Nielsen was responsible for the making of many a young Diesel engineer, for it was on the boats of the infant Golden Gate Ferry Co. that American merchant seamen were able to get Diesel experience. In World War II Chris went back to sea in Diesel ships, this time for Uncle Sam as chief engineer of the Army Transport *Pueblo*.

The transition from steam to Diesel was sometimes all but impossible for the ferry engineers to make. "For the first six months," said Albert Leslie

Smith, who preferred the steam, "even my soup tasted like Diesel oil to me." The first engines had overhead valves operated by a camshaft with a great jerky motion, which caused Chief Engineer Charles Kircher to remark, when time came to start the engine, "All right, boys, let's feed the chickens." The sharp valve action made the linkage look like a brood of chickens pecking up grain.

One ferry engineer, sentenced to an ignominious end among the Diesels, wrote a letter to his brother which expressed the sentiments of the ferrymen quite well. It read, "Dear Bill: This engine I have to operate reluctantly was invented by a Dr. Rudolph Diesel. Although I think he invented it without any malicious intent, I cannot prove it. To start the engine takes some knowledge, steady nerves and a certain amount of bravery. First you turn on the starting air and let the engine turn several revolutions this way. The primary purpose of this act is to clear the cylinders, but truthfully, it helps the engineer gain a little self confidence before giving it the works. It also adds prestige to the act in the minds of the observers.

"After closing the indicator cocks, turn on the fuel, shut your eyes and open the starting valve wide open. If everything is as it should be, the relief valve will pop with considerable noise and everything about you will begin to shake and tremble. This means that the engine has started, so shut off the starting air. When the smoke has cleared away and the audience has returned, look wisely at the gauge board as if you really understood what the instruments are and how to read them.

"It is strongly recommended that an engineer not spend too much time thinking about these engines. It has been noted that once this happens, it is virtually impossible to get the mind onto any other subject. The best way to avoid this psychic derangement is to go ashore as often as possible. A dimly lighted bar as far from the dock as is conceivable provides the best treatment!"

In spite of all the types of engines used on the boats, all gave a good account of themselves when it came to reliability. Some of the electrically-propelled ferries came out with pilothouse control of engines, but this feature was probably far ahead of its time, for it was not accepted. In all other respects the ferryboat was functionally sound, equipped to do an enormous job and do it efficiently, and its effectiveness can be attested to by the millions of patrons who shared their time with the ferryboats of San Francisco Bay.

The San Francisco & North Pacific's *Tiburon* was badly damaged by an 1893 fire with the sad results seen below. The golden eagles still perch triumphantly on the pilot-houses with double steering wheels visible inside. In the hazy distance can be seen the Mission Rock terminal, at the left, and Goat Island. The *Tiburon* was rebuilt and by 1898 appeared as in the picture above, the golden eagles now atop square pilothouses. The ship is the *City of Pueblo*, loaded with troops for the Philippines. (Both: *San Francisco Maritime Museum*)

IV
Fires, Fogs and Fractures

THE SAFETY RECORD of the ferryboats on San Francisco Bay is truly imposing, considering the potential hazards on the crowded Bay, the number of boats in service and their innumerable trips. For over two decades the boats carried between 50 and 55 million passengers a year, with minimal injuries and negligible loss of life. In light of this record one can only conclude that the safest place to be was aboard a ferryboat. This over-all record of safety should be borne in mind in reading this chapter describing the limited number of incidents which marred the record.

The first of these on record was on April 3, 1859, when the boilers exploded on the Contra Costa Steam Navigation Co.'s ferry, *Contra Costa*. Six persons were killed and many injured and there was considerable loss of horses and property as a result of this calamity. The steamer was out of service for several months.

"Among those killed was the steamer's barkeeper," recalled George A. Clinton, one of the passengers on board. "Talking about barkeepers, it was a jolly crowd we used to have on those trips. Everyone knew everyone else. There was no sitting down in those days to read the newspapers. All the boys used to get together somewhere near the bar. When we got stuck on the bar of sand silt at the entrance to the creek, there was always the bar on the boat with its knot of pleasant gossipers to while away the time when we were delayed. There was no ticket officer then, or men in uniform to punch the slips of cardboard. A collector used to come around and get our two-bit pieces, bringing a deck hand with him to make sure he missed no one."

Boiler explosions were quite common in the early days of steamboating, and although boiler pressures were low, the large volume of water carried in the boilers was a potential bomb if fires were not properly attended. Boilers were constructed of iron plates; there were no facilities for testing metals and they blew up with such regularity that this one factor alone was the cause of Congress passing laws to establish a Steamboat Inspection Service.

In 1872, Captain John Leale recalled in his logbook that the California Pacific Steamer *Capital* was sunk. Sinkings were frequent occurrences when the wooden boats were tied to the slip unattended and most of the ferries experienced major bilge flooding.

The first collision recorded on San Francisco Bay was when the North Pacific Coast Railroad's steamer *Petaluma of Saucelito* struck the *Clinton* of the Contra Costa Steam Navigation Company off Yellow Bluff (Fort Baker), on the 27th of October 1877. The cause of the collision is not known, but the impact was so great that the *Petaluma* cut the *Clinton* in two. The section containing the engines sank immediately at the scene of the accident and Chief Engineer Manning was trapped in the machinery space and went down with his ship. The other section which remained afloat was towed to Sausalito, but was surveyed as a total loss. With the sinking of this vessel, the final act in Charles Minturn's stormy career with his Contra Costa Steam Navigation Co. came to a close.

The second collision occurred on February 19th, 1879, involving two Central Pacific ferries operating between San Francisco and Oakland Mole. The old *Alameda* rammed the *El Capitan*, and although there is no record of any injuries or loss of life as a result of this accident, the *El Capitan* had to be extensively reconditioned following the mishap. The *Alameda*, however, did not even lose a day of service. The collision occurred in a heavy

On this page are the participants in the unhappy drama that took place in the early evening fog off Alcatraz Island, an incident that inspired the opening episode of Jack London's novel, *The Sea Wolf*. The graceful little *San Rafael* was struck in the dining room by the *Sausalito*. By the time the picture below was taken the *Sausalito* had been remodeled as a passenger boat capable of seating over 2000 persons. *(Below: Northwestern Pacific)*

morning fog and was perhaps due to the inability of the captain of either vessel to tell how far away the other boat happened to be. It is to be noted that fog dampens whistle sounds making it extremely difficult to interpret their direction and closeness.

To the accident-prone narrow gauge North Pacific Coast Railroad came the first disastrous fire in Bay ferry annals. On February 25, 1884, aboard the *Saucelito*, moored at the company wharf at Point San Quentin, a fire started which was soon out of control and burned the ferryboat to the water line. This accident not only removed the *Saucelito* from the company roster, but also damaged the Point San Quentin pier to such an extent that the landing was abandoned and ferry service between Point San Quentin and San Francisco was never resumed.

Another in the long series of North Pacific Coast accidents (which were not by any means confined to marine activities) occurred January 14, 1886. The steamer *San Rafael*, San Francisco bound, left the slip in Sausalito at 4:30 p.m. Soon the San Francisco & North Pacific's ferry *Tiburon* was sighted coming down Raccoon Strait, black smoke pouring from her tall stack in an air of defiant challenge. The *San Rafael* met the challenge and the race was on. The two boats jockeyed for position all the way to the Ferry Building until, approaching their respective landings at a 27 degree angle, they ran a collision course. The *San Rafael* came out of the accident second best; her front railing, flagstaffs and lifeboats were smashed while the *Tiburon* escaped with a broken window. With the exception of this damage to the superstructure, there were no other injurious results. Thereafter, racing between these two rival lines was stripped of its glory and the managements bestowed some well-chosen profanity on the respective captains.

On February 27th, 1888, the Southern Pacific's *Julia*, just recently converted to a double-end ferry and placed on the run between South Vallejo and Vallejo Junction, blew up while tied to the pier at South Vallejo. This vessel's boilers had been modified to burn crude oil, the first such application on San Francisco Bay and it was reported that difficulties with the oil burning were the cause of the explosion. Unfortunately not a fragment of the boilers or the firemen who tended them remained to tell the story of the demise of the *Julia*. It was not until the second *Tamalpais* appeared in 1901, with more successful oil burners, that fuel oil came into general use on the ferryboats.

On New Year's Day, 1893, the steamer *Tiburon* burned in the slip at the old Ferry Building in San Francisco. Most of the upper cabin was destroyed by the blaze and the boat had to be rebuilt. Following the fire, and while the underwriters were viewing the *Tiburon's* smoking remains, the unfortunate watch engineer was questioned as to how much water was in the hold. He contemplated the soupy, murky, oil-slicked water in the dank hulk, pondered a minute as though making some mental calculations, and then dove in, fully clothed. He disappeared from sight then reappeared to contribute the sagacious intelligence that the water was over his head.

Although the following story does not relate to any particular incident, the rivalry between the deck and engine crews on the ferryboats was as significant as it was on deep sea ships. The tall tale goes that the Captain and the Chief Engineer, arguing about the merits of their respective professions, claimed that they not only could handle each other's jobs as need be, but they could handle them better than the incumbent. One day they agreed to trade assignments, and scarcely five minutes had gone by when the Captain called the Chief Engineer from his new vantage point in the engine room, "Chief, I have to admit you're a better man than I am, I can't turn a wheel." "Of course not, you silly fool," replied the Chief from the wheel house, "we're on the beach."

On November 30th, 1901, the fog settled, heavy and black upon San Francisco Bay; it was ten minutes after six in the evening and Captain John Taylor McKenzie looked down on the foredeck from the round pilothouse on the North Pacific Coast Railroad's steamer *San Rafael*. He consulted his watch, but no word came from shore until 12 minutes past departure time, that the last of the passengers and express were aboard and the boat could depart. The white haired old captain rang down on the telegraph to Chief Engineer James Jones to back out of the slip, and the paddles churned as the graceful little steamer vanished into the fog.

Here is Old Dick on a happier day, being led off the *San Rafael* by First Officer James Brooks. In the wheelhouse at the time of the collision was her highly respected master, Captain John Taylor McKenzie. He went on to command the second *Tamalpais* until he retired in 1909. Immediately after the 1906 earthquake and fire the Southern Pacific set up emergency dining facilities in the Ferry Building. Thousands of meals were served by the railroad free of charge to workers and refugees. Many of the disaster relief operations were personally directed by President E. H. Harriman of the S.P. and the Union Pacific. Bespectacled and derby hatted, he is the seated figure at the left of the picture below. *(Two pictures above: Roy D. Graves collection; below: Southern Pacific)*

On board the *San Rafael* at the time was Miss Fannie Shoobert of Sausalito, a young lady of 24. Fifty years later, to the day, she generously recalled for the author her memories of that momentous occasion.

"We proceeded across the Bay wondering how Captain McKenzie made his way, but he had done it thousands of times before and no one doubted that this would be another passage without incident. When the boat reached Alcatraz Island, we heard a tremendous crash forward, and the boat stopped immediately. I was sitting in the after cabin on the upper deck and one of the passengers came back and told us ladies that there was nothing to worry about, that there had been a collision with the steamer *Sausalito*, but that everything would be all right in a few minutes. Then a deck hand came along and told us that the captain wanted us to put on life preservers just as a precaution, although he assured us that no one would have to get into the water.

"We sat there in the cabin with our life jackets on for about 15 minutes and I must say that there was no panic among the passengers. A plank was arranged between the decks of the two ferries and most passengers were able to walk across to the *Sausalito*. Being a sort of a daredevil young girl, I jumped into the water and was picked up in a minute or two by the *Sausalito's* crew. Of course we had to return with the *Sausalito* to San Francisco and you can bet my family had many an anxious moment before they learned that I was safe."

As the *San Rafael* began to settle in the water, the crew remembered "Old Dick," the horse kept on board to haul express carts on and off the steamer at the terminals. They gave him every opportunity to cross the plank to the *Sausalito*, but he could not be induced or coaxed to abandon his ship, nor would he try to swim from the wreckage. Like the legendary sailor "Old Dick" went to a watery grave on a ship that had been his home as long as he could remember.

The gallant little queen sank with her golden eagles, her gaily-decorated paddle boxes, her glamour, her grace, all gone but not to be forgotten. Newspapers of the time claimed anywhere from two to three human deaths as results of the accident. No record, of course, was ever made of the names of passengers who boarded ferryboats and one cannot be certain as to how many persons were lost in this collision. Captain John Tribble of the *Sausalito* was held responsible for the accident and was discharged by the North Pacific Coast following the investigation.

Of San Francisco's great earthquake on April 18, 1906, much has been written. As if the earthquake itself had not done enough damage it was followed by three days of raging fires. During these first days of disaster, no one was allowed into the city without a pass. Ferry travel to San Francisco was very slight at first and only persons with authorized credentials or the need to come to the aid of relatives were allowed off the boats.

The boats carried many refugees away from the City to the Marin and Oakland shores. All movement of evacuees was accomplished without charge. On April 19, 1906, the Southern Pacific alone transported 1,073 carloads of homeless persons to destinations where they would be safe with relatives and friends. The company's warehouse facilities were offered free of charge by the Southern Pacific to the homeless, and explosives and stores of gasoline were issued free of charge to the city authorities.

It was the ferryboats, and the rail lines which fed the ferry terminals, which hauled in fire-fighting equipment, relief supplies of food, clothing and medicines. The ferries themselves did not escape unscathed. The Key Route ferry *Claremont* was on the ways at the John W. Dickie yard in Alameda, completed up to the main deck level. When the workmen came to work that morning they found the 190-foot hull toppled off the building ways and severely damaged. But it was the ferries that provided the vital transportation for San Francisco during this, her greatest hour of need, and the ferries played a vital part in rebuilding the City by the Golden Gate.

On Sunday December 6, 1908, the steamer *Newark* was on the run from the Ferry Building to Oakland Pier. The fog had been very thick all afternoon and evening and ferry service generally was both disrupted and curtailed. The Oakland Creek Route boat had been withdrawn for the night. The *Newark* was lying at Oakland Pier about 10 p.m. loading passengers from a train. Just before leaving the slip her captain received

The sorry spectacle at the left was all that remained of the Key Route's first ferry, the *San Jose*, after her fire. Sold to the Six Minute Ferry and remodeled for her new career, she was drastically altered. The picture above was evidently taken in 1922, soon after she entered the service of the Rodeo-Vallejo Ferry, for close scrutiny of the original photograph reveals traces of the Six Minute Ferry's herald under the fresh white paint of the pilothouse. A deckhand on the foredeck is attending to the rudder pin. The single-ended boat in the lower picture is the Monticello ferryboat *General Frisbie* executing a turn, off the Ferry Building, while the *Piedmont* waits in her slip and the *Oakland* comes in from the left. (Above: San Francisco Maritime Museum; below: Ed Zelinsky collection)

word from the dispatcher that the steamer *Oakland* had been put on as an extra boat and that he should be alert to listen for her. The *Newark* blew a long whistle on leaving the slip and this was responded to by a whistle from the other vessel. The captain remarked to his first officer that the *Oakland* appeared to be far to the south and therefore would not be of concern to the *Newark*. The next whistle from the *Oakland* caused the *Newark* to stop and a few seconds later the *Oakland* struck the *Newark* just forward of the port paddle wheel, and the whole wheel was damaged. Fortunately, although the *Oakland* punctured the hull of the other boat, all damage was above the water line. The *Newark* backed away and both boats proceeded to fulfill their missions, but the *Newark* had to go to the Southern Pacific shipyard for extensive repairs.

In 1911, the little steamer *Requa* of the Northwestern Pacific burned at the wharf in Tiburon, the fire completely gutting the craft. The superstructure was then redesigned, the steam machinery removed and a standard gasoline engine installed to replace it. The boat was then rechristened *Marin*.

The Panama Pacific International Exposition in San Francisco in 1915, left its mark upon all who were privileged to witness the spectacle, for the display of lights on its many buildings of fantasy were not only a sight to behold from the fairground itself, but they took on an even more intriguing appearance when viewed from the ferryboats. Special excursion boats were run by various ferry lines, the Southern Pacific, the Northwestern Pacific and the Key System, to give the fairgoers an opportunity to witness this breath-taking sight. For the Southern Pacific steamer *Amador* the fair held no delights for it was at this exposition that her funeral pyre was built and the faithful ferry veteran was deliberately ignited and destroyed in a night fireboat demonstration. Amid a glow of colored lights while the band played on, came the spectacular ending for a long-standing servant of the Bay of San Francisco.

On December 14, 1918 the Monticello Steamship Co. ferry *General Frisbie* was cautiously proceeding through the fog abreast of Point Pinole. The steamers of this line operated on compass courses with a set speed and a set time for each leg of the varied courses through San Pablo Bay. Times and places for meeting their own steamers were well known to the Monticello ferry captains, and the master of the *General Frisbie* was expecting a meet with the same company's steamer, *Sehome*. Periodically he sounded the whistle and listened for the answering whistle through the fog. Aboard the *Sehome* the same routine was going on. Both boats stopped and sounded their whistles, unfortunately at the same moment, so that neither one was able to hear the sound of the other. Hearing no answering whistle, the *General Frisbie* got under way again, only to collide with the *Sehome*.

The *Frisbie* dealt the *Sehome* a mortal blow in the engine room, cutting a monstrous hole through her side. Nobody was injured and an orderly transfer of passengers to the *General Frisbie* was made before the stricken steamer went down. It happened that a Marine band from the Mare Island Navy Yard was aboard the *Frisbie* on the way to San Francisco, in uniform and with instruments. To reassure the other passengers, the bandmaster struck up "K-K-K-Katy," "There's a Long Long Trail a Winding" and other favorite songs of World War I. This action is credited with having averted a panic on the two boats.

In 1919 the Key System steamer *San Jose* burned at the Key Route Pier in Oakland and much of the offshore portion of the pier was damaged as well. The boat was declared a total loss, was towed into shallow water and never used by the Key System again. She did not long lie idle, however, for the Mare Island Employees' Association bought her and converted her to an auto boat and she was to run for three more companies before her little triple expansion engine was stilled forever.

The Richmond-San Rafael ferry *Charles Van Damme* spent a memorable Christmas in 1921. Under the command of Captain Ray Clarke, she left Point San Quentin at 9 a.m. with 25 cars on board, including the limousine of the warden of the state prison. The boat had gone only a short way from the slip when a wild gale broke, rendering the vessel quite unmanageable for the half-day that followed. The 300 horsepower engine and sidewheels of the little red steamer were entirely ineffective against the southeaster with which the ferry had to contend. Captain Clarke

The fierce heat of the fire that burned the Key Route pier and the *Peralta*, then only six years old, left her fine steel superstructure in this grotesque twisted mess above The beautiful mahogany pilothouses were completely burned away. Below, fireboats are extinguishing the blaze that destroyed the *Oakland* at the Alameda terminal and ended an eighty-year career, the longest on San Francisco Bay. *(Above: San Francisco Maritime Museum)*

tried to reach Red Rock but his efforts failed. The strong seas broke the rudder loose and carried it away and the automobile deck became awash. Many of the passengers were terrified and most of them strapped on life preservers. The machinery hatches had to be secured with canvas to prevent the water from swamping the craft. One farmer with an automobile, perhaps not worth more than fifty dollars, strapped a life preserver around it with loving care, apparently hoping to keep the car afloat if it were washed overboard. Fortunately he did not have to test this arrangement. In the confusion that ensued, the gale blew a life boat out of the davits, smashing the warden's limousine, a sight which several thousand convicts would have loved to behold. At two o'clock in the afternoon, Captain Clarke finally beached his vessel at Winehaven near the Richmond terminal without any loss of life.

One foggy Sunday evening, April 24th, 1927, the Golden Gate Ferry's *Golden City*, formerly the *Aven J. Hanford*, was returning to Sausalito from the Hyde Street terminal with only three cars on board. Her newly-installed Diesel engines rumbled smoothly as she scurried with her light load to the Marin shore to pick up a full pay load of week end returnees. Fog was very dense over the channel; suddenly in the murk loomed the bow of the little steamer *Newport*, coming in from sea. She rammed and sank the *Golden City* with a single blow. Passengers and crew had barely five minutes to abandon ship. All that was saved from the *Golden City* was the cash register from the newsstand which the faithful attendant refused to abandon.

On the afternoon of February 17, 1928, the beautiful new *Peralta* was heavily loaded with commuters homeward bound from San Francisco. As the ferryboat approached the Key System's Oakland terminal, passengers began moving forward to be ready to disembark when the gangplank was lowered. Soon water began to cover the lower foredeck until it was awash and thirty persons were in the Bay. Five of them were drowned,

the greatest toll of lives in any ferry disaster on San Francisco Bay since 1859, when six people perished as a result of a boiler explosion on the *Contra Costa*. The *Peralta's* bow had dipped under the weight of passengers moving forward because the forward ballast tank was full, ballast not having been pumped to the after tank for this trip as required by instructions. The elaborate counter-balancing system on the *Peralta* and the *Yerba Buena* was not used after this disaster and there were no more such accidents.

But this was by no means the end of troubled days for the *Peralta*. On May 6, 1933, the boat was stored in the slip at the Key terminal in Oakland when a disastrous fire broke out which enveloped terminal and ferryboat alike. The *Peralta* was completely gutted by fire and was towed to Moore Dry Dock, her birthplace, for survey. The Key System, in conjunction with the insurance company, totaled the boat out, however the insurors were able to sell the hull to Puget Sound Navigation Co., Seattle, Washington, who rebuilt her with new Diesel engines as the streamlined ferry *Kalakala*, and at this writing she is still in service for the Washington State Ferries. The Key Route Pier was so badly damaged that service could not be resumed for days.

When the windup came and the bridges had supplanted the boats, there were many forty- to sixty-year veteran vessels for which there was no market. The ferry *Oakland* burned in 1940 in an accidental fire while stored at the Alameda Mole of the Southern Pacific. The fire simplified the task of scrapping the *Oakland* and subsequently a great number of the old timers which had outlived their usefulness—including the *Tamalpais*, the *Alameda* and the *Santa Clara*—were destroyed in this way.

Although the mishaps described in this chapter are not all-inclusive, they do encompass all the fatal accidents experienced in the hundred-year history of local navigation on the Bay. All in all, the calamities which beset the San Francisco Bay ferries were few and far between, leaving an unequalled record of safety.

In 1935 the San Francisco-Oakland Bay Bridge was still more than a year from completion that would mean the end for most of the ferries. *(Southern Pacific)*

V

History of the Ferry Companies

~~~~~~~~~~~~~~~~~~~~~~~~~~~~~~~~~~~

T HE HISTORY of the firms that operated ferries on San Francisco Bay is complicated. Some operations continued for many decades; others died after a few years or were involved in combinations or consolidations. To assist the reader in understanding the continuity of this history, the stories of the companies are grouped in five sections, each with its own chronology.

The earliest regular ferry operation on the Bay began in 1847 on Carquinez Strait; independent ferry operations that started before 1914 in that region are discussed in Section I. Section II is the story of the vast ferry system of the Southern Pacific and its antecedents. The other passenger lines between San Francisco and the East Bay are the subject of Section III, and of Section IV, the passenger ferries across the Golden Gate. Finally in Section V is the story of the automobile ferry lines organized after 1914. Although these histories are brief, they include pertinent facts on development of the lines, boats and routes operated and peculiarities in their operation.

Some of the ferryboats sailed under more than "two flags," were rebuilt, renamed, reconfigured and considerably altered in appearance. The attempt here is to keep the record of the various ownerships and changes clear enough that a student of maritime history can trace the life of each craft, even though it may have been transferred many times before being broken up. Some of the enterprises were quite large. The Southern Pacific at one time had 42 boats in operation as a single ferry enterprise. In such a vast operation, which hauled 50,000,000 passengers a year, the direct livelihood of many Bay Area residents depended on the ferries. As the reader reviews the history of these 27 major ferry companies, he will come to grasp the significance of this operation and justly

to appreciate the magnitude of the job that was accomplished.

SECTION I

NORTH BAY LINES

The first ferry service on San Francisco Bay was on Carquinez Strait; nearby is the only passenger ferry that has survived through the years to the time of the present writing. Altogether, ten ferry lines operated in the Bay at or beyond Carquinez Strait. Six of them, not a part of the Central Pacific story and founded before the days of the automobile, are discussed in this section. Two belong more properly in Section II of this chapter, the other two in Section V.

MARTINEZ-BENICIA FERRY

In 1847 Robert Semple, founder of Benicia, began a ferry between that community and Martinez, across Carquinez Strait, a service which was intermittently maintained for over a century until completion of the highway bridge between those cities in 1962. In 1851 Captain O. C. Coffin put a flat-bottomed boat, the *Ione,* in this trade. In 1859 he joined his brothers, Charles and Henry, in building at Benicia a small steamer of 97 gross tons and 75 horsepower, the *Carquinez.* For the next 21 years they ran her in service to Martinez until she was condemned by the steamboat inspectors in 1881. The operators at once began plans for another boat and the next year, at Martinez, completed the 144-ton *Benicia.* While somewhat larger than her predecessor, the new boat was still small for a ferry, and was in competition with the largest ferryboat in the world, the train ferry *Solano,* that carried foot passengers from Benicia to Port Costa, a few miles west of Martinez. In 1888 the Martinez ferry discontinued

This post card view of the *Benicia*, taken at San Diego in 1902, is the only known picture of the little vessel, with her housed-in walking beam. The *City of Martinez*, once she was weighted enough that her paddle wheels reached the water, performed her duties for almost twenty years, but was never noted for beauty. Passengers on the *Vallejo* had only a few minutes to enjoy the sun on her spacious hurricane deck during the short crossing of Mare Island Strait. *(Below: San Francisco Maritime Museum; above: Roy D. Graves photo; top: his collection)*

service and sold the *Benicia* to the San Diego & Coronado Ferry, where she had the distinction of the only walking beam engine to operate regularly on San Diego Bay. She made her last trip July 4, 1903, and was dismantled in 1904.

With the advent of the automobile, the need for a vehicular ferry became apparent, for the *Solano* carried only trains and foot passengers. In 1911 and 1912 the City of Martinez improved the water front and put in a new ferry slip. The following year, J. H. McNamara, James McClellan, Judson Colton, Dr. Edwin Merrithew and others founded the Martinez-Benicia Ferry & Transportation Co., and procured the little steamer *City of Seattle* from Puget Sound to carry automobiles.

In 1917 the company built a new steamer, the *City of Martinez* at Antioch. When she was launched, her displacement was so light that her paddle wheels failed to touch the water, much to the chagrin of her builder and the naval architect who had calculated her line of flotation. With some additional lead for ballast, she was finally ready to earn some revenue for her owners. After the Rodeo-Vallejo Ferry gave way to the Carquinez Bridge in 1927, the company obtained the *Issaquah* from that line.

Never an outstanding success, the twin-stacked *City of Martinez* was condemned in 1936, while still the line's newest boat. She was burned on the Martinez water front by the city fire department. The ferry company wound up its business on December 31, 1940 and on New Year's Day, 1941, the properties passed into the hands of the City of Martinez without cost. In 1943 the city acquired the *Charles Van Damme* from the Richmond-San Rafael Ferry and sold the two smaller boats to the Mare Island Ferry. In 1944 it bought the *City of San Rafael* from the Army.

Martinez went out of the ferry business in 1956, and the State of California succeeded it, already planning a bridge to be incorporated into the State Highway system. The *Van Damme* ran a few months before being withdrawn from service by the State for inability to pass the annual Coast Guard inspection. For a period of nearly four months, no service was maintained pending the completion of a new boat, the second *Carquinez,* which operated for the balance of the ferry days.

The last trip was Saturday, September 14, 1962, with Captain John Mattheson, commanding. Souvenir rides followed regular service, and when the day was over, the "Little Toot," as the *Carquinez* was affectionately known, went to Bethlehem Steel Co.'s yard for preparation for a long journey to Florida for future ferry service. And with her departure went the last opportunity to ride an auto ferry on the Bay.

MARE ISLAND FERRY

As the Navy Yard at Mare Island was isolated from the Vallejo shore, it was necessary to establish ferry service between these two points. The yard opened in 1854, and in 1855, the government steamer *Huron* was placed in service, followed some four months later by the launch, *Ion,* not to be confused with the *Ione* of the Martinez-Benicia line. Commercial operation of the ferry did not begin until the late 1860s with the incorporation of the Mare Island-Vallejo Ferry Co., which began operation with a tiny steamer called the *Lizzie,* named for the first American child born in the city of Benicia.

In 1870 the first regular ferryboat was put in operation, a small double-ended boat, the *Mare Island.* Old yard records indicate that this steamer could haul 1500 passengers, but this many people must have been jammed in like sardines! It took only a few minutes to cross Mare Island Channel and, although the boat had seats, it was standing room only at the start of the day and at quitting time. In 1879 the Mare Island Company added the *Vallejo* to the fleet, another double-end ferryboat built that year in Portland.

This brought about the sale of the *Mare Island* to a land development company that flourished in West Berkeley for a scant few years. The vessel was used to haul people to and from the development at no charge to prospective purchasers or landholders, but with a fare for visitors. In San Francisco the ferry landed at Meiggs Wharf at the foot of Powell Street. The land development scheme did not prosper and the ferry service passed unnoticed into oblivion. The *Mare Island* spent her last days of record at the mouth of the Yukon during the Alaska gold rush.

The Mare Island Ferry Co. built another boat in 1883 to operate in conjunction with the *Vallejo,*

For most of her career the *Ellen* worked in her native Vallejo, but some errand brought her to a military section of the San Francisco water front for the top picture. In the dock at the end of 2000-foot-long Meiggs Wharf, can be seen the tiny *Mare Island* when she was running between here and West Berkeley. The *Sehome* is shown while still a paddle steamer. *(Below: C. Ferry Hatch collection; two photos: Roy D. Graves collection)*

the little double-ended steamer *Ellen*. She plied Mare Island Strait until 1915, then was leased to the Richmond-San Rafael Ferry. She served this line for only a month before she failed to satisfy the steamboat inspectors, and so was retired and finally broken up in 1919.

During World War I the ferry enterprise fell from popularity with the yard employees. Some of those who were particularly dissatisfied organized the Solano Aquatic Club on a membership basis. The members were entitled to participate in excursions, two of which were operated daily from Vallejo to the Yard in the morning, and from the Yard to Vallejo at night. Writhing in the pinch of competition, the Mare Island Ferry Co. obtained an injunction against the club to restrain it from operating a ferry within a mile and a half of the terminals of the established concern. This injunction failed to disturb the Aquatic Club, for the terminals were removed to beyond the mile and a half limit set by the decision of the Court, and the members added hiking to their repertoire at the start and conclusion of each day. The business of the Mare Island Ferry Co. dwindled to such an extent that it was forced to sell out to the Club, which was then incorporated as the Association of Mare Island Employees.

The new ferry owners not only prospered with the ferry to the Yard, but they commenced an automobile ferry across Carquinez Strait, the Six Minute Ferry, which carried 467,320 passengers in 1921. The government frowned on a federal employees' activities group competing with commercial enterprise outside of the Yard, and this factor, plus other circumstances, led to the dissolution of the Association. The two ferry lines were purchased by the Rodeo-Vallejo Ferry Co., which immediately sold the Mare Island-Vallejo ferry to local interests. Victor Rauhauge is the current operator of the line.

In World War II, the *City of Seattle* and the *Issaquah* were purchased from the Martinez-Benicia Ferry Co. and added to the fleet. The old *Vallejo* still carried on and in June of 1946 was the last double-end ferry to run across Mare Island Strait. Launch service, at this writing, is still provided on one of the last continuous ferry operations on the Bay.

CALIFORNIA PACIFIC RAILROAD

The first Vallejo-San Francisco direct ferry was begun by the California Pacific, a railroad north and east from Vallejo, organized at about the time when the "Big Four" were forming the Central Pacific. After a stormy beginning, beset with monetary woes, the road opened for business in November, 1868. Milton S. Latham, a San Francisco financier, pulled the road out of the financial doldrums, and a line from Vallejo to Calistoga was constructed as well as one to Sacramento up the west side of the Sacramento River. This line was extended from Davis to Marysville in 1870.

The railroad began ferry service in 1869, from its terminal in South Vallejo to San Francisco. The famous steamer, *New World*, whose stormy passage around the Horn in 1850 electrified the maritime world, was one of the river craft used by the California Pacific for this service. The company also acquired the *Capital* and the *Sacramento*, two other river veterans, and with these swift vessels maintained a most adequate service, connecting with all mainline trains. Not only did the company's own boats serve the line, but boats in river service also called regularly at the South Vallejo wharf on both up-river and down-river trips.

In 1871 the California Pacific again experienced financial troubles, and thoughts of further expansion had to be tabled. Probably the only reason for the faltering line's continued existence was that its owners, knowing its potential value to the Central Pacific, were willing to feed in more money in the hope of recouping it through an outright sale. At the time, the Central Pacific line ran from Sacramento to Stockton and into Oakland through Niles Canyon or via Martinez on the south shore of Carquinez Strait. If the Central could only run over the California Pacific's tracks, the distance between Oakland and Sacramento could be shortened markedly.

The two roads finally reached an agreement in 1876 and the California Pacific was no more. Its trackage between Sacramento and Suisun became the Central Pacific's main line in 1879, with completion of the train ferry *Solano* and of a new line connecting Suisun with the ferry's northern terminus at Benicia. Ferries now began operating from the former California Pacific terminal at

The picture above was taken at the Monticello Steamship Co.'s home dock in Vallejo July 4, 1905, the day the Vallejo, Benicia & Napa Valley Railroad made its first connection with the Monticello steamers. Below is the *Napa Valley* at the line's San Francisco terminal, just north of the Ferry Building. A goodly crowd is on board. *(Above: C. Ferry Hatch collection; below: Society of California Pioneers)*

South Vallejo to Vallejo Junction on the Central Pacific main line near Crockett. The direct ferry service from South Vallejo to San Francisco ended in 1883.

ADEN BROTHERS FERRY CO.

In 1890, Martin, John and Joseph Aden had a stern-wheel steamer, the *Sunol*, constructed for them in San Francisco and were soon operating a daily round trip between the Vallejo water front and San Francisco. This was the first such service from Vallejo proper, although in the 1870s there had been ferry service from the railroad terminal at South Vallejo to San Francisco, operated first by the California Pacific and later by the Central Pacific, which soon shortened the run to extend only across Carquinez Strait to Vallejo Junction, on the main line between Crockett and Rodeo. A ferry passenger from Vallejo could here board the train for Oakland Pier, there to transfer to the ferry for San Francisco. Now in 1890 the Vallejo people once more enjoyed direct ferry service to the City.

The Aden Brothers scheduled the *Sunol* with a running time of 3 hours, 45 minutes, not exactly record time between the two communities. This service did not permit practical commuting, and in 1895 competition arrived with the tiny *Monticello*, flying the banner of the Hatch Brothers Steamship Co. This little speedster could make the trip in about two hours, so the Adens answered the challenge in 1898 by chartering a larger, faster vessel, the *H. J. Corcoran** which kept competition alive with her monstrous stern wheel until the *General Frisbie* and the *Arrow* arrived on the Hatch Brothers' roster.

In 1905 the three Adens gave up their passenger business, sold their little *Sunol* to a fourth brother, R. J. R. Aden, who operated the vessel until 1913, hauling freight only. He sold the *Sunol* to the Leslie Salt Co. which rechristened her the *Pyramid*. Eventually she came home to Vallejo and disintegrated on the bank of the Napa River, from which she once proudly sailed.

MONTICELLO STEAMSHIP CO.

Zepheniah Jefferson Hatch was the master and owner of a little steamer named the *Monticello*,

---

*The *H. J. Corcoran* will long be remembered by Bay historians as the *Crockett* of the California & Hawaii Sugar Refinery.

built in Ballard, Washington in 1892. The vessel was named for his home town in New York State, and the nameboard carried the figure of a horse from the weather vane of the Hatch farm. In 1895 he sailed his steamer from Puget Sound to San Francisco Bay, experiencing a breakdown on the way which disabled the boat. It was salvaged by the Pacific Mail Steamship Co., but the owner was able to pay off the libel and inaugurate ferry service between the foot of Maine Street in Vallejo and the San Francisco Ferry Building on August 10, 1895. At the time the ferry line was known as the Hatch Brothers Steamship Co., since a younger brother, Charles N. Hatch had joined the venture.

By 1900, the business had grown to such an extent that the company had a new vessel built, the *General Frisbie*, named for the son-in-law of General M. G. Vallejo and the first person to settle Mare Island. The *Frisbie* was a speedy craft, and with her the Hatches sparked a lively competition with the Aden Brothers who had been operating between Vallejo and San Francisco since 1890. Following this success, still another boat was required, and in order to finance it, the brothers were in 1904 obliged to incorporate and accept capital from outside the family. Their new Monticello Steamship Co. was soon able to purchase from the National Bank of Commerce in Seattle, at a foreclosure sale, the swift little steamer *Arrow* to add to this growing fleet of racers on San Francisco Bay.

1905 was a banner year for the company, for the Vallejo, Benicia & Napa Valley Railroad (Napa Valley Line) connected at the Maine Street dock with the Monticello boats on July 4, and the two companies were able to offer combined service from San Francisco to Calistoga. This same year, Samuel Sutton became port engineer for the steamship company, and his talents were a contributing factor to the success of the enterprise over the ensuing years. It was also in this same year that the Aden Brothers withdrew their passenger service, leaving the Vallejo trade solely to the Monticello Steamship Co.

The company bought its only paddle steamer in 1909, the *Sehome*. Built in 1877 at The Dalles, Oregon as the stern-wheeler *Mountain Queen*, she had been rebuilt as a side-wheeler in 1889. In 1914 Monticello had her converted to propeller opera-

The grand stairway of the *Asbury Park* was more customary on Eastern steamboats of consequence than on the ferryboats on San Francisco Bay. She was indeed a steamer of note, a famous racer for the Central Railroad of New Jersey, the pride of the Sandy Hook fleet. In eastern waters she carried two stacks. She took the long trip west in 1919, sailing through the Panama Canal with a Vallejo crew, and was converted to ferry service by the Monticello Steamship Co., losing her forward stack in the process. It was nearly six years before she was rechristened *City of Sacramento*. (*Left: Robert Parkinson photo; below: C. Ferry Hatch collection*)

tion which served her until she was rammed and sunk in 1918 by the *General Frisbie*.

After the purchase of the *Sehome*, the company was still in need of a larger boat, so it got together with the bank and the Union Iron Works and worked out a way of financing one. As a result, the first large ferry of the company's "big three" was built in 1910, the steamer *Napa Valley*, which proved to be a most effective member of the Vallejo fleet. When World War I and the resulting increase in activity at the Navy Yard brought workers from all sections of the Bay Area to Mare Island, the yard management urged the Monticello line to obtain more boats the size of the *Napa Valley*.

To start this trend, the *General Frisbie* was lengthened at the Barnes & Tibbets yard in Oakland in 1918, and in the same year Tremaine Hatch and Sam Sutton went East to look for a suitable craft. They found the *Asbury Park* of the Central Railroad of New Jersey lying idle in New York Harbor. This flyer had once been the queen of the Sandy Hook fleet, a speedy vessel of tremendous horsepower. She was purchased and made ready for the trip to the Pacific Coast. Coal was even carried in the main cabin for the journey. She left Jersey City September 15, 1918, stopped for coal in Havana and Panama, and in 24 days was greeted on the Vallejo water front by a cheering throng who did not let her coal-streaked sides dampen the glamour of the occasion.

The *Asbury Park* was so fast that her wash broke every mooring in the Mare Island Channel on her inaugural trip on November 20, 1919. She and the *Napa Valley* were converted to accommodate automobiles in 1922, but even this speedy pair was not enough to carry the heavy traffic. In 1924, Sam Sutton found the *Florida* of the Old Bay Line in Baltimore, Maryland to his liking. He purchased the boat, made the trip from Baltimore to Vallejo in 18 days, and she was refitted and placed in service October 9, 1924. She was re-christened *Calistoga* in a gala celebration that led to the re-christening of the *Asbury Park* the following year as the *City of Sacramento*, more in keeping with the locale where this steamer sailed.

In February of 1927, the two sons of Charles N. Hatch, Tremaine and C. Ferry Hatch, sold the Monticello Steamship Co. to the Golden Gate Ferry, which had given the Monticello group some challenging competition by building a toll road which greatly shortened the route to Sausalito, with a mere twenty minute Bay crossing from there to Hyde Street.

The Vallejo-San Francisco direct ferry was continued in operation by both the Golden Gate Ferry Co. and its successor, the Southern Pacific-Golden Gate Ferries, Ltd., until 1936, when bridge crossing eliminated its need. In many respects it was the grandest line on the Bay, it had the longest run, the fastest and largest of the single-end ships, and a passage which was the most difficult for the captains and navigators. There were six compass course changes in the thirty odd miles, and these were made by co-ordinating compass and watch. Even in fog, the same breakneck speed was run, for only steady running and a correct course located the buoys in these wide expanses of water with limited channels. Only the *Frisbie-Sehome* collision marred the otherwise perfect navigational record of the line, and to the oldtimer in Vallejo, the days of the Monticello Steamship Co. are a fond remembrance.

SACRAMENTO NORTHERN RAILWAY

In 1910, the Oakland & Antioch Railroad constructed a line from Bay Point through Concord, Walnut Creek and way points, reaching Lafayette in 1912. On April 3, 1913, the rails had reached Oakland, and the road was reorganized as the Oakland, Antioch & Eastern Railway. Construction continued and reached Sacramento in September of the same year. In order to get the trains across the delta area, a ferry was established between Mallard, near Pittsburg, and Chipps on the northern shore. Service began September 3, 1913.

The first boat of the new company was the *Bridgit*, so named because it was hoped that at some time in the future the crossing would be avoided by "bridging it." This ferry could handle six of the short electric cars and was powered with a gasoline engine, an extremely early application of this form of power to ferries. The boat was built of wood by Moore & Scott in Oakland and was ready for the new company in April of 1913. After a short thirteen months' life, only nine of which had been productive, the *Bridgit* burned at the southern terminal, apparently the victim of a

In the photograph above, taken before 1875, the original *Alameda* with her towering "jam factory" stack approaches the dock at Davis Street Wharf, San Francisco's original terminal for Oakland ferries. Coal bunkers on adjoining piers are for ocean steamers. The woodcut of the City from Goat Island is from *Our Native Land*, an illustrated 1882 travel book. That the artist has taken license is evident in San Francisco's magnified hills, the closeness of the vessels to the island and in the absence of a walking beam on the ferryboat, which may have been inspired by the *Oakland*, judging from her general lines. The sail boats in the foreground are depicted in loving detail. The fog bell silhouetted intriguingly on the island at the right is a predecessor of the steam whistle and later the diaphone that have since served the same purpose. The most conspicuous structure in the City is the brand new Palace Hotel; also identifiable are the tall shot tower at Second and Howard Streets, Saint Patrick's Church and the twin onion towers of Temple Emanu-El. (*Above: San Francisco Maritime Museum*)

faulty fuel system, and on that date, May 17, 1914, Fireman's Fund had another insurance claim and the electric line had no boat.

The second vessel, the *Ramon*, was a steel boat, also gasoline powered, with the capacity to carry six electric railway cars. She was constructed by the railroad, on its own premises at Pittsburg, and began service late in 1914, to continue as long as the railroad operated a ferry. The line was known variously as the San Francisco-Sacramento Railway and the Sacramento Short Line until January 1, 1929, when it was reorganized and rechartered as the Sacramento Northern Railway. This resulted from a merger with what had been the Northern Electric Railway from Sacramento to Chico. The new company was a wholly-owned subsidiary of the Western Pacific Railroad.

Passenger service was discontinued in 1941 and the olive-green *Ramon's* work for the next eleven years was entirely with freight cars. Cost of maintaining the ferryboat, slips and approaches presented a constant drain on the treasury and all ferry service was discontinued in 1952.

SECTION II

THE SOUTHERN PACIFIC AND ITS ANTECEDENTS

The earliest daily ferry service between Oakland and San Francisco presently became part of a coordinated railroad and ferry operation. Along with several similar enterprises, this in turn became part of the biggest rail-ferry system of all, one that operated not only between San Francisco and the East Bay, but also on Carquinez Strait, as will be seen in this section.

CONTRA COSTA STEAM NAVIGATION CO.

Faced with infrequent, undependable and expensive boat service to San Francisco, the town council of Oakland in 1852 decided to improve this situation by granting the Contra Costa Steam Navigation Co., organized by H. W. Carpentier and Charles Minturn, a twenty-year exclusive right to operate a ferry to the City. Service began with two veteran river boats, the *Kate Hayes* and the *Erastus Corning* to a West Oakland landing which avoided the hazards of San Antonio Creek (Oakland Estuary). This channel was dredged in

1853 and the ferry was then able to use the Creek Route, with a landing near the present foot of Broadway, much more convenient to the site of the little town of Oakland. That same year the ferry steamer *Clinton* was completed at the shipyard of John G. North, going into service on the Creek Route the day after Christmas under the command of Captain L. B. Edwards. She made three trips daily at a fare of fifty cents per person per trip; the monthly commutation rate was twenty dollars.

The two river boats were soon returned to service on the rivers and in 1857 the company had another boat built at the North yard, the *Contra Costa*. She made her maiden voyage on September 15, and by the time she was placed on the route, commutation fares had been lowered to ten dollars a month. The *Contra Costa* was fitted out with spacious pens for cattle and hogs, a necessity of the day.

All went well with the Contra Costa Steam Navigation Co. until James B. LaRue challenged it with the competition of his San Antonio Steam Navigation Co. This company had the old river steamer *Confidence* converted into the ferry vessel *San Antonio*, and on April 8, 1858 began its own service between Oakland and San Francisco with Captain John B. Fouratt as master. A rate war was followed by a court fight in which Carpentier and Minturn sought to enjoin their rival from infringing on the franchise they had received from the Town of Oakland. Pending the outcome of the litigation, the ferry captains of the two companies kept rifles in their pilothouses ready to shoot at each other while jockeying for position in the Creek. Finally the court ruled against Carpentier and Minturn on the ground that Oakland had no exclusive ferry right to grant.

During these hectic days LaRue launched a small ferry, the *Oakland*, that was so much better than Minturn's boats that the rival companies agreed to split the traffic while retaining their separate identities. This joint operation began August 2, 1859. In 1862 Minturn took the little *Clinton* off of the Estuary run and used her independently in service to Point San Quentin and up Petaluma Creek.

The opening of the San Francisco & Oakland Railroad in 1863 brought train service to West

Oakland has long described herself as the city "where rail and water meet." This slogan originated with the Oakland Long Wharf which accommodated railroad trains, seagoing ships, passenger ferries and car ferries. The artist who made the woodcut for *Our Native Land* depicted a ferryboat with high-peaked pilothouses of a type far more common in the East and on the Mississippi than on San Francisco Bay. San Francisco's original ferry terminal at the foot of Market Street, with its low clock tower, was built by Central Pacific. *(Below: Roy D. Graves collection)*

Oakland with a ferry route to San Francisco much shorter than the Creek Route. The combination train and ferry ride to San Francisco took less time than the all-ferry trip from the foot of Broadway. Minturn leased the *Contra Costa* to the new operation, which used her on its inaugural trip September 2, 1863.

The following July, both the *Clinton* and the *Contra Costa* were leased to Minturn's new Petaluma & Haystack Railroad to operate between San Francisco and Haystack Landing on Petaluma Creek. This operation lasted about two years.

The two boats were later leased to the San Rafael & San Quentin Railroad and on March 21, 1870 began meeting trains at Point San Quentin and carrying passengers from there to San Francisco. Four years later they were reconveyed by the estate of Charles Minturn to the Contra Costa Steam Navigation Co. which was no longer in the ferry business. The *Clinton* was leased in January 1875 to the North Pacific Coast Railroad and used as a ferry until October 27, 1877 when she sank following a collision with the *Petaluma of Saucelito* off Yellow Bluff. The *Contra Costa* saw no further ferry service, but she was rented for excursions until she was retired and broken up in 1885.

SAN FRANCISCO & OAKLAND RAILROAD

By 1857 Oakland had grown to the legal status of a city. It now had regular ferry service to San Francisco direct from the foot of Broadway down three miles of San Antonio Creek and then across the Bay to San Francisco, a total distance of nearly six and one-half miles. It had no railroad service as yet, but that year the City Council adopted a resolution granting Joseph Black, John Caperton and their associates the right to construct a railroad through the streets of Oakland. The line was to commence at the site of a proposed bridge over San Antonio Creek from Alameda and proceed down Seventh Street to a promontory known as Gibbons' Point (later the site of Oakland Mole).

The project was regarded with enthusiasm by the citizenry of Oakland, but it lay dormant until 1861 when the San Francisco & Oakland Railroad was incorporated to operate a combined rail and ferry line to San Francisco. John B. Felton, one of Oakland's most prominent citizens, and later its

mayor, was the company's first president. The original incorporators included George Goss, Redmond Gibbons, Charles W. Stevens, William Hillegass, R. E. Cole, Samuel Wood and Joseph Black. The enterprise was financed with French capital.

Work began at Gibbons' Point August 8, 1862. A wharf was built there, three-quarters of a mile into the Bay, to accommodate ferries. When it opened August 2, 1863 the road was only four miles long from Broadway, down Seventh Street to the end of the pier in the Bay. Davis Street Wharf, the San Francisco terminus, was over three and a half miles away. Six trips a day were provided by the *Contra Costa*, leased from Minturn, and the *Oakland*, bought from LaRue.

In October 1865 the San Francisco & Oakland Railroad was purchased by the San Francisco & Alameda Railroad.

SAN FRANCISCO & ALAMEDA RAILROAD

In the 1860s there was no direct rail connection between Alameda and Oakland. It was not until 1873 that the two cities were joined by a bridge across the Estuary. On March 25, 1863 a new company was incorporated by Alfred A. Cohen, F. D. Atherton, E. B. Mastick, Charles Minturn, J. D. Farwell, J. C. Kellogg and John W. Dwinelle to build and operate a railroad and ferry service between Alameda and San Francisco. It came to be known as the "Encinal Line" but its official name was the San Francisco & Alameda Railroad.

The railroad was built from Alameda Wharf at the foot of Pacific Avenue via Lincoln Avenue to the eastern boundary of Alameda and thence to the mainland near 47th Avenue in Melrose, which did not become a part of the City of Oakland until 1909. The first scheduled rail trip was on August 25, 1864.

The San Francisco & Alameda had no ferryboat of its own when rail service began, but later that same year the company was able to avail itself of the opportunity afforded by an explosion, October 26, 1864 in Suisun Bay, on the river boat *Sophie MacLane*, resulting in the death of three people. The Encinal Line bought the remains of this vessel, rebuilt her and used her in ferry service between San Francisco and Alameda beginning March 1, 1865. That same year, the road was pushed on to San Leandro and Hayward.

The painting of Oakland Long Wharf, as seen from the Bay in about 1875, shows the *Thoroughfare* and the *El Capitan* in the slips. Off the picture to the right would be Oakland Mole, of which the great train shed is depicted in the architect's sketch, dated 1880, above. At the right is shown a suburban locomotive of the type used on Oakland and Berkeley local passenger trains. In later years the suburban trains always used the tracks at the left. When the Central Pacific rebuilt the river steamer *Chrysopolis* at the Oakland Point shipyard, she emerged as the steamer *Oakland*, shown below. *(Three pictures: Southern Pacific)*

In October, 1865, apparently under the influence of the Central Pacific, the San Francisco & Alameda purchased the San Francisco & Oakland Railroad. The next year the company had the beam-engined ferry *Alameda* built for its route. She is said to have been the first ferryboat constructed as a double-ender for service on the Bay. Meanwhile the Central Pacific was quietly acquiring stock in this company until August 1868, when it publicly announced that it had finally gained control.

CENTRAL PACIFIC RAILROAD

While the Central Pacific was building eastward in the late 1860s toward its meeting with the Union Pacific, which was to span the continent with steel for the first time, it used three river veterans to haul passengers and express to San Francisco from the railroad's depot on the levee in Sacramento. These vessels were the *Washoe*, the *Yosemite* and the *Chrysopolis*, a speedster with the record for the fastest passage between Sacramento and San Francisco, to the time.

The Central Pacific had no intention of keeping its western terminal at Sacramento. It was headed for San Francisco Bay, where in 1868 it had already established a shipyard and built the double-end passenger ferry *El Capitan*. It was busy constructing a line from the Bay to Sacramento and purchasing smaller roads to speed its work. Thus, it quietly purchased stock of the San Francisco & Alameda and the San Francisco & Oakland railroads until, in 1868, it had control of them and their steamers, the first *Alameda,* the first *Oakland* and the former river boat *Sophie MacLane.*

On May 10, 1869 the Central Pacific and Union Pacific rails were united at Promontory Point, Utah, and transcontinental trains were able to come to California, but passengers from the East still had to transfer to the river boats in Sacramento to complete the trip to San Francisco. Soon the connection with the San Francisco & Alameda line was completed and so on September 6, 1869, the first transcontinental train to reach San Francisco rolled on to Alameda Wharf where it was met by the steamer *Sophie MacLane*, according to contemporary records.

This arrangement did not last long. The service to Alameda continued while alterations were made to the Oakland wharf of the San Francisco & Oakland Railroad to accommodate the larger trains. By November 8, 1869 this work was completed and an 88-year procession of trains from the East began using the facility. Oakland Pier was rebuilt in 1881 to the configuration familiar to transcontinental travelers until 1957. The old landmark finally succumbed to the wreckers in March, 1966.

The shoal water off the eastern shore of the Bay presented no natural harborage without dredging. To permit ocean-going ships to discharge cargo to freight cars, Oakland Long Wharf was built and opened to traffic on January 16, 1871. When the ships came in from the sea, silk and other precious commodities from the Orient could be transshipped to fast express cars for the journey to the eastern seaboard. For freight car transfer from the Long Wharf to San Francisco the Central Pacific had slips for car ferries, and at its Oakland Point yard constructed the car ferry *Thoroughfare*, first vessel of that name and second product of the yard. Five years later it augmented this service by building the larger car ferry *Transit*, also a product of Central Pacific construction. The Long Wharf continued in freight service until after the turn of the century.

When the mainline train connection was moved to Oakland in 1869, local ferry service continued to Alameda, but in 1873 the wharf of the San Francisco & Alameda Railroad was abandoned and all rail activity was centered at the Long Wharf and Oakland Pier. The next year the little ferry *Oakland* was broken up and the Central Pacific passed her name on to the river speedster *Chrysopolis*, which they had purchased outright and rebuilt into a double-end ferryboat. She began her new career as the second *Oakland* on June 2, 1875. At this time the passenger ferry fleet also consisted of the first *Alameda*, the *El Capitan* and two rebuilt river veterans, the *Amelia* and the *Julia.*

Until 1875 the Central Pacific's ferry landing in San Francisco was the Davis Street Wharf. The railroad's own terminal, predecessor to the State of California's famous Ferry Building, was opened to traffic on September 4 of that year. Slips for other ferry lines were built by the State along East Street, now the Embarcadero, adjoining the Central Pacific terminal between Market and Clay

The South Pacific Coast Railroad's *Bay City* leaving the wharf at Alameda Point passes the coal tipple that served the narrow gauge locomotives. *(Southern Pacific)*

Streets. Adjacent to these were slips for the river boats and for the steamers of the California Pacific.

The Central Pacific's acquisition of the California Pacific in 1876 has been discussed in a previous section. This transaction added the steamer *Capital* to the company's fleet.

On July 1, 1876 the Central Pacific instituted a ferry run from San Francisco up the Estuary to the foot of Broadway in Oakland. Because of its convenience to downtown Oakland and because it did not meet mainline trains, this Creek Route handled teams, freight wagons and other vehicles. For many years this was the principal carrier of vehicular traffic between Oakland and San Francisco.

After the purchase of the California Pacific in 1876, the Central Pacific began to construct a line from Suisun to Benicia with ferry and car transfer facilities at Benicia, on the northern shore of the strait, and Port Costa, on the main line to Stockton. At the Central Pacific's shipyard at Oakland Point, the huge *Solano* was built to ferry the trains. This gigantic vessel was 420 feet long and had two walking beam engines, one for each of her great paddle wheels. She began her ponderous task at 3 p.m. September 24, 1879, carrying a train southbound from Benicia to Port Costa. For many years thereafter, both freight and passenger trains kept her in continuous operation.

Concurrently with placing the *Solano* in train ferry service, the Central Pacific commenced passenger ferry service a few miles down Carquinez Strait, between the California Pacific terminal at South Vallejo and Vallejo Junction on the southern shore. Although a great reduction in train operation resulted from the Central's purchase of the California Pacific, ferry service was maintained between South Vallejo and San Francisco until the spring of 1883.

The *Amelia* and the *Julia* were assigned to the short run across the strait and, to augment service to Oakland Pier, the new steamer *Piedmont* was built at the Central Pacific's Oakland Point yard. This was the only boat built with an engine of mammoth dimensions without benefit of a walking beam. The huge single cylinder was horizontal, directly connected to the crank. Although the boat was in service for over half a century, this type of engine was never duplicated, suggesting that its operators were somewhat less than happy with it.

On February 17, 1885, the Central Pacific ceased to be an operating company, and the entire railway and ferry operations were taken over by the newly organized Southern Pacific Co., without any change in the composition of the stockholders.

The Central Pacific was a pioneer in Bay ferry operation. It had more routes than any other company up to that time, operated more steamers, hauled more passengers and built more boats with railroad employees than did any other company. Few people think of Huntington, Stanford, Hopkins and Crocker, the "Big Four" of the Central, as steamboat men, but their marine operation was one of the most significant in the tale of "crossing the Bay."

SOUTH PACIFIC COAST RAILROAD

In the 1870s, everyone who could command capital, it seemed, was bitten by the railroad bug; no exception to this rule was Bonanza King James G. Fair, who projected a railway from Alameda to the Colorado River to be called the South Pacific Coast Railroad. Initial plans called for building the line to Santa Cruz, which was not exactly on a direct line to the Colorado River. Construction on this narrow gauge project began in May, 1876.

On April 18, 1877, the first ferry was launched for the new company, the big steamer *Newark*, for many years conspicuous on the Bay for her enormous paddle boxes which housed 42-foot wheels. Her master was Captain John Leale, whose memoirs are among the few that have been preserved for historians in ferry research. As the boat was completed before the railroad was open for business, she was first used for hauling ties and rails to Dumbarton Point during construction of the line. She also carried occasional excursions.

In San Francisco the terminal for the South Pacific Coast was at the foot of Market Street; in the East Bay it was at Alameda Point, where a new station and ferry slip were fitted out. The line was open for business on March 20, 1878. Two months later, on May 18, the new steamer *Bay City* was launched for the company. Rail service was now available between Alameda, San Jose and Los Gatos. A third steamer, the *Garden City*, was launched June 20, 1879.

The Southern Pacific's much-rebuilt *El Capitan* steams down Mare Island Strait in service between Vallejo Junction and South Vallejo. Below is an old photo along San Francisco's water front from south of the Ferry Building.

The South Pacific Coast's *Bay City* is heading out of the slip for Alameda while the North Pacific Coast's *San Rafael* heads in from Sausalito. *(Above: Roy D. Graves photo; below his collection)*

The following year the railroad was completed to Santa Cruz, which was as far as it was ever to get. On May 23, 1880, a picnic train officially opened the railroad, but the train unfortunately jumped the track, spilling everyone out of the cars and killing fourteen, so the South Pacific Coast mountain line did not exactly begin life "in the grand manner." This narrow gauge railroad was subject to all the mishaps of a three-footer and in its time had its share of trouble.

When a fourth boat, the steamer *Encinal*, was still under construction in 1887, the Southern Pacific bought the line for a reported $6,000,000, and the South Pacific Coast emblem of a track disappearing into the setting sun was adopted as the emblem of the Southern Pacific.

During the early 1900s a third rail was laid to permit conversion to standard gauge operation, but the narrow gauge was not to wind up its activities in anything other than a blaze of glory. On April 18, 1906, the engine waited on the turntable to be steamed for the last passenger run to Santa Cruz. On the following day the standard gauge service was scheduled to begin, using the new rail which had been laid beside the narrow gauge track. But when the hostler came to attend to his iron horse that morning, he found her resting in the turntable pit, in no condition to make the trip. She was a sorry victim of the great San Francisco earthquake.

The Alameda ferry line continued under Southern Pacific management, becoming one of the most popular of the routes. It was on the Alameda ferries that the straw hat celebration was held annually, marking the end of the summer, when the more prosperous commuters would toss their straws into the Bay in honor of the occasion. It was also on the Alameda ferry that the commuters held their annual bathing beauty contest. Said Earle Heath, famed publicist for the Southern Pacific, "It seemed as though the committee always chose a frosty morning for these contests. The commuters selected a "Miss Alameda" from a bevy of bathing girls, whose chief interest at the moment was to change to warm clothing and get a hot cup of coffee.

Alamedans loved their ferry with a passion and when the ferry line was scheduled for discontinuance, following completion of the Bay Bridge, the commuters threatened to buy the boats and run them themselves. Alameda did not yield without a fight, but, inevitably, the ferry service had to come to an end January 14, 1939.

SOUTHERN PACIFIC CO.

On February 17, 1885, the Southern Pacific Co. succeeded to the rail and ferry operation of the Central Pacific. This service not only included connections with mainline trains, but also with the steam-operated local service which the Central Pacific had built up in the East Bay. At the time of the transfer, ferry service was operated from San Francisco to the foot of Broadway in Oakland, from San Francisco to Oakland Pier, from Vallejo Junction to South Vallejo and the train ferries from San Francisco to Oakland Long Wharf and from Port Costa to Benicia. At the time of the transfer, the Central Pacific had ten boats: the first *Alameda, Amador, El Capitan*, the second *Oakland* and *Piedmont* on the run to the Mole, the *Capital* on the Creek Route, the *Julia* between South Vallejo and Vallejo Junction, the first *Thoroughfare* and the *Transit* between the Long Wharf and San Francisco and the *Solano* on the train ferry run across the strait.

Two years later the company took over the South Pacific Coast Railroad and its San Francisco-Alameda ferry. This route and the ferryboats *Newark, Bay City, Garden City* and *Encinal* were now operated as part of the Southern Pacific.

The steamer *Berkeley* was added to the fleet as a new boat in 1898, the first screw propeller ferry on the Southern Pacific. Ten years later the sidewheeler *Melrose* was added to carry automobiles on the Creek Route, and by 1911, the interurban lines in the East Bay were being converted from steam service as the last step in the modernization and electrification of Bay commuting. After 1906 the car transfer operation at the Long Wharf was discontinued and the original *Thoroughfare* retired. Her running mate, the *Transit* continued hauling cars to various piers until 1934. A new *Thoroughfare* was added to the fleet in 1912; she and the *Melrose* were the first ferryboats on the Bay designed especially for automobiles. In 1914, two radically new vessels were built for passenger service, the second *Alameda* and the *Santa Clara*, with machinery located outboard, below decks,

The *Garden City* drifts into her slip at the south end of the Ferry Building after a run on the Creek Route from the foot of Broadway, Oakland. A group of foot passengers, enjoying a five-cent ride across the Bay, will walk ashore before the automobiles chug off the boat. Approaching from the left is the auto ferry *Shasta*, to the right, the *Sacramento*. All three are Southern Pacific steamers. The center photograph depicts the upper cabin on the *Berkeley* in the later, post-commuting years, with the refreshment stand appearing at the left. Port Costa had two slips in its later years as a ferry terminal. The view below shows them occupied by both the *Solano*, with her twin walking beams, and the *Contra Costa*. The overpass across the main line tracks was to accommodate foot passengers between Port Costa and Benicia. This tremendous operation of ferrying entire trains, while not unique, was novel enough and big enough to attract wide attention wherever it was practiced. *(All: Southern Pacific)*

adjacent to the independently operated paddle wheels. This permitted a large central alleyway for express carts and trucks, and the ferries were sometimes used to haul express and mail on extra trips which were not passenger runs.

Every November there was a big day for local traffic when the University of California and Stanford played their annual "Big Game." Whether this contest was held in Berkeley or in Palo Alto, the Southern Pacific and the Key System would be taxed to the limit hauling fans of the Red and the Blue, with trains and boats dispatched as rapidly as they could be loaded. Before the game, the crowd, colorful with pennants and chrysanthemums, was always good natured and orderly, trying to grab a sober bite to eat before the frenzy of the game overtook them. The return trip, no matter which side won, was invariably marked by the hilarity of the celebrants, many of whom had tasted victory—or drowned defeat—by virtue of the bottles on their hips.

In 1914 the Southern Pacific built another ferry for the Carquinez train crossing to relieve and augment the Solano's ponderous chore. This was the Contra Costa, with outboard machinery similar to that on the new Alameda and Santa Clara, to leave the decks clear for more railroad cars.

Many older ferries were rebuilt in the S.P. yard during the years to come, but only one passenger boat brought a new name to the fleet. From the bones of the old Newark in 1923 emerged the gleaming new Sacramento—transformed, but she still bore the Newark's old official number.

In 1922 the Southern Pacific bought the three new automobile boats that were on the ways of the Union Iron Works, under construction for the Six Minute Ferry when it came to its ignominious end. The new screw steamers, auto ferryboats, were named Shasta, San Mateo and Yosemite and their success prompted construction of three larger sisters with capacity for more automobiles. These were the El Paso and the New Orleans, delivered in 1924, and in 1925 the Klamath. Two years later the Fresno, Stockton and Lake Tahoe joined the fleet, the first Diesel-electrics on the Southern Pacific roster. In 1929 these boats were transferred to a separate company, the Southern Pacific-Golden Gate Ferries, Ltd. The Southern

Pacific itself retained the passenger and train ferry operations.

Ferry service from South Vallejo to Vallejo Junction was discontinued in 1927, on completion of the Carquinez Bridge, and the train ferries were supplanted by the Southern Pacific railway bridge from Martinez to Benicia on November 30, 1930. In 1933 a fine 20-year-old ferryboat joined the S.P. fleet, the Sierra Nevada, which had served the Western Pacific as the Edward T. Jeffery and the Feather River. The latter railroad received trackage rights on Oakland Pier and its passengers were transported on Southern Pacific ferries in exchange for this boat which now became the mainstay of the passenger ferry between Alameda and San Francisco.

All commuter ferry service to the East Bay ceased January 14, 1939 when the "Red Trains" began rolling over the San Francisco-Oakland Bay Bridge. Later that year the Sierra Nevada, Oakland and Piedmont were leased to the Key System for operation to the Golden Gate International Exposition on Treasure Island. During the years of World War II the Sierra Nevada was joined by the Alameda and Santa Clara in War Shipping Administration service, operating to Bay Area shipyards from the Transport Building at the foot of Mission Street.

The Southern Pacific fleet in 1951 consisted of the Berkeley, the Sacramento, the Eureka, acquired from the Northwestern Pacific in 1941, and the San Leandro, purchased from the Maritime Commission. This was a remarkable assortment of boats: two beam engine ferries, one turbo-electric and one triple expansion. With only the mainline trains to meet, and with American railroads steadily losing passengers to the airlines, the business of these ferries was not overwhelming. Tourists, sightseers and nostalgic Bay Area residents sometimes went on the boats just for the ride, which was also a great entertainment for children. There was a brief, pallid revival of commuting on the boats in 1947 when Key System trains and busses were tied up in a long strike and some commuters found it convenient to take mainline trains and the boats to San Francisco, but this was only for the duration of the strike. Use of the remaining ferryboats declined as rapidly as did the use of railroads for mass transportation. The two walking

In the upper picture, opposite, autos line up to buy tickets for the Oakland Mole auto ferry. These will be surrendered to the ticket-taker, shown in the lower view among the cars to expedite loading the boat when it is ready for them. His shanty is in the foreground while the ticket-seller's shack is in the distance. In later years this double process was shortened by the installation of toll booths. The dusty road above leads to the Alameda Point auto terminal, to which the steamer *Melrose* has brought the cars whose blurred images are more due to long exposure than to great speed. Across the water to the right can be seen the long Key System pier from Oakland. The picture below could not have been taken much later than it was, for the *Piedmont* will soon be put out of business by the newly completed Bay Bridge under which she will presently pass. Meanwhile the *Delta King* heads south along the water front to pick up cargo for her night run to Sacramento, after which she will return to her dock to receive passengers. *(Below: Ted Wurm photo, courtesy Roy D. Graves; three pictures: Southern Pacific)*

Following World War II hundreds of thousands of servicemen from the Pacific and the Far East were demobilized through military installations on San Francisco Bay. Many harbor craft bore messages of welcome for them. The inscription on the *Eureka* said, "Welcome Home Veterans — We Are Proud of You!" On July 30, 1958 the steamer *San Leandro* made her last revenue run and closed not only her own career but that of the once-mighty Southern Pacific ferry fleet. The San Francisco Municipal Band, with Maestro Arthur Fiedler as guest conductor, played a farewell concert aboard the ferryboat and San Francisco's fireboat *Phoenix* celebrated the occasion with a display from her monitor nozzles. *(Above: William Knorp photo; two photos: Southern Pacific)*

beam boats were retired during the 1950s and the *San Leandro* became the regular boat with the *Berkeley* as spare. These two remained in operation until July 29, 1958, when all train service to Oakland Mole was discontinued.

Thus ended the oldest ferry route on San Francisco Bay, the one with the most boats and by far the most passengers. Of particular pride to the management that rules the Southern Pacific from 65 Market Street, San Francisco, where top priority has always been given to safety, is the remarkably enviable record on that score during the many decades when S.P. ferryboats carried millions of passengers safely across the Bay.

SECTION III

SAN FRANCISCO-EAST BAY COMPETITION

Ferry traffic between San Francisco and the East Bay was a Southern Pacific monopoly from the time it acquired the South Pacific Coast Railroad for several years until a local firm challenged it with competition. It was further challenged by another local firm and then by two major railroads with transcontinental connections, before the automobile came and brought revolutionary changes to transportation on San Francisco Bay, as everywhere else in the United States. These four companies will be discussed in this section, in the order of their appearance on the ferry lanes of San Francisco Bay.

NICKEL FERRY

In 1893, a group of disgruntled Oaklanders, determined to break the Southern Pacific's monopoly in ferry business to San Francisco organized a new company to provide service for foot passengers between Oakland and San Francisco at the lowest possible price. This group, headed by John L. Davie—later mayor of Oakland—purchased a small single-end screw steamer, the *Rosalie*, which was built by the Hay & Wright yard in Alameda, presumably just before purchase of the yard by John W. Dickie.

Terminals were secured close enough to the Southern Pacific's "Creek Route" so that operation was parallel. In Oakland the Nickel Ferry's pier was at the foot of Franklin Street, a block east of the Southern Pacific's terminal at the foot of Broadway. In San Francisco the new line rented a dock at the foot of Mission Street, a block south of the Ferry Building.

The Nickel Ferry was named for its one-way fare. The Southern Pacific was obliged to reduce its fare to meet the competition, but its ferryboats far outclassed the speed and capacity of the *Rosalie*. The Nickel Ferry sold her and leased the stern-wheel river boat *Alvira*, which had more speed but shared the *Rosalie's* disadvantage of having to turn around at the end of each run. Neither the *Alvira* nor her occasionally-rented replacement, the *Frank Silva* could keep up with the competition. The nickels of the passengers were not enough to sustain the line and in two short years the original Nickel Ferry had vanished.

The Southern Pacific maintained the five-cent fare for passengers on its Creek Route and thus inherited the nickname of its onetime rival. While fares elsewhere went up, the S.P.'s "Nickel Ferry" remained for decades the cheapest way to cross the Bay. It was not until the 1930s that the fare was raised to a dime.

After she left the Estuary, the *Rosalie* was taken by her new owners, the Alaska Steamship Co., to the Inland Passage, where she ran in local service.

ATCHISON, TOPEKA & SANTA FE RAILWAY

The struggling Atlantic & Pacific and San Francisco & San Joaquin railroads were slowly and deliberately swallowed up by the Santa Fe, and before Californians could realize it the longest railway in the nation was halfway to San Francisco. Although the projected terminal was Stockton, on deep water of the San Joaquin River, nobody expected the Santa Fe to stop there, nor did the railroad do so.

The Santa Fe procured land at Point Richmond and constructed its new western terminal there. In anticipation of its completion a new ferryboat was ordered from the Union Iron Works in 1899, but this new vessel's construction did not keep pace with the completion of the railroad, and it was apparent that an interim boat was required. W. A. Bissell, traffic manager for the Santa Fe, approached Captain John Leale of the Southern Pacific, saying, "Jack, we are about to start operations to Point Richmond very soon and we haven't time to build a boat. There is nothing in these waters to suit. What's the matter with your get-

The Santa Fe's first San Francisco Bay ferryboat was the graceful single-ended *Ocean Wave,* shown below near Goat Island, with a barkentine at anchor in the background. Beneath the slatted semicircle of her paddle box is the lettering, "Santa Fe Route" in white letters on a blue background. Above is the railroad's second boat, the *San Pablo* departing the passenger slip at Ferry Point, Richmond, while a transfer barge and tugboat are in the freight slip. This terminal was not too well known to San Franciscans, for it was reached through a tunnel in the hills at Point Richmond and was seldom visited by others than railroad employees and patrons. *(Above: Roy D. Graves collection; below: San Francisco Maritime Museum)*

ting a month's vacation and see what you can find?"

Captain Leale's reply was conditional on getting a release from "my people" (the Southern Pacific), with the express knowledge that he would be acting as agent for the rival railroad. This was obtained without difficulty. The two roads had recently consummated a mutual pact which permitted the Santa Fe trackage rights in Tehachapi Pass, and the S.P. management understood the proposal and agreed to it, with the ferry captain retaining full rights to his regular job when the task was completed.

Captain Leale took off for the Pacific Northwest where he found the steamer *Ocean Wave* at New Westminster, British Columbia. She had been originally built for Columbia River service for the narrow gauge Ilwaco Railway & Transportation Co. in 1891 and had outlived her builder's requirements. Captain Leale had her drydocked, or "hauled out," as they put it in those days, examined the ship and pronounced her sound. The little side-wheeler was admirably built and very suitable for the Santa Fe's requirements, so she was duly purchased, boarded up for the voyage, and towed by the tug *Holyoke* to San Francisco Bay. The tow began May 20, 1899 and the vessel arrived at the Richmond terminal four days later without incident. Captain Leale's service with the Santa Fe was now complete; he returned to the Southern Pacific's Oakland run two days later.

The *Ocean Wave* was used at first to take supplies to Richmond from San Francisco, then she was refitted for passenger service which did not commence for a year because of construction difficulties with the rail line. On the morning of July 6, 1900, the little steamer was ready for the inaugural trip in the berth at the Ferry Building in San Francisco. Captain John Lauritzen, in his new blue uniform with the Santa Fe emblems on his lapels, rang down on the telegraph to Chief Engineer Ed Mahoney promptly at 8:00 a.m., and the steamer *Ocean Wave* took off for Point Richmond adding yet another ferry line to the already crowded waters of the Bay.

Toward the latter part of 1900, the new boat ordered the previous year from the Union Iron Works and christened *San Pablo*, made her trial trip and was placed in service in December of that year. The *Ocean Wave* then became the spare, or relief boat, a role she played until 1911 when a new double-end vessel similar to the *San Pablo*, but 39 feet longer, the *San Pedro*, was added to the fleet. This boat, also a Union Iron Works product, had twin smokestacks, one of the few Bay vessels so equipped, but she was graceful to say the least, and one of the most picturesque of the ferry flotilla that brought color to the Bay.

During World War I, the United States Railroad Administration required the Santa Fe to operate passenger trains from the Southern Pacific's Oakland Pier, in order to consolidate facilities. The Santa Fe ferries were used intermittently during this period as extra boats between the Ferry Building and Oakland Pier. Ferry service to Richmond was resumed in 1919 and continued until April 22, 1933, when the Santa Fe concluded its own agreement with the Southern Pacific again to operate the passenger trains from Oakland Pier.

The *San Pablo* was sold for scrap in 1937 and ended her days as part of a fish reduction operation on the Bay for which she was named. The *San Pedro* was sold to the Key System and renamed *Treasure Island*. In 1938 she was used to haul construction workers to the Golden Gate International Exposition on Treasure Island and in 1939 and 1940, she was in continuous passenger service to the Fair.

KEY SYSTEM

The transportation company which became known as the Key System was a combination of all the small independent lines that had flourished in the East Bay prior to 1901. The interurban operations were incorporated in 1902 for $2,400,-000 as the San Francisco, Oakland & San Jose Railway Co., since it was then contemplated that the electric lines would be extended to San Jose. In 1908 the corporate name was changed to San Francisco, Oakland & San Jose Consolidated Railway. By 1912 the aspirations to reach San Jose were shelved and the company was again reorganized, this time as the San Francisco-Oakland Terminal Railways. Through all these changes in corporate name, the company's advertising and emblem featured the key and the words "Key Route." The key finally gained recognition in the corporate title when the company was reorgan-

The first Key Route ferry, the *San Jose*, gleamed with fresh orange paint and with gold-leaf lettering on her black nameboards as she made her trial trip on Oakland Estuary in 1903. A party of well-dressed company officials was on board to admire her many advanced features. The temporary whistle, wired to one side of her stack, will presently be replaced by a pair of graceful brass ones, placed fore-and-aft on it. Although this fine glass negative is unfortunately cracked, it was taped together for this print. By 1931 the Key System Pier was an impressive complex with a double train shed and two main slips in which the *Peralta* and the second *Yerba Buena* are moored, above. The trains now approached the pier over the long rock causeway at the left; only a stub, used for car storage, remains of the original wooden trestle on which trains ran over the shoals to the shore. The approach and toll plaza for the Bay Bridge are now to the north of the rock fill. (*Above: Alameda-Contra Costa Transit District; below: Kenneth Jenkins collection, courtesy Marshall F. Silverthorn*)

ized in 1923 as the Key System Transit Co. After another reorganization the transbay operations emerged in 1929 as Key System, Ltd. In 1935 this name was shortened to Key System. Through the years, however, the average Bay ferry user referred to the line as "Key Route" or "Key System."

The new organization operated electric trains in Berkeley and Oakland, which terminated on a pier in San Francisco Bay near what is now the eastern approach to the San Francisco-Oakland Bay Bridge. The service was continued by ferry to San Francisco's Ferry Building. The first un-official trip was made September 24, 1903, on the new ferry *San Jose*, which, with the *Yerba Buena*, had been built for the line by John W. Dickie. Both were screw propeller steamers, as were all the boats that were built for the company.

To the *Yerba Buena* went the honor of carrying the first revenue passengers on October 26, 1903. The first train arrived at the Oakland pier at 9:52 a.m. and Captain William A. Rasmussen and Chief Engineer August Musshardt got their boat under way. The Key Route theme dominated the dec-orations for this gala occasion and even the officers' license frames were adorned with little golden keys. The rail route, terminating at the finger pier, resembled a key when delineated on a map, hence the emblem and name.

The ferry *San Francisco* was added to the fleet two years later, making her maiden voyage on April 18, 1905. Next to follow was the *Claremont* on March 14, 1907. This boat was scheduled to be delivered somewhat earlier, but had been jarred from the building ways while under construction at the Dickie yard during the famous 1906 quake. A fifth boat, the *Fernwood,* joined the orange fleet February 2, 1908. This group of ferries performed magnificently for the line, and operated without mishap until 1919 when a fire partially destroyed the Oakland terminal and gutted the *San Jose*. She was then sold to the Six Minute Ferry Co., and rebuilt as an auto boat.

In 1922 the two turbo-electric ferries *Hayward* and *San Leandro* joined the company fleet, the first steel-hulled vessels on the line. The four little wooden boats were placed in reserve and in time were leased to the Golden Gate Ferry Co. for con-version to automobile ferries.

In March, 1927, the turbo-electric *Peralta* was delivered to the Key System, and a month later she was joined by her sister, the second *Yerba Buena*. These resplendent vessels had been on the Bay less than a year when the *Peralta* earned her reputation as the hard-luck ferryboat by dipping her main deck under water when crowded with passengers, with the loss of five lives. This reputa-tion was confirmed on May 6, 1933, when she was caught in a fire which destroyed her together with the old Key Route Pier. The pier was rebuilt but the boat was totalled out and sold to a scrap con-cern, which in turn sold the hulk to the Black Ball Line on Puget Sound. There she was rebuilt, re-configured and rechristened *Kalakala,* and her new life under Diesel power has lasted through this writing as she still operates for the Washington State Ferries.

In an era when the Bay was thronged with snow-white ferryboats, particularly in the concen-tration of steamers which operated from San Fran-cisco's Ferry Building, the Key Route boats pre-sented a dash of color in their brilliant orange painting—attractive or not, according to one's taste. They were frustrating to early photo-graphers who had to use film stock that was singularly non-sensitive to oranges and reds. In their build-ers' finery, the *Peralta* and the second *Yerba Buena* were particularly colorful with orange, white, brass and cream-colored stripes to make them even more distinctive. All this was capped with mahogany pilothouses reminiscent of the wheel-houses on early ocean steamers in the days when the woodworker's craft was the symbol of mag-nificence on both inland and ocean waters.

The Key System ferries went out of the com-muter business on January 14, 1939, when trackage on the lower deck of the San Francisco-Oakland Bay Bridge was completed. The Key System's orange electric trains, together with the dark green ones of the Sacramento Northern and the massive red ones of the Southern Pacific's Interurban Elec-tric Railway Co. now ran to the Bridge Terminal in San Francisco, but this was not quite the end of ferryboats for the Key. The company had pur-chased the *San Pedro* from the Santa Fe in April, 1938, and it served the fairgrounds on Treasure Island to transport workers constructing the Golden Gate International Exposition. When the fair

The Key Route Pier, when first opened, was a jolly place, orange and white with a gold key and a neat black-and-gold sign above the train shed entrance. The fine new orange electric trains were finelined, lettered and numbered in gold leaf. The cavernous interior was lit by arc lights. Potted palms and banana trees added a touch of elegance to the passengers' waiting room with its fence of turned wooden rods. Several pictures of the old terminal here and in Chapter I are from the collection of Swedish-born Captain Adolph Nilsson, an officer on the very first Key Route boats, who became captain of the *San Jose*. The fire on the night of May 6, 1933 left the havoc above, from which the cremated remains of the *Peralta* have already been towed away. Artfully fabricated from corrugated steel, the new terminal and train shed were quickly built for an anticipated short life; first construction of the East Bay section of the Bay Bridge appears beyond it. The twin-stacked boat is the second *Yerba Buena*, surviving sister of the *Peralta*. (*Five photos: Alameda-Contra Costa Transit District*)

At the left is a view, from the west terminal on Treasure Island, of the *Hayward* departing for San Francisco to fetch another load of fairgoers for the 1939-1940 Golden Gate International Exposition. During and immediately after World War II the *Yerba Buena* carried many thousands of troops between the Army staging area at Camp Stoneman near Pittsburg and the San Francisco Port of Embarcation. The Western Pacific's stern-wheel passenger ferry *Telephone* is seen below making the landing at the Ferry Building about 1910. *(Top: Brian Thompson photo; bottom: Western Pacific)*

opened February 18, 1939, Key boats served both sides of the island, operating to the west side from San Francisco's Ferry Building and to the east side from the Key System pier in Oakland.

The ferries *Sierra Nevada*, *Oakland* and *Piedmont* were leased to augment the Key's own fleet, the *San Pedro*, rechristened the *Treasure Island*, the second *Yerba Buena*, *Hayward* and *San Leandro*. During the fair's second season, 1940, busses were substituted for the ferry service to Oakland, but boats still operated between the fair's west terminal and San Francisco. After the fair closed the *Treasure Island* was sold to the Navy and the Key's other boats to the Maritime Commission.

The *Yerba Buena* was transferred to the Army Transportation Corps during World War II and operated between Camp Stoneman and the Army piers on San Francisco Bay. For a time she was renamed *Ernie Pyle*, but the Transportation Corps reconsidered and restored her maiden name in 1946. The *Hayward* was retired in 1947, after a disastrous fire which destroyed her main generators, and was later scrapped. The *San Leandro* was also leased to the Army and then went on to a new career with the Southern Pacific, being the last boat to be operated in regular service by that company.

The Key Route was one of the most prolific carriers of passengers on San Francisco Bay, second only to the Southern Pacific. In 1921, the Key carried nearly 15,000,000 persons compared with the Southern Pacific's 27,000,000 (over all routes), and the third place Northwestern Pacific's 7,000,-000. The Key had one of the shorter routes across the Bay, but no doubt one of the most comfortable, for their steel, turbo-electric boats were the smoothest operating ferries under way that ever sailed on this magnificent inland harbor.

WESTERN PACIFIC RAILROAD

The last of the transcontinental railroads to come to San Francisco Bay was the Western Pacific, which connected with the Denver & Rio Grande Railroad at Salt Lake City, crossed the Bonneville Salt Flat, headed west across Nevada, crossed the Sierra Nevada and descended the Feather River Canyon to California's Central Valley, then through Niles Canyon to Oakland, where it built a new terminal where the Estuary entered the Bay, south of the Southern Pacific's Oakland Mole.

The last spike was driven at Keddie, in the Feather River Canyon, on November 2, 1909 and on August 22, 1910, the first train rolled into the new Western Pacific Mole on Oakland Point.

It was met by the Key System's *Yerba Buena*, which the company had borrowed to provide suitably elegant accommodations for the inaugural trip. According to Roy Graves, engineer on that occasion, the management was disappointed that many of the passengers on the first transcontinental train decided to omit the ferry trip entirely.

The Western Pacific borrowed the fine Key boat for the occasion because the company was not very proud of its own boat, the stern-wheel steamer *Telephone*, built in Portland, Oregon in 1903. The vessel was one of the fastest boats on the Bay, but her appointments were rather on the Spartan side and it is reported that many of her structural timbers had not even been debarked. Even her speed was negated by the time-consuming necessity of turning around at each end of the route, a handicap she shared with all other single-enders. Clearly, a more satisfactory craft was required.

The Western Pacific management was intrigued with the Key Route boats, the *Claremont* and the *Fernwood* in particular. They ordered a new boat to be built at Moore & Scott Iron Works in Oakland. This vessel, delivered in 1913, was named the *Edward T. Jeffery* in honor of the president of the Western Pacific, who was also president of the Denver & Rio Grande. The ferry resembled the Key boats in many respects, even to the four-cylinder double compound engine. Painted Tuscan red as long as she was named the *Jeffery*, the vessel was a success from the outset.

During World War I she operated for the United States Railroad Administration between the Southern Pacific's Alameda Mole and the Ferry Building, since the Western Pacific's trains operated during that period out of the Southern Pacific's Oakland Pier. After the war, service was resumed to the Western Pacific's Oakland Mole. Toward 1930, the vessel was painted white and re-christened *Feather River* in keeping with the railroad's advertising. In May, 1933, in exchange for trackage rights for passenger trains into Oakland Pier,

The Western Pacific's Oakland Mole was a neat yellow-and-white example of 1910 classicism. It is photographed, above, from the deck of the departing ferryboat, presumably the *Feather River* since the railing and lifeboat are white. The company's new car ferry, *Las Plumas,* is seen on the Willamette River in the 1957 photograph, leaving the Albina Engine & Machine Works in Portland, Oregon, bound for San Francisco Bay. Railroad cars served as quarters for the crew. *(Above: Roy D. Graves collection)*

the vessel was conveyed to the Southern Pacific and relettered *Sierra Nevada.*

After a 24-year lapse of ferry operation, the Western Pacific had built for it in Portland, Oregon, the steel car ferry *Las Plumas* in 1957. The ferry was designed to transfer freight cars to the various freight slips about the Bay from the Western Pacific's Oakland freight yards. The completion of the vessel was climaxed by a voyage down the Pacific Coast under the boat's own power. Since accommodations for sleeping were not a part of the configuration of the *Las Plumas,* two standard Pullmans were carried on deck for quarters, together with a business car and a tank car for extra fuel. While the vessel can operate in either direction, for a sustained run it is designed primarily for one direction only and has an auxiliary bow propulsion motor for maneuverability. At this writing, the *Las Plumas* is the only operating ferryboat on San Francisco Bay.

SECTION IV

ACROSS THE GOLDEN GATE

To the north of San Francisco, separated from the City by the waters of the Golden Gate, lies Marin County, a region of wooded hills and valleys and dominated by Mount Tamalpais. The people who lived here depended on the ferryboats to get to San Francisco.

To trace the history of ferry operation across the Golden Gate, it is necessary to begin once more in the 1860s. Two different railroad systems developed in this region, each headed for the redwood country of California's northern coast, each with its own ferry system connecting with San Francisco. They developed in distinctive ways, but ultimately merged into a unified train and ferry operation that for three decades served well to connect the City with its beautiful suburbs in Marin County.

SAUSALITO LAND & FERRY CO.

The beauties and possibilities of the southern Marin peninsula as a site for suburban development within easy reach of San Francisco were evident a century ago. A group of businessmen in 1868 organized the Sausalito Land & Ferry Co., incorporated October 4, 1869, with the purpose

of acquiring the southern sector of Captain William A. Richardson's Rancho Saucelito and selling residential lots to persons seeking "a quiet rural home in a lovely place." As the corporate title suggests, operation of a ferry was vital to the undertaking, for no other regular ferry service was available between Sausalito and San Francisco. With the purchase of a lot, a landholder was given a pass on the ferry; all other passengers were subject to a published tariff.

The company built a general office building and a ferry dock in Sausalito at the foot of Princess Street, which was named for the company's first boat, the little steamer *Princess.* In San Francisco, a terminal was leased for a monthly rental of $75 on Meiggs Wharf, at the foot of Powell Street.

The inaugural trip of the *Princess* was made May 10, 1868 with Captain James Brooks in command. The chief engineer was Thomas Wosser, grandsire of a dynasty of ferryboat engineers who would serve five companies over the years to come. At first, five trips a day were made with the *Princess,* but on June 28, 1870 they were reduced to three. The company also bought a yacht, the *Diana,* for use when the ferryboat was undergoing repairs, which was often.

The land development depended on the availability of ferry service to San Francisco, but the minutes of the company make it clear that the management had little enthusiasm for this phase of the business. By 1874 it had become a downright chore and the next year the company directors were happy to relinquish their rights of ferry operation to the North Pacific Coast Railroad and even purchased $25,000 worth of that company's stock.

This development scheme had established permanent ferry service between San Francisco and the Marin shore, a service that was to continue for more than seven decades. The *Princess* saw no further service and was broken up in 1881.

NORTH PACIFIC COAST RAILROAD

The company which now obtained the franchise to operate ferries out of Sausalito had been incorporated December 19, 1871 and was chartered to build a narrow gauge railroad from San Francisco to redwood country on the Russian River and ultimately on to Humboldt Bay. James Shafter

As the pictures on this page suggest, the ferry operations of the North Pacific Coast were carried on amid symbols of 19th century deep-sea navigation. In the top picture, the graceful *San Rafael* steams along the San Francisco waterfront past windjammers, one under sail. In the foreground is Captain Whitelaw's salvage yard at Bay and Kearny Streets, boasting an advertisement for a famous sandy mechanic's soap. At the left are a pair of steamers with auxiliary sail—or vice versa. Polluting the atmosphere with coal smoke is the big N.P.C. car ferry *Sausalito*, in the background. The view of 1892 Sausalito features the black-hulled revenue cutter *Bear* early in her long and distinguished career. In one of the N.P.C. side slips can be seen the first *Tamalpais*. The mountain of the same name looms high in the right background. (*Above: San Francisco Maritime Museum; left: Marshall Silverthorn collection*)

was the first president and among the original directors were Milton S. Latham, James B. Stetson and William T. Coleman.

The principal terminal was in Sausalito, where shops, general offices and ferry wharves were constructed. By 1875, when the ferry franchise was obligingly relinquished by the Sausalito Land & Ferry Co. to the North Pacific Coast, the railroad line reached Tomales, and service began that year. Two new boats were ordered by the company to be built in New York and delivered on San Francisco Bay, but for immediate ferry service other arrangements had to be made. The *Princess* was in need of extensive repairs and not adequate for the railroad's needs, so the single-ended *Petaluma* was refitted and renamed *Petaluma of Saucelito*, then put into the ferry service. This boat had two engine rooms, one operating each paddle. All too often one of the engines would be entirely out of operation, making it necessary to cross the Bay on one paddle, a most annoying occurrence for the passengers.

Meanwhile, in 1875 the road bought out the standard gauge San Rafael & San Quentin Railroad that operated trains to meet Charles Minturn's boats at Point San Quentin. It leased the *Clinton* from Minturn to continue this service, until she collided with the *Petaluma of Saucelito* and sank October 27, 1877. After the N.P.C. converted the S. R. & S. Q. tracks to conform to its own three-foot gauge, it now had two ferry lines between San Francisco and Marin County. It operated this "horseshoe service" until 1884.

The two new boats ordered from New York were at length completed, then disassembled and loaded on freight cars for shipment to the Bay. It is reported that each boat required 120 cars and came in several special trains to San Francisco, where they were reassembled. On August 11, 1877, the *San Rafael*, a resplendent little single-ender, made the run from San Francisco to San Quentin. Her twin vessel, the *Saucelito*, made her maiden voyage October 16, 1877. Although the life of the *Saucelito* was short, she had the distinction, on September 21, 1880, of carrying President Rutherford B. Hayes from San Francisco for the first visit of a President to the Mare Island Navy Yard.

After the arrival of the two newcomers, the *Petaluma* was again rebuilt, this time sporting a new name, *Tamalpais*, the first of two vessels to be so christened.

The *Saucelito* and the San Quentin wharf both burned in 1884. As the ferryboat was a total loss, it was not possible to continue boat service to San Quentin and thereafter only the Sausalito terminal was maintained. The *Tamalpais* and the *San Rafael* shared the company's ferry chores until 1894 when the big new *Sausalito* was built to ferry passengers and to transfer narrow gauge cars. This double-ender proved to be a very useful piece of equipment.

Settlement of Marin County had by now progressed to the point that commute trade began to boom, and the boats were filled on the morning and evening trips six days a week. Picnic crowds to Camp Taylor in the summertime added to the burden, and the boats had to be augmented by renting extra ferries from other companies. To help with the increasing business and to replace the aging *Tamalpais*, the company proceeded to order a new boat.

Prosperity was not quite the word to describe the affairs of the North Pacific Coast. Rail accidents levied a heavy toll on the company, and when the new ferry arrived, the second *Tamalpais*, the line's treasury was all but drained. The final blow came with the sinking of the *San Rafael* in 1901, and there was nothing left to do but sell the line to someone who could invest fresh capital in the tottering venture.

After some months of negotiation, the properties were taken over by a new syndicate, the North Shore Railroad, on March 7, 1902. The Marin County suburban lines were modernized during ensuing years, but the last segment of the narrow gauge line from Fairfax to Cazadero continued for nearly thirty years. This was one of the most picturesque railroad lines through the redwood groves and on the coastal shores and it was finally abandoned on Saturday, March 29, 1930.

NORTH SHORE RAILROAD

While the North Pacific Coast Railroad was wallowing in debt occasioned by train wrecks, ferry sinkings and litigation enough to discourage the bravest of investors, a dynamic salesman of electrical products could see in it a great opportunity. This man was John Martin, Pacific Coast

Windjammers dominate these scenes of the ferry operations of the North Shore Railroad, successor of the North Pacific Coast. The rail and ferry terminal in Sausalito was rebuilt in 1903, as part of the new management's modernization of the line. A stern wheeler, below, brings building supplies for the building contractor. Above, the second *Tamalpais*, lettered for the North Shore, departs the Sausalito slip on an afternoon trip to San Francisco in 1904. In both pictures, beyond Richardson Bay, always a haven for sailing ships, rises Belvedere island, now heavily wooded and dotted with fine homes but then very sparsely wooded and settled.

representative for the Stanley Electric & Manufacturing Co.

William Stanley, who founded this firm with the financial assistance of George Westinghouse, is credited with the invention of a generator and multiple system of transmission for alternating current, which made the flexibility of transformed voltage available to electric railroads. Stanley wanted to outfit an operating railway with his equipment to demonstrate its value, so he sent John Martin, with the financial backing of Romulus Riggs Colgate, the soap manufacturer, in search of a railroad to electrify.

Despite the woes of the North Pacific Coast, Martin and his associates toured the line in Milton S. Latham's private car *Millwood,* and when their journey was abruptly ended by a derailment in Austin Creek Canyon near Cazadero, John Martin's 200-pound frame was found dangling from a tree in ungraceful helplessness. "Let's buy the line now," he told his companions, "before it kills somebody."

On March 7, 1902, the narrow gauge North Pacific Coast was taken over by the North Shore Railroad with John Martin as president, Eugene J. DeSabla, vice president, W. M. Rank, general manager and A. H. Babcock, electrical engineer. The new firm rebuilt the Marin County suburban lines to standard gauge and electrified them. Part of the line was kept dual gauge so that the narrow gauge steam service could continue to Cazadero.

The company also inherited the ferry service from Water Street, Sausalito, to the Ferry Building in San Francisco. As the steamer *San Rafael* had recently been sunk, only the *Sausalito* and the *Tamalpais,* both second boats of their names, were in operation. A third boat was badly needed.

In 1903 two boats were added to the ferry roster, the double-end passenger ferry *Cazadero,* named for the line's northern terminus, and the stern-wheeled car float *Lagunitas.* Both the boats were built by John W. Dickie and neither was a particular credit to the designer. The *Lagunitas* was badly underpowered and the *Cazadero* had a permanent list to port. Some well-placed fixed ballast solved the *Cazadero's* trouble, but the *Lagunitas* was never re-engined and lived out a short and not-too-useful life of some 15 years trying to struggle across the Bay as best she could.

Electrification of the line was completed by 1905, with generous technical assistance from the Southern Pacific and financial backing provided by the Santa Fe. Both of these major railroads coveted the properties and acquired ownership of this and the other North Bay railway system. By 1907, a new operating entity was to take over both systems.

The regime of the North Shore was short, but in its brief years it transformed a decrepit narrow gauge steam road into a modern electric system which was a model of this type of operation for years thereafter. John Martin faded rapidly from the transportation picture and by 1912 his career was ended by an ill-advised venture in generation of electric power by internal combustion engines. His progressive ideas applied to the North Shore will always be remembered as a vital part of the electrical history of San Francisco Bay.

SAN FRANCISCO & NORTH PACIFIC RAILWAY

Marin county's other railway system was organized by Peter Donahue, one of the most brilliant and energetic men in San Francisco. Incorporated on November 17, 1869, the San Francisco North Pacific Railway succeeded to the properties of the San Francisco & Humboldt Bay Railroad, which had also been organized to build from the Bay Area to the redwood country. The San Francisco & North Pacific began service from its terminal at Donahue Landing on Petaluma Creek on October 31, 1870, at first going only as far as Santa Rosa. By the next year it extended north to Cloverdale.

Ferry service from San Francisco to Donahue Landing began in 1870, the Steamer *Antelope* being brought down from the Sacramento River for the purpose. A new single-ender, the *James M. Donahue,* was built for the company in 1875 and named for the founder's 15-year-old son. The route from Donahue Landing, three miles south of Petaluma, down the creek and across many miles of the Bay was a lengthy one; adding to its perils were the hazards of low tule fogs which frequented the marshy mouth of Petaluma Creek as well as San Pablo Bay. So Peter Donahue extended the line from Petaluma to San Rafael in 1882 and, by 1884, the railroad had reached the shore of the Bay at Point Tiburon.

From 1884 until the coming of the *Ukiah* in 1890, the *Tiburon* was queen of the San Francisco & North Pacific's ferry fleet. There was no smog control board to frown on the emission of coal smoke, when her picture was taken from the deck of the *San Rafael*, above. Below she is seen with her older sister, the *James M. Donahue* at the S.F. & N.P.'s terminal in Tiburon. The photograph at the left is evidence that by 1906, during the California Northwestern regime, the *Tiburon* had entered the age of the automobile. There were no wheel blocks available, but a convenient substitute was found on board. *(Left: Ted Wurm collection, courtesy Roy D. Graves; below: Northwestern Pacific)*

The terminal at Donahue Landing was dismantled and the buildings were brought down to Tiburon on barges. Station, offices of the company, shops, carbarns, enginehouse—they all came and were re-erected almost precisely in the relative positions they had been assigned at Donahue, so historians encounter some difficulty in trying to identify photographs of the two locations.

The *Antelope* was retired and, to establish the new service, the San Francisco & North Pacific built a new boat, the *Tiburon*. It was powered by a beam engine, built for Peter Donahue at the Union Iron Works in 1860 and stored for 24 years in a barn before it was finally installed in the ferryboat.

Late in 1885 Peter Donahue died and his holdings were inherited by his son, James Mervyn Donahue, who now became president of the railway. The company extended its main line to Ukiah, the final track construction under Donahue ownership. To commemorate this achievement, in 1890 it built another ferry at its Tiburon shops, the *Ukiah*, a combination freight car ferry and passenger boat. This vessel became famous for its service on picnics and excursions to El Campo and Paradise Cove.

President James M. Donahue died at the age of thirty in 1890. In the process of settling his estate, which included the majority of shares in the San Francisco & North Pacific Railway, the road was sold on the block in 1893 to a syndicate formed by Andrew Markham, Sydney V. Smith and Arthur W. Foster. The *James M. Donahue*, the *Tiburon* and the *Ukiah* comprised the ferry fleet transferred to the new owners, who continued operations under the old corporate name, but experienced financial difficulties. In 1898 the railroad was sold by the Marin County sheriff.

CALIFORNIA NORTHWESTERN RAILWAY

The California Northwestern Railway Co., which in 1898 purchased the assets of the San Francisco & North Pacific from the auction block on the steps of the Marin County Court House in San Rafael, was formed by a syndicate which included the same three men who had purchased its predecessor in 1893, but this time Arthur Foster was the leading light, apparently with something more

tangible than good will from the Southern Pacific to back him.

The new company continued to operate the same boats as had its predecessor, in the same ferry service from Tiburon to the Ferry Building, San Francisco. There is no record that the name of the new company was ever lettered on the paddle boxes or that the ownership of the boats was ever changed on Custom House records.

The rail line was extended from Ukiah to Laughlin in 1901, to Willits in 1902 and to Sherwood in 1904. Service was increased and the timecard read, "California Northwestern Railway, lessee of the San Francisco & North Pacific Railway." The operation was short-lived, for the properties of this company, together with those of several other roads, fell into the hands of the Southern Pacific and the Atchison, Topeka & Santa Fe in 1907.

NORTHWESTERN PACIFIC RAILROAD

This was a joint venture, financed by both the Southern Pacific and the Santa Fe* with a dedicated purpose of building a through line from San Francisco to Eureka. It absorbed about a dozen different rail lines, including the North Shore and the California Northwestern and their ferry routes, beginning operation as the Northwestern Pacific on January 8, 1907.

The new company consolidated facilities so that interurban trains soon operated only from Sausalito. By April 1, 1909 the California Northwestern's ferry line from Tiburon to San Francisco was eliminated and in its place was a new ferry to connect Tiburon and Belvedere with Sausalito. It was a sad day for those commuters who had formerly enjoyed the direct trip from Tiburon to San Francisco.

The Northwestern Pacific inherited the car ferries *Ukiah* (standard gauge), *Lagunitas* (narrow gauge) and the passenger ferries *James M. Donahue*, *Tiburon*, *Sausalito*, *Cazadero* and *Tamalpais*. The *Donahue* was the only single-ender and, since she was a semi-menace to navigation on the crowded San Francisco water front with her requirement for turning around, she was seldom used on this route and operated between Tiburon, Belvedere and Sausalito. Another disadvantage of

---

*This joint arrangement lasted until 1929 when the Southern Pacific bought out the Santa Fe's interest.

Automobiles of somewhat later date, probably well into the Northwestern Pacific period, are seen on the foredeck of the *Sausalito* as she drifts into the slip. The many trees and residences visible on Belvedere Island beyond the *Cazadero*, below, suggest that the picture was taken many years later than the view from across Richardson Bay, a few pages back. *(Above: Roy D. Graves collection)*

the *Donahue* was that her paddle shaft was almost four feet above the main deck level, preventing express and baggage carts from being pulled clear through the vessel, although this was not too much of an impediment in a single-ender. The shaft provided Marin County small fry with a wonderful place to take a belly-flop ride, particularly if no deck hand were looking.

The *Donahue* was really too large for the Tiburon run, so the company bought a small steamer, the *Requa*, for this service. Fitted with a tiny triple-expansion engine, when she arrived in 1909 she was the darling of the fleet. The *Requa* burned to the waterline in 1911 and was rebuilt by the company as the gasoline ferry *Marin*. This little craft connected with all San Francisco boats, a service which was continued until 1933, when bus transportation deprived the good citizens of Tiburon and Belvedere of the ride they had come to love dearly.

By the fall of 1914 the railroad was driven through to Eureka, but formal opening of the new sector was delayed for over a year. During World War I, the United States Railroad Administration operated the line, using the ferry *Ukiah* to handle so many freight cars, of the Northwestern Pacific and of other lines as well, that the railroad claimed that this heavy usage had broken the *Ukiah's* back and funds were obtained from the U.S.R.A. to rebuild the vessel. As a car ferry was no longer required, she was rebuilt at the Southern Pacific Shipyard as the passenger ferry *Eureka*, with a seating capacity for 2300 persons and life-jackets for over 3000.

With the advent of the *Eureka*, the *James M. Donahue* was ready for disposal, and she was towed to Point San Quentin where she was used as a fishing facility until she disintegrated. The *Tiburon* was the next to go, rounding out service in 1924. The A-frame for her walking beam had become so unstable due to continual stress on its massive timbers that it was no longer rigid. A tremendous rebuilding job was indicated, and as the *Tiburon* was a small boat with limited seating capacity, she was retired.

Four boats remained as the familiar fleet of the Northwestern Pacific until 1927, when the company recognized the motor car. Up to that time, automobiles were carried at sufferance, on a space-permitting basis. In 1922, the vehicular Golden Gate Ferry had started competition which cut and cut into the Northwestern Pacific's ferry revenues, and now the time had come to fight back.

Three new Diesel-electric ferries were built, the *Santa Rosa* at General Engineering and Drydock Co., the *Mendocino* at Bethlehem Steel (Union Iron Works) and the *Redwood Empire* at Moore Dry Dock Co. These were the only Northwestern Pacific ferries to have the beautiful company emblem painted on the stack: The Bay, Mount Tamalpais and a redwood tree. But this addition to the fleet was too late; the Golden Gate Ferry had gained the good will of the motorist and never relinquished it. In 1929, the three Diesel boats were transferred to the Southern Pacific-Golden Ferries, Ltd., and the Northwestern Pacific concentrated on foot passengers for the train connections.

In 1934 the *Sausalito* was condemned and her engine scrapped. The hulk was towed to Antioch where it was made into a clubhouse for a rod and gun club.

With the opening of the Golden Gate Bridge in May, 1937, the end grew closer. The Northwestern Pacific went to a two-boat operation with limited train schedules in an effort to cut costs, but even this economy move failed. On February 28, 1941, the electric trains and ferries made their farewell runs on one of the stormiest days the Bay had known.

Thomas Wosser had been the engineer on the first Marin ferry, the *Princess* of the Sausalito Land & Ferry Co. His son Richard Wosser was, for years until his retirement in 1927, chief engineer of the *Tamalpais*. And as the *Eureka* pulled away from the Ferry Building at midnight, Chief Engineer Andrew Disher winked at Lawrence Wosser, his first assistant engineer. Lawrence, son of Richard and grandson of Thomas, took the bar as Chief Engineer Disher said, "Larry, on this occasion, I think you had better handle the engine." With this nostalgic touch and magnanimous gesture on the part of Andy Disher, a fine gentleman and a great engineer, the curtain rang down on not the oldest, but one of the grandest of ferry services, conducted with elegance and with overtones of nobility.

Auto congestion was severe at Sausalito in the early 1920s, as shown by the picture above, taken before opening of the Golden Gate Ferry. The bus with "4" on the trunk is the Santa Rosa Auto Stage. The N.W.P.'s ungainly *Lagunitas* was seldom photographed, but is depicted, top, opposite, at the spare berth in Sausalito. The only stern-wheel car ferry on the Bay, she was in service but 14 years; her wooden hull, lacking the copper sheathing given most wooden vessels, soon fell victim to decay. Below her is the fine steel auto ferry *Redwood Empire*, one of three built to meet Golden Gate Ferry competition. She and her sisters, the *Santa Rosa* and the *Mendocino*, were the only boats of this company to display its beautiful emblem on the stack. The little *Marin* crosses the bow of the docked *Sausalito* as she leaves for Belvedere and Tiburon in the beautiful 1920 scene at Sausalito. The view of the *Cazadero*, below, was taken from the deck of the *Tamalpais* as fog billows over her namesake mountain. *(Opposite, top to bottom: Southern Pacific; Northwestern Pacific; San Francisco Maritime Museum)*

The Richmond-San Rafael Ferry & Transportation Co.'s general office building at Castro Point in Richmond bore the line's three-link trade mark, symbolizing how it linked the two communities of its name. Below is the *Charles Van Damme*, the line's first boat after the short career of the *Ellen*, in the slip at Point San Quentin. At the bottom, the *Klamath* loads vehicles while the *Sonoma Valley*, ex-*San Jose*, is moored in the storage slip. This was during the transition period when the wooden boats were retired and the steel boats bought from the Southern Pacific-Golden Gate Ferries, Ltd. were going into service. (*Above: Southern Pacific; two photos by Marshall Silverthorn*)

SECTION V

FERRIES FOR AUTOMOBILES

When the first automobiles sought to cross the Bay, they naturally used the ferry accommodations already available to animal-drawn vehicles. As long as automobiles were rare and roads outside the cities were primitive, this arrangement was reasonably adequate, but the rapid increase in the number of cars in the 1900s brought their special needs to the attention of ferry operators.

As has been seen in earlier sections of this chapter, various of the ferry lines accommodated automobiles and it is understandable that the *Melrose*, first ferryboat built expressly for motor vehicles, operated on the Creek Route, for many years a principal vehicular crossing. But as the number of automobiles multiplied and as the highways of the Bay Area were extended and improved for their use, more ferry lines were needed to meet their need.

In this section are the stories of the five ferry companies which were organized to handle automobile traffic across various parts of San Francisco Bay.

RICHMOND-SAN RAFAEL FERRY

In 1911 an early-day motorist pulled up at Point Richmond and looked across the three miles of San Pablo Bay toward the hills of Marin. "How do I get over there?" he asked of young Raymond H. Clarke who was fishing from the Richmond shore.

Clarke replied, "Well, you go to Oakland, to the foot of Broadway; they will take cars on the boat. Then when you get to San Francisco, take the Northwestern Pacific ferry to Sausalito. Sometimes they will permit cars on the boat." Then, pointing across the water to the Marin hills, he added, "If you're lucky, you can do that three miles in three hours."

The motorist muttered something akin to "Forget it!" and Ray Clarke went on fishing. As he watched his line which drew no response from the finny tribe, he thought to himself, "How could I get a boat or maybe a barge and pull cars across the water?" The idea stuck with him, and he could not let go of it. He talked boat and barge to anyone who would listen.

Finally he went to live with his wife's uncle, Charles Van Damme, Secretary of the Olson & Mahoney Lumber Co. Ray Clarke talked boat morning, noon and night. Charles Van Damme listened only casually at first but the longer he heard the tune, the more he knew the music. One day he proposed the ferry from Richmond to San Rafael to Andrew F. Mahoney, partner of the firm. There was no argument, and few questions were asked. Van Damme came home that evening and told Ray Clarke to go look for a boat.

Ray found the *Ellen* of the Mare Island Ferry Co. and leased her for $250 per month in 1915. The Northwestern Pacific had the pier at Point San Quentin where in 1884 the *Saucelito* had burned in her slip. This was sometimes used as a railroad terminal, but had accommodated no ferries since the fire. Ray leased this pier and a waterfront site at Castro Point in Richmond. The company was capitalized for $25,000, and on May 1, 1915, service commenced with Captain Hiram Knight at the wheel. The new enterprise did not operate for long; steamboat inspectors condemned the *Ellen* after a month of service, and the company had to start all over again. This time a new boat, the side-wheeler *Charles Van Damme*, was ordered from James Robertson, the Benicia builder, and in July 1916 service was resumed on a six-trips-daily basis by the Richmond-San Rafael Ferry & Transportation Co., a division of the Olson & Mahoney Co.

Ray Clarke always wanted to be captain of his own boat, but he had only a small boat operator's license and had to begin as a deck hand and work his way to the top. He accomplished this and was master of the *Charles Van Damme* even before the fleet was augmented in 1921 by a second side-wheeler, the *City of Richmond*. She was followed in 1924 by the *City of San Rafael*, the last side-wheeler to be built on the Bay.

Traditionally the Richmond-San Rafael boats were painted a barn red which was greatly in contrast to the white boats of most of the other ferry operators. The partners, Oliver Olson and Andrew Mahoney, who annually alternated as chief executive of the company, could not agree whether the boats should be painted red or white, so there was a long time during the 1920s when the boats were red only every other year. The company's link-

The bottom picture, of the Richmond-San Rafael Ferry's Richmond terminal can be easily dated as during the 1920s by the vintage long-nosed automobile at the right and by the red-painted corner of the *City of San Rafael* appearing at the right. The "Next Boat Leaves" clock was no longer in operation by the time the above view of the *Sierra Nevada* was taken approaching Point San Quentin terminal. The year was 1955 and the Richmond-San Rafael Bridge was nearly completed. After September, 1956, the boats were needed no more and, with stacks draped in canvas, the *Klamath* and the *Russian River* stand silent and forlorn in the view below; a bit of the *Sierra Nevada* is visible at the left.   (Bottom: Southern Pacific)

chain emblem continued to decorate the sides of the vessels.

With the demise of the Rodeo-Vallejo Ferry the *San Jose* was purchased from that line and in 1928 joined the Richmond-San Rafael roster, extensively refitted as the *Sonoma Valley*.

When the Southern Pacific-Golden Gate Ferries ceased to operate in 1939, the Richmond-San Rafael Ferry purchased the *El Paso, Klamath* and the *New Orleans*, which was rechristened *Russian River*. On May 30, 1947, the *Sierra Nevada*, the boat of many owners, was purchased from the Southern Pacific and converted to automobile service. With these four vessels, service continued until September 1, 1956, when the new State-owned bridge eliminated the need for the fleet which was painted the traditional white during all of its last years.

Although not quite the last of the auto ferries to operate, this was the last major company to run some of the old familiar ferryboats on the Bay. Termination of the line seemed so final. True, there were a few brief years while it was still possible, by driving all the way to Martinez, to take the short crossing to Benicia; otherwise San Francisco ferry fans had lost their last opportunity to ride a local ferryboat. The only remaining way to ride on the Bay was aboard a private craft, or among the crowds of tourists on the spacious harbor sightseeing boats.

RODEO-VALLEJO FERRY

In 1915 the Carquinez Ferry Co. offered launch service of short duration across Carquinez Strait, and the Southern Pacific continued to carry passengers between South Vallejo and Vallejo Junction, but no facilities existed for vehicles until the organization of the Rodeo-Vallejo Ferry Co. by three grocery men who felt that a need existed for the transportation of automobiles and trucks across Carquinez Strait. Aven J. Hanford had a grocery store in Calistoga, and was a farsighted dynamic businessman. Oscar H. Klatt and his father-in-law, Gentry, worked for Tillman & Bentle, wholesale grocers, and these two became well acquainted with Hanford. Between them they founded the Rodeo-Vallejo Ferry Co. in 1918, secured terminal space in the two cities named in the corporate title, and then began looking about for a boat.

The little steamer *Issaquah* had been built in Seattle in 1914 and was now operating on Puget Sound. There Hanford purchased the boat, hired a crew and was about to take the train home when the captain suggested that he ride down the coast on the ferryboat. It would take only a couple of days and the train fare would be saved. Hanford did not notify his family of the change in plans and everybody at home began to worry when neither the *Issaquah* nor its new owner appeared in five days. Finally the little vessel arrived in Vallejo after having ridden out a violent Pacific storm. Despite her need for repairs, she was immediately placed in service on July 4, 1918, in time for the rush of holiday traffic.

The "*Squash*," as the *Issaquah* was affectionately known, did the bulk of the work on the Rodeo-Vallejo Ferry and was the boat which operated during the hectic years when the line was hard-pressed by the rival Six Minute Ferry. This competition all but spelled the finish for the Rodeo-Vallejo Co. for the *Issaquah* had to travel three times as far as did the Six Minute Ferry's *San Jose*.

Aven J. Hanford fought back by building a fast new vessel, named for himself, with engines and boilers from the old Navy destroyer *Farragut*. Although she stuck on the ways when launched at James Robertson's Benicia shipyard and had to be pulled into the water by tugs, the *Aven J. Hanford* was soon in service and ran a month between Rodeo and Vallejo before outside circumstances removed the Six Minute Ferry from the picture.

The Rodeo-Vallejo Ferry Co. purchased its defunct rival's franchise, ferryboat and other assets for $400,000 in March 1922. They put the *San Jose* on the run from Rodeo to Vallejo opposite the *Issaquah*, and transferred the *Aven J. Hanford* to the Golden Gate Ferry, since Hanford, Klatt and Gentry had by now acquired control of that company.

In 1923, Aven J. Hanford and Oscar H. Klatt incorporated the American Toll Bridge Co. and had the Carquinez Bridge engineered for them. It is interesting to note that these progressive ferrymen built the first major bridge that replaced a ferry line across the Bay. The bridge was opened to traffic in May 1927 and the Rodeo-Vallejo Ferry ceased operations. The *Issaquah* was sold to the Martinez-Benicia Ferry, and the *San Jose* to the

The rare picture of the *San Jose*, above, is the only known photograph of the Six Minute Ferry in operation. The Golden Gate Ferry's Hyde Street terminal looks rather primitive in the 1923 picture, below, as compared with its later appearance. In her original white paint, the motor vessel *Golden West* is in the dock receiving motor cars; the army water boat, *El Aguador*, is in the distance. *(Above: Roy D. Graves collection; below: Harry E. Speas collection)*

Richmond-San Rafael Ferry, which had her remodeled and rechristened *Sonoma Valley*.

SIX MINUTE FERRY

In 1919 the Association of Mare Island Employees, successful in its operation of the Vallejo-Mare Island Ferry, decided to expand its operations and help employes who lived across Carquinez Strait from Vallejo. Noting the success of the Rodeo-Vallejo Ferry in the automobile trade, the Association's promoters, Forbes H. Brown and C. V. Stewart, obtained a terminal at Morrow Cove on the north shore and another terminal directly opposite at Crockett. They now had a route about a third as long as that of their rival.

The Key Route ferry *San Jose* had burned earlier that year. The Association purchased her and had her rebuilt as an auto boat at James Robertson's Benicia shipyard. To publicize the brief running time of the new line they adopted the name Six Minute Ferry. The immediate success of this venture almost ruined the Rodeo-Vallejo Ferry. Brown and Stewart were able to interest Mayor James Rolph of San Francisco in the enterprise. Recently the successful operator of wooden sailing ships during World War I, Rolph helped finance the building of three new ferryboats for the Six Minute run; these were begun on the ways of the Bethlehem Steel Co. (Union Iron Works) in San Francisco.

Trouble now came to the Six Minute Ferry. An earthslide wiped out the Morrow Cove terminal and the government began investigating the legality of the Association's operation in competition with private enterprise in a locality not adjacent to the Federal premises. The Southern Pacific, which had seen the company as potential competition now bought the three new boats that were still on the ways. The Association was dissolved and its only active ferry, the *San Jose* was sold to the Rodeo-Vallejo Ferry Co. The short life of a short ferry was ended in 1922.

GOLDEN GATE FERRY

The Golden Gate Ferry was the brain child of an early-day motorist who lived in San Francisco but loved to take his Sunday ride in the hills of Marin and Sonoma Counties to the north. The motorist was Harry E. Speas, and he was sick and tired of the long wait required to board, if lucky, the passenger ferries of the Northwestern Pacific. The latter company accepted automobiles as an accommodation, but was not always in the mood to accommodate. One Sunday evening, Harry Speas and his family missed the last boat from Sausalito to San Francisco, and as he spent the night in a local hostelry, he convinced himself that a second ferry line for automobiles was required.

In 1920, Harry E. Speas incorporated the Golden Gate Ferry Co. for $1,000,000 and obtained approval from the State Railroad Commission to sell stock. After much personal effort, he obtained the lease of property at the foot of Hyde Street in San Francisco for a terminal, and waterfront property on deep water in Sausalito was made available to him by Captain Randolph Pettersen. In this period of ferry expansion on San Francisco Bay, there were no boats available with which to commence service, and stock sales had been insufficient to finance the immediate construction of a new vessel.

Speas went to Aven J. Hanford, president of the Rodeo-Vallejo Ferry Co. for assistance, and an agreement was consummated whereby Hanford, Klatt and Gentry of the latter corporation were made directors of the Golden Gate Ferry Co., and the new Rodeo-Vallejo ferryboat, *Aven J. Hanford*, was transferred to the Sausalito-Hyde Street run. On May 28, 1922, blue-uniformed Captain John Lorentzen rang down "full speed ahead" on the engine telegraph, and one of the most lucrative enterprises on San Francisco Bay was launched with minimal fanfare.

On July 4, 1922, the second boat, the *Golden Gate*, the first Diesel-electric ferry on San Francisco Bay went into operation, and the *Golden West* followed in 1923. These first three boats were painted white originally, but in early 1924, the standard colors for the company consisted of bright yellow hulls and superstructure trimmed in black, in keeping with the "golden" theme of this monetarily golden enterprise. In 1924, the company leased the Key Route's wooden steamer *Yerba Buena*, converted her to carry automobiles and rechristened her the *Harry E. Speas*. Other Key boats were leased and added to the fleet within the next two years, the Key's *San Francisco* becoming the *Golden Dawn*, the *Fernwood*

An even earlier picture of the Golden Gate Ferry, in its first year of operation, appears below. The *Aven J. Hanford* is tied to the side dolphins as the new *Golden Gate* leaves the pier. They are offering stiff competition to the Northwestern Pacific's *Tamalpais*, which can be seen in the distance. Above are two other views of the line's Sausalito terminal after the *Harry E. Speas*, the former Key Route *Yerba Buena*, had been added to the fleet and painted golden yellow. The end pilings of the slip in the top picture are canted from battering of the boats while docking. *(Top: James Milani collection)*

being refitted as the *Golden Era* and the *Claremont* as the *Golden Way.*

Aven Hanford, having become interested in other activities, sold his stock and retired from the ferry company in March, 1925. He was succeeded as president by A. C. Stewart, who had an eye for the Vallejo trade. In order to compete with the Monticello Steamship Co., the Golden Gate Ferry built a toll road from Vallejo to Sears Point to divert automobiles to the Sausalito-San Francisco auto ferry. This venture was neither profitable nor did it remove the competition. The big, swift Monticello boats continued their grip on Bay auto trade.

More hulls in golden yellow appeared on the Bay. The *Golden State* was built in 1926 and four boats to be much like her were ordered from the General Engineering & Drydock Co. The *Aven J. Hanford* was converted to straight Diesel drive and renamed *Golden City,* only to operate a mere two days before she was sunk in a collision with the steamer *Newport.*

A second service, between Hyde Street, San Francisco, and the foot of University Avenue, Berkeley, commenced in 1927. The Berkeley shoal was crossed by a three-mile pier which both shortened the ferry trip and provided a convenient parking place for waiting automobiles. In time for the opening of this service, three of the almost identical new Diesel-electric vessels, the *Golden Bear, Golden Poppy* and *Golden Shore* were on hand. This year Harry E. Speas withdrew from active participation in the company and the boat named for him became the *Golden Coast.*

Also in 1927 the Golden Gate Ferry Co. bought out the Monticello Steamship Co. from Tremaine Hatch and C. Ferry Hatch for $2,000,000. This would suggest that the opening of the Sears Point toll road in 1925 had not exactly crushed the Monticello competition. The great ferries *Napa Valley, City of Sacramento* and *Calistoga* added substantially to the carrying capacity of the Golden Gate fleet. These fast boats could carry over 100 automobiles each, as compared with the 62-car capacity of the "Golden" class ferries.

In 1928 the *Golden Age,* last boat to be built for the Golden Gate Ferry, joined the fleet. This year, too, a new auto ferry was inaugurated from Point Richmond, near the Santa Fe ferry terminal,

to San Francisco, where an additional slip was added adjacent to the newly-acquired Monticello lease at the north end of the Ferry Building. The growth of the new company was phenomenal, a constant concern to the Southern Pacific, the Golden Gate Ferry's only rival. Profits were increasing at a steady rate of 26% per year on the capital investment, and the piers and boats were choked with traffic. Ferry police on the Berkeley pier were urging motorists to drive at least sixty miles per hour to keep the boats filled and running.

The greatest demand for additional boats was on the Sausalito run on Sunday nights. When the auto traffic taxed the capacities of the Diesels, the steamers were broken out to supplement the schedule. The timecard was ignored with boats arriving and departing as soon as they could be unloaded and then refilled. The deck hands would squeeze every possible car onto the ferries in every imaginable position, then off they would go to Hyde Street, and return nearly empty to repeat the process. If the smaller steamers could not handle the demand, the *City of Sacramento* would be taken off the Vallejo run, devour cars in her gaping hold and beat the time it took the Diesel ferries to make the crossing, even if she did have to turn around at each terminal.

In 1929, the Southern Pacific and the Golden Gate Ferries concluded an agreement for joint operation wherein the name of the Golden Gate Ferry was preserved, but the stock of the young company was bought outright by the S. P. The merger was a sensible solution to a highly competitive operation, and economies could be realized and parallel services eliminated. Thus ended the meteoric seven-year career of a ferry company whose tremendous expansion reflected the growth in use of automobiles and highways during the same period. The Golden Gate Ferries were absorbed in an organization which handled masses of vehicles of proportions that only the great bridges could surpass.

SOUTHERN PACIFIC-GOLDEN GATE FERRIES, LTD.

As the vehicular ferries became vital links in the Bay Area's highway system, reflecting the new universality of the family car, this company was organized in 1929 as a joint operation of all auto-

By June, 1931, the Hyde Street terminal had developed dramatically since the 1922 view shown on an earlier page. The only boat that can be positively identified is the *Yosemite*, which can be seen loading cars for Sausalito. One of the wooden Diesels is unloading cars from Berkeley; a steamer, probably one of the Key Route conversions, is leaving the other Berkeley slip, and one of the steel Diesels approaches from Sausalito, at the left. Above, much mutilated in appearance to facilitate loading automobiles, the *City of Sacramento* is packed with young people on a 1932 Christian Endeavor excursion. *(Above: Southern Pacific; below: San Francisco Maritime Museum)*

mobile ferries controlled by the Southern Pacific, the Golden Gate Ferry and the Northwestern Pacific. Carl F. Fennema, formerly of the latter company, became general manager of the new company; all the stock was owned by the Southern Pacific. The number of ferryboats afloat on the Bay was near an all-time high but the end of this new ferry line was contemplated from its beginning, so to speak, for two great bridges were on the drawing boards of engineers, bridges which would soon span the Bay from San Francisco to Oakland and from San Francisco across the Golden Gate.

Billboards advertised the new line on Califronia highways; "Nine Routes, Twenty-Seven Boats," they said. This was true enough, if one knew how to count the routes. Three of them fanned out from the foot of Mission Street in San Francisco to Alameda, to Oakland Pier and up the Estuary to the foot of Broadway in Oakland. From the north end of the Ferry Building were the lines to Richmond and Vallejo. The lines to Berkeley and Sausalito landed at the foot of Hyde Street. These were the seven routes on boats actually operated by the new company. The other two routes were from the Ferry Building, from which passenger ferries of the Southern Pacific and the Northwestern Pacific sometimes took automobiles to Oakland Pier and Sausalito, respectively. This practice was soon discontinued and the number of routes remained at seven until the opening of the San Francisco-Oakland Bay Bridge in November, 1936.

The boats were easier to count: Thirteen were from the Golden Gate Ferry, eleven from the Southern Pacific and three from the Northwestern Pacific, for a total of 27. The *Melrose* was retired in 1931 and the *Thoroughfare* in 1935. The ex-Key Route boats, *Golden Era*, *Golden Dawn*, and *Golden Coast* were used mostly as spares and in times of peak traffic.

Until the San Francisco-Oakland Bay Bridge was opened to traffic, the company flourished; this new route on which automobiles could drive across the Bay at a toll lower than the fare on the automobile ferries of course brought an immediate and drastic loss of traffic on the transbay boats. Opening of the Golden Gate Bridge the following May did the same thing for auto ferries between

The Southern Pacific-Golden Gate Ferries, Ltd. abandoned the auto ferry service between Sausalito and Hyde Street, San Francisco, on July 24, 1938. In the wheelhouse of the steamer *Yosemite* for the last trip were Captain Edward Hallin, right, and First Officer Carl Nielsen. The captain had started as a deck hand on the *Aven J. Hanford* and devoted his entire ferry career to the Golden Gate Ferry and its S.P.G.G. successor.

San Francisco and Sausalito. Of the once vast ferry empire, only the Sausalito-Hyde Street and Oakland Pier-San Francisco services remained in operation. In order to compete with the bridges, fares were greatly reduced, but traffic fell off day by day and it was evident that automobile ferry operation to San Francisco was doomed.

Less than fourteen months after the opening of the Golden Gate Bridge, the last boat went from Hyde Street to Sausalito on July 24, 1938, the *Yosemite*, with Captain Edward Hallin at the helm. The service to Oakland Pier lingered about a year longer before the *Lake Tahoe* made the last revenue run for the Southern Pacific-Golden Gate Ferries, Ltd., with the same Captain Hallin in command. He had started as a deck hand on the *Aven J. Hanford* on the initial trip of the Golden Gate Ferry. And so it ended in 1939, quietly and without fanfare. Of the company that had enjoyed

FOR SALE

6 Automobile and Passenger Ferry Boats, now on San Francisco Bay

STEEL HULL—OIL BURNING

Ferry Steamers	Auto Capacity	Passenger Capacity	Vehicle Clearance	Length		Width		Brake Horse Power	Tonnage	
				Keel	Deck	Beam	Guards		Gross	Net
City of Sacramento	103	2,027	11′ 6″	298′ 0″	308′ 0″	50′ 0″	67′ 4″	2,600	3,016	1,829
Calistoga	103	1,526	9′ 6″	298′ 2″	308′ 5″	45′ 0″	65′ 0″	2,600	2,680	1,516
Napa Valley (1)	85	1,528	11′ 6″	231′ 2″	242′ 0″	48′ 7″	62′ 5″	2,600	2,189	1,289
Shasta (2)	62	2,200	11′ 6″	206′ 0″	230′ 0″	42′ 0″	63′ 6″	1,230	1,782	1,120
Yosemite (2)	62	1,400	11′ 4″	206′ 0″	230′ 0″	42′ 0″	63′ 6″	1,230	1,782	1,120
San Mateo (2)	62	1,175	11′ 6″	206′ 0″	230′ 0″	42′ 0″	63′ 6″	1,230	1,782	1,120
(1) Similar in type to Calistoga. (2) Sisterships.										6/1/39

For Further Information Write:

Southern Pacific Golden Gate Ferries, Ltd.
65 Market Street, San Francisco, California

seven years of spectacular success, there remained only a small organization to dispose of the boats.

Following the bridge opening the *Golden West* was sold to the San Diego & Coronado Ferry and the former Key Route steamers were retired to the shore of Oakland Estuary. The *Golden Age* and the *Golden State* went to the Kitsap County Transportation Co. in Washington for service on Puget Sound, while the Black Ball Line (Puget Sound Navigation Co.) received the *Shasta, San Mateo, Golden Poppy, Golden Shore, Lake Tahoe, Mendocino, Redwood Empire, Stockton, Santa Rosa, Fresno* and — later — the *Napa Valley*. The Black Ball had also bought the *Golden Bear*, but during the course of the tow northward, this ferryboat was wrecked beyond economical repair in a storm and was towed into Empire, Oregon. The only portion left intact was a pilothouse, which was purchased by Hans A. B. Sneve, a Sausalito marine manufacturer's representative, returned on a truck and for years used as his office above his Sausalito home. In 1943 the Black Ball Line purchased the *City of Sacramento* from the War Shipping Administration which had bought it from Southern Pacific-Golden Gate Ferries.

For its new assignment, the steamer *Yosemite* had much the farthest to go. It was sold to a line in South America to run on the Rio de la Plata from Colonia, Uruguay, to Buenos Aires, thirty miles away. The little steamer was all boarded up for the trip with a tremendous bulkhead installed on the foredeck to protect the ship from the seas. She made the passage in something like forty days, going down the west coast to the Panama Canal, then down the east coast of South America. Her crew reported an uneventful trip, for the ocean was smooth and the weather fine all the way.

The former *Yosemite* is shown on a trial run prior to her departure for Uruguay on February 9, 1940. One propeller has been removed to increase efficiency and the vessel is operating stack forward. Her new owners went out of business after a couple of years and the *Argentina* was converted to a barge. After a number of years in this capacity she was finally abandoned and sunk. *(Below: Robert W. Parkinson photo; opposite: his collection)*

These excursion boats offer visitors to San Francisco an opportunity to travel on the Bay, and also provide commute service between Tiburon and San Francisco. *(Below: Orie Damewood photo; both: courtesy Harbor Tours, Inc.)*

VI
Ferryboats Today

THE BEAUTIES of San Francisco Bay, in all sorts of weather, day and night, remain undiminished as the years go by. The details of the picture are ever changing as new buildings rise on the San Francisco and Oakland skylines and new residential districts spread over the hills around the Bay. The stately ferryboats are no longer part of the scene on the water, but in their place are countless small pleasure boats and on a fine day the Bay is dotted with thousands of white and colored sails. It is still possible to get out on the Bay to enjoy the beauty and exhilaration that was once the daily privilege of ferry passengers, but no longer on a full-sized ferryboat, with or without walking beam and paddle wheel. Vestiges of old services remain; commuters once more ride on an old ferry route nearly sixty years abandoned; excursion boats are available. Some of the ferryboats themselves can still be seen at the edge of the Bay and, on distant waters, others are still traveling.

The last remaining of the historic *routes* has been continuously in operation for well over a century. Since 1851 boats have shuttled across Mare Island Strait, carrying people between Vallejo and the Navy Yard. Launches now run on this route every working day from 6:30 to 7:30 a.m. and from 3:30 to 4:30 p.m. The boats are open to the public, although admittance to the Yard itself is subject to Naval security regulations.

The easiest way for someone without a private boat to enjoy a ride on the Bay is on an excursion boat. The red-and-white craft of Harbor Tours, Inc. land at Pier 43½ on the Embarcadero, near San Francisco's Fisherman's Wharf. The boats themselves, of course, are no more like the old ferryboats than the 1960s are like the 1920s. They are built in a different age and for a different purpose. Nevertheless, they do make life on the Bay

accessible to people of the 1960s and thousands of Bay Area residents and visitors enjoy riding the *Harbor King*, the *Harbor Prince*, and the *Harbor Queen* or the other vessels of this fleet.

Next to Pier 43½ is Pier 43 where there is a rail ferry slip that accommodates the only large ferryboat currently in service, the Western Pacific's car ferry, *Las Plumas*. Loaded with freight cars, she shuttles between here and the railroad's 25th Street San Francisco yard, its Oakland Mole, and Encinal Terminal in Alameda. This graceful but utilitarian craft was built in Portland, Oregon and came to the Bay almost thirty years after the last of the older ferryboats was constructed. In 1967 she will pass her tenth birthday.

About a mile south along the Embarcadero is San Francisco's famed landmark, the Ferry Building. Its tall gray tower was for years regarded as the symbol of the City, standing as it did over the City's "front door" through which countless travelers and suburbanites entered San Francisco. Now fronted with a two-level elevated concrete freeway, the building itself looks much as it always did, although its northern half has been extensively remodeled to accommodate the headquarters of the San Francisco World Trade Center Authority.

A number of the ferry slips have been destroyed by fires. One in the mid-1950s destroyed an attractive landmark familiar to commuters on the Key System and Northwestern Pacific boats. It was a small white bell tower that stood on the finger between the two slips. From its gilded dome, supported on graceful pillars, once hung the big bell that guided ferry pilots trying to find the slip in the fog. It had long since been succeeded in this purpose by more modern bells and foghorns.

Most of the rest of the slips are being removed as construction proceeds on the Bay Area Rapid

These boats all went to Puget Sound after the opening of the big bridges on San Francisco Bay. The *Golden Poppy* became the *Chetzemoka*, above, now an extra boat on the San Juan Islands route. The *Fresno* was single ended and remodeled as the *Willapa*, below; she is on the Seattle-Bremerton run. The *Shasta* has now been retired to serve as a restaurant at Portland. (*Above: Jack Whitmeyer photo; two photos: courtesy Washington State Ferries*)

Transit District's transbay tube, through which trains will speed back and forth between the City and Oakland in the 1970s. The eastern end of this underwater line will be at the site of the vast yellow-and-brown train shed that stood until 1966 on the Southern Pacific's Oakland Pier. Soon it will be possible, in the cool darkness of the tunnel at the bottom of the Bay, to travel in about eight minutes the same trip that once took twenty minutes on a ferryboat, in fog or rain or sparkling sunshine, with sea gulls, passing watercraft and distant views of cities and hills to distract attention from the grim urgency of getting from one side of the Bay to the other.

Just north of the Ferry Building is a landing where, on the morning of every business day, the *Harbor Queen* or one of her sister vessels arrives to discharge a boatload of well-dressed latter-day commuters from Marin County. This is a revival of the old ferry route of the San Francisco & North Pacific Railway that used to run the *James M. Donahue*, the *Tiburon* and the *Ukiah* between the Ferry Building and the railroad's Tiburon terminal. Service on this route was discontinued in 1907 when the Northwestern Pacific consolidated all San Francisco-Marin County services in its Sausalito terminal. The current revival of this service now departs from a dock in Tiburon not far from the old S. F. & N. P. terminal at 7:30 a.m. for the forty minute crossing to the Ferry Building. The return trip leaves San Francisco at 5:30 p.m. As freeways and bridges become more and more clogged with traffic, it is possible that this type of commuting may become more common in the future.

Moored at Slip 10 is the neat white *San Leandro*, last of the Southern Pacific ferries to travel the once busy route from the Ferry Building to Oakland Pier. Painted orange, she arrived on the Bay in 1923 and served the Key System for 17 years, then engaged in five years of home-front war work before the Southern Pacific acquired her. She spent her last 13 active years carrying mainline passengers, baggage and express between Oakland and San Francisco. Her last run was in July, 1958. She was overhauled in 1965 and is maintained in a serviceable condition, ready for immediate use—the last of the old Bay ferryboats still in this condition. She is registered to the Em-pire Shipping Corporation of Oakland and her agent is the Franklin Machine Works of San Francisco, willing to lease her to any concern wishing to start a ferry line.

Of the San Francisco Bay ferryboats still in operation, most will be found in the Puget Sound fleet of the Washington State Ferries, which inherited the operations of the Black Ball Line and the Kitsap County Transportation Co. The only steamer still in use is the *San Mateo*. On completion of four new ferries, she may perhaps be retired; it has been proposed that she then be made a marine museum. Her Californian name contrasts oddly with the Indian names conferred on most Puget Sound ferries. She was one of the oldest of the San Francisco Bay ferries that went there soon after the opening of the Bay and Golden Gate Bridges. Presumably her new owners planned to retire her soon and did not bother to change her name. The *San Mateo* proved so durable that she is still on the job after thirty years in the Northwest and little changed in appearance, except for painting.

The Diesels that went to the Sound were all renamed and have been visibly modified in some degree. They are equipped with radar and enclosed against the cooler climate of the Northwest. The wooden Diesels *Klahanie* (ex-*Golden Age*), *Kehloken* (ex-*Golden State*) and *Chetzemoka* (ex-*Golden Poppy*) are generally used on the less-traveled routes; on the major routes are the larger and finer steel Diesels: *Willapa* (ex-*Fresno*), *Klickitat* (ex-*Stockton*), *Nisqually* (ex-*Mendocino*), *Enetai* (ex-*Santa Rosa*), *Illahee* (ex-*Lake Tahoe*) and *Quinault* (ex-*Redwood Empire*).

These boats are readily recognizable to the discerning San Francisco Bay ferryboat fancier, even though some are now single-enders or have other fairly radical changes. Completely unrecognizable is the flamboyantly streamlined *Kalakala*, built on the hull of the Key System's fine *Peralta* after her brief unhappy career was ended by fire in 1933. Apparently the flames consumed any "jinx" that might once have haunted her, for the *Kalakala* has operated successfully on the Sound for more than thirty years.

Farther to the north is another old favorite from San Francisco Bay in a new guise, the *Langdale Queen*, a Diesel operated by the British Columbia

After her disastrous 1933 fire, the hulk of the *Peralta* was towed to Puget Sound where she was rebuilt as the "World's First Streamlined Ferry," the silvery motor vessel *Kalakala*, above. On San Diego Bay the *Golden Shore* now operates as the *Silver Strand*, the *Golden West* as the *North Island*. (Above: courtesy Washington State Ferries; two photos: Bishop Newsphotos: courtesy San Diego & Coronado Ferry Co.)

Government on a ferry route from Horseshoe Bay, north of Vancouver, across the mouth of Howe Sound to Port Langdale on the Sechelt Peninsula. She was built in 1903 at the Philadelphia yard of William Cramp & Sons as the steamer *Asbury Park*. In 1918 she came through the Panama Canal to join the fleet of the Monticello Steamship Co. on San Francisco Bay, where she broke all speed records. She was renamed *City of Sacramento* and served the Golden Gate Ferry and the Southern Pacific-Golden Gate Ferries, Ltd. before she was put out of the auto ferry business by the bridges. After a tour of duty with the War Shipping Administration, she went in 1942 to Puget Sound where she joined the Black Ball fleet. In 1952 she was stripped to the waterline, given a Diesel engine and named *Kahloke*. In 1961 the British Columbia Government bought her, and in 1964 named her *Langdale Queen*. One wonders whether the workers at the Cramp yard in Philadelphia expected that the steel hull they built so soundly in 1903 would last for more than sixty years and be still operating in British Columbia waters as late as 1967.

More than a thousand miles down the Pacific Coast from British Columbia, in San Diego Bay, are two wooden Diesel ferryboats built for the Golden Gate Ferry. When the Southern Pacific-Golden Gate Ferries, Ltd. ended service they sold the *Golden West* to the San Diego & Coronado Ferry Co., who rebuilt her with the wide-open automobile deck appropriate to San Diego's balmy climate, and renamed her *North Island*. She is now that line's stand-by vessel.

In 1944 the company bought the *Elwha* from the Puget Sound Navigation Co. She had operated ten years on San Francisco Bay as the *Golden Shore*; in San Diego she got her third name, *Silver Strand*, but was not noticeably remodeled. She will pass her fortieth birthday in 1967 and still operates regularly. Aside from her white coloring, she still looks much as she did when in 1927, painted golden yellow, she made her debut with the opening of the Berkeley ferry. An incident in her career moved the Drake Navigators Guild of Point Reyes, California to address the following letter to the company under date of June 17, 1954:

Three hundred and seventy-five years ago, on June 17, 1579, Francis Drake landed on the

West Coast of what is now the United States, at Drakes Bay, Marin County, California. There at *Nova Albion* (New England), he built a fort and remained 36 days while he careened and repaired his ship the *Golden Hind*. This camp predated the first English colony on our East Coast, Fort Raleigh, by six years, the colony at Jamestown by 28 years, and the colony at Plymouth by 41 years.

The Drake Navigators Guild is pleased to present to the Motorship *Silver Strand*, through the San Diego Historical Society, this flag to be flown in San Diego's observance of this important date in American history.

In selecting the *Silver Strand* as our "flagship" on San Diego Bay, we are especially mindful of the fact that in May 1938, while being towed from San Francisco Bay to Puget Sound, she was taken into Drakes Bay for shelter from heavy seas. We are mindful also that this vessel has served well in the three great harbors of our West Coast: on San Francisco Bay as the *Golden Shore*; on Puget Sound as the *Elwha*; and on San Diego Bay as the *Silver Strand*.

As of this writing, 14 boats are known to be still running; another is in condition to be put back into immediate operation if needed. Almost as many of the boats are at or near the shore, still intact and recognizable and, in many instances, in use.

Most glamorous of these, perhaps, is the *Klamath*. She was launched two days after Christmas in 1924 as a workaday, no-nonsense auto ferry to round out the Southern Pacific's fleet of six on the then-new vehicular route between Oakland Pier and the Ferry Building. Efficient she was, sturdy and staunch, and she gave the Southern Pacific and Southern Pacific-Golden Gate Ferries, Ltd. 14 years of dependable service. In 1938 she was sold. According to her log:

November 1, 1938—This day commences as *Klamath* joins Richmond-San Rafael Ferry line. Crew variously employed at their trades. Evening port made at Point San Quentin.

Another wartime log entry is of interest:

July 2, 1944—Heavy westerly swell developed during morning hours. 4:23 p.m., *Klamath* proceeding under all prudent steam when U. S. Navy submarine crossed her bow, the same being rammed by the *Klamath*. Damage light to both vessels.

This was the most imposing war record of any of the ferries on San Francisco Bay. It is not recorded that the *Klamath* received the Purple Heart following this incident, nor that the Navy launched

(Gabriel Moulin photo courtesy Walter Landor & Associates)

any reprisal attack. She continued her placid operations for another dozen years, then, says the log:

> September 1, 1956—*Klamath* commences her retirement. All flags struck.

For the second time in her career the *Klamath* was out of a job because of the completion of a bridge.

She was laid up at the edge of Oakland Estuary for a few years until the industrial designer, Walter Landor, learned she was available and saw the possibility of using her as a floating studio and addition to his existing offices at Pier 5 in San Francisco. He had her taken to the Bethlehem shipyard, where she was first built; there she was completely remodeled. Most of her machinery, including the propeller, was removed and for six months the process of reconstruction proceeded under the supervision of Alexis Tellis of the Landor organization. Partitions, ceilings, heating, air conditioning, plumbing, lighting, telephones and other types of equipment were added to make her an attractive and well-equipped studio and office for an industrial design firm. The purpose was to restore the *Klamath's* best features and introduce glamour that would have been foreign to an automobile ferry. Finally the day came when she was towed from the shipyard to her new berth:

> July 9, 1964—This day commences with crew in disarray. Recommissioning ceremony at appointed hour. The Old Man comes aboard and sets sail for triumphant return to the Ferry Building. Cargo becomes slightly wet en route, but all flags are flying.

She is now permanently moored at Pier 5, just north of the Ferry Building, a visible blending of the romance of San Francisco's ferryboat past with the future-oriented profession of industrial design, as exemplified by Walter Landor & Associates. As Mr. Landor expressed it: "We felt that the imaginations and spirits of our group would be stimulated by a studio that is beautiful and imaginative as well as functional."

One of the old Northwestern Pacific ferry slips in Sausalito has a permanent occupant in the fine 1898 Southern Pacific ferry *Berkeley*. She looks almost exactly as she did during her nearly sixty years of service for the Southern Pacific, but now serves as a floating store, the "Trade Fair." After the S.P. discontinued its ferry service between Oakland Pier and the Ferry Building in 1958, she was purchased by Luther W. Conover, a merchant and ferryboat fancier who was then in business ashore. He brought her to Sausalito and fitted her main deck up as a store, with wind shelters on the fore and afterdecks. The beautiful Victorian upper cabin with stained glass and carved woodwork has been left intact, as has all the machinery. According to Mr. Conover, she could be refitted and made ready to go back into ferry operation with a minimum of difficulty. In the meanwhile Sausalito residents and visitors like to go aboard the *Berkeley*, to shop and browse amid the attractive merchandise, most of which, appropriately, is garnered from the seven seas. Motion of the moored vessel, noticeable in heavy weather, has never deranged the displays nor broken fragile merchandise. The only problem it ever creates is for the occasional seasick customer!

Five other ferryboats are drawn up on the edge of Richardson Bay, among many houseboats north of Sausalito on the site of the Marinship yards where, during World War II, many merchant ships were built. All are owned by C. L. Arques. Most prominent is the *City of San Rafael*, used as a dwelling on its upper deck. The *Vallejo* and the *City of Seattle* have been rather extensively remodeled as dwellings. The rapidly deteriorating *Issaquah* is, at this writing, untenanted.

Here also is the *Charles Van Damme*. Since she left the service of the Martinez-Benicia Ferry, she has been leased to various restaurant concerns, first at Jack London Square in Oakland and later here north of Sausalito. Currently her tenant is a night club or restaurant called The Ark. The paddle boxes have been cut out for a view of the wheels and the machinery is removed and stored in the basement of the San Francisco Maritime Museum.

At the foot of Broadway in Oakland, near where the Creek Route boats of Charles Minturn, James B. LaRue, the Central Pacific, the Southern Pacific and the Nickel Ferry used to dock, is Jack London Square, named in honor of the famous author who was born in Oakland and became a familiar figure on the Estuary as a youth. Moored off this square is a floating restaurant called the Showboat, where

With a vermilion stack, the *City of Sacramento* looked like this when she was in the fleet of the Puget Sound Navigation Co. Remodeled for her new duties as a shopping center, the *Sierra Nevada* is being moved to her new berth at Ports of Call Village, San Pedro. During the 1966-67 winter the *Sacramento* was repainted in a new color scheme and readied for her 1967 fishing season off Redondo Beach. (*Above: courtesy Washington State Ferries; below: courtesy William Knott; bottom: Gary G. Allen photo*)

lunches, dinners and banquets may be enjoyed in a nautical atmosphere and with a fine view of the busy maritime life on the Estuary. This establishment is on the *General Frank M. Coxe*, a single-ended boat that saw many years of ferry service on the Bay for the United States Army.

Built for the Army in 1921 at Charleston, West Virginia, she traveled to San Francisco Bay on a lengthy route down the Kanawha, Ohio and Mississippi Rivers to the Gulf of Mexico, through the Panama Canal and up the Pacific Coast to the Golden Gate. On the Bay she shuttled between Fort McDowell on Angel Island, Fort Mason in San Francisco and other Army posts on the Bay. More than two million troops rode on her during World War II. In 1946 she began several years of service as an excursion boat on the Bay. Then in 1955 she went to Stockton, on the San Joaquin River, to begin her career as a floating restaurant. She came to her present berth at Jack London Square in 1958.

Another floating restaurant is to be found at the edge of the Willamette River, not far from Portland's Union Station. This is the *River Queen*, latest incarnation of the *Shasta*. After 17 years on San Francisco Bay, she went to Puget Sound where she gave many more years of service as the *Shasta*. Perhaps this Californian name sounded Indian enough to satisfy Washingtonians.

After retirement on the Sound, she was taken down to Portland and remodeled to accommodate the restaurant. While the alterations have not greatly changed her, the windows on the main deck have been modified to resemble the type on the *Sacramento* or the *Berkeley*. Previously the windows of the *Shasta's* main deck were small and infrequent, like those in a barn or garage. The new windows allow patrons to enjoy the fine view of the river, mountains and the Oregon metropolis.

In San Pedro, nestled against the shore of the Main Channel into Los Angeles Harbor, can be found the familiar white form of the *Sierra Nevada*, moored at an attractive and picturesque shopping center, Ports of Call Village. On her hurricane deck is now a promenade from which visitors may view the harbor activity, and a glassed-in sea food restaurant has been added here. Aside from the topside additions and prominent ladders

leading to the hurricane deck, the present *Sierra Nevada* still displays the distinguished lines that Moore & Scott in 1913 built into the Tuscan red *Edward T. Jeffery* for the Western Pacific. Much of the atmosphere of her passenger accommodations has been preserved in the shops on her main and cabin decks.

A dozen or so miles to the northwest, farther by sea around Palos Verdes Peninsula, is the city of Redondo Beach. Anchored about 3½ miles offshore, from May to September each year, is the *Sacramento*, minus machinery but fitted out as a de luxe fishing barge and anchored at the edge of the Redondo Submarine Canyon, where a wide variety of fish abound.

She made her last run for the Southern Pacific on November 22, 1954, and was sold the next year to the Pacific Shipbreaking & Salvage Co. to be cut up for scrap. Gordon McRae, owner of Redondo Sportfishing Co., heard about the *Sacramento's* impending fate and sent a crew to San Francisco to buy the big vessel and tow her to Redondo Beach. She left the Golden Gate on New Year's Eve of 1956 and the old hulk's timbers groaned and strained as they kept just ahead of a storm all the way down the coast. Once in King Harbor, Redondo Beach, she was outfitted with generators, live bait tanks, galley and tackle store and began her new career as a sport fishing barge in her 80th year.

Her winter quarters are in the Bethlehem Shipyard, San Pedro, where annual maintenance chores are done. When May comes again she is towed back to her spot off Redondo Beach. She can be seen from shore all the way from El Segundo to Palos Verdes Peninsula.

1967 will mark the 90th year since she was launched as the *Newark*, a combination car float and passenger ferry for the South Pacific Coast Railroad. She remained the *Newark* for 46 years through several remodelings, in one of which her famed 42-foot wheels were replaced with 29-foot ones. Then in 1923 she was thoroughly rebuilt and renamed the *Sacramento*, to serve the Southern Pacific's Oakland-San Francisco route for more than 31 years. Despite her advanced age, she seems to be doing well in her new employment. In 1966 she played host to over 30,000 deep sea anglers and seems set for many seasons to come.

Another of the old ferryboats is being used as a fishing resort just east of Crockett on the picturesque south shore of Carquinez Strait. Here is the *Garden City*, devoid of machinery and not too badly dilapidated. This once-proud queen was built for the South Pacific Coast Railroad in 1879 as a combination passenger ferry and dual-gauge car afloat; she was rebuilt at the Southern Pacific shipyard in 1902, after which she served as an early version of the automobile ferry, mostly on the Creek Route, until she retired in 1929. She is open to the public and can be viewed as a typical example of the San Francisco-Oakland or the San Francisco-Alameda ferry in the heyday of ferry service on the Bay.

About forty miles up the shore of the Bay and into the mouth of the San Joaquin River is the former Northwestern Pacific ferry *Sausalito*, on the shore near the Antioch Bridge. She is now a clubhouse for a gun club, in good preservation but without her machinery. She is not open to the general public. As originally built in 1894 by John

The *Berkeley* is being eased into the Sausalito slip where she now serves as a floating Trade Fair. *(Two photos: Richard Weymouth Brooks, courtesy Luther W. Conover)*

W. Dickie, for the North Pacific Coast Railroad, she too was a combination passenger and car ferry, but in her case the tracks were narrow gauge. She experienced many minor rebuildings during her service with the N.P.C., the North Shore and the Northwestern Pacific. Her retirement began in 1933.

The San Francisco Maritime State Historical Monument maintains at the Hyde Street Pier an excellent exhibit of four samples of wooden shipbuilding on the Pacific Coast. Here are a two-masted lumber schooner, a steam lumber schooner, a hay barge and the ferryboat *Eureka*. She is in excellent condition, carefully restored to give the visitor an accurate idea of what she was like and how she operated.

The *Eureka* was originally built in 1890 at Tiburon by the San Francisco & North Pacific Railway as the car ferry *Ukiah*. After World War I the Northwestern Pacific had her completely modernized and rebuilt at the Southern Pacific shipyard and she emerged in 1923 as the *Eureka*, flagship of the N.W.P. fleet until ferry service was discontinued in 1941.

Her machinery is the *Ukiah's* original machinery, partially modernized. The fine beam engine is a splendid example of the main propulsion equipment for so many San Francisco Bay ferryboats, carefully restored so that visitors may see how such an engine appeared, but no longer operable because of a broken crank.

Her paint décor indicates Northwestern Pacific ownership; she is white with the colorful redwood tree-Tamalpais-Bay emblem on the paddle box; not typical of N.W.P. practice are the gray canvas decks and the white interiors of the ventilators. Before the Southern Pacific took over this vessel, the decks were buff and the ventilators were red inside.

While she operated on the Northwestern Pacific, her only master of record was Victor L. Verdellet, who was at the helm on her maiden voyage in 1923 and who rang up "Finished With Engines" on her last N.W.P. trip in February, 1941.

An outstanding example of the San Francisco Bay ferryboat, the *Eureka* is preserved for posterity visually in close to mint condition, a maritime museum piece of the highest order, preserved and maintained by a staff dedicated to keeping her pristine. That her walking beam, forever stilled, faces out over the Bay and the Golden Gate, where the glories of the ferries were gained in a hundred years of faithful service, is a reminder of an era of grandeur in the past of a colorful city.

An air view of the San Francisco Maritime State Historical Monument shows the *Eureka* in her slip at the foot of Hyde Street beside her sister ships in the permanent exhibit there. The public is welcome to explore the ferryboat as well as the steam lumber schooner *Wapama*, to her right, and, behind her, the three masted schooner *C. A. Thayer*. On the water front at the extreme right is the San Francisco Maritime Museum. *(Aeromarine Photo Service, courtesy San Francisco Maritime State Historical Monument)*

Glossary of Ferryboat Terms

The following is a brief glossary of terms frequently used in connection with ferry vessels on San Francisco Bay:

ABEAM — at right angles to the keel.

AFT — toward the stern of the vessel. Between the stern and the amidship section of the vessel.

A-FRAME — main structure of a beam type of engine, usually constructed of wood or steel upon which the walking beam is housed.

AMIDSHIP — in the longitudinal, or fore-and-aft center of the vessel.

APRON — that portion of the runway for boarding a ferry vessel which is used at the apex of the slip for adjusting to tidal conditions.

ATHWART — across, from side to side; transverse, at right angles to the keel.

BALLAST — either solid or liquid weight added to a vessel to improve trim or stability.

BEAM — the extreme width of a ship's hull. Also, a transverse horizontal member for supporting a deck.

BILGE — the lower, rounded portion of a vessel's hull joining the bottom with the sides.

BITT — iron heads fixed on a deck for belaying hawsers, warps, or ropes.

BITTER END — the inboard end of a cable or rope.

BOOBY HATCH — the cover of a scuttleway or small hatchway such as that which leads to the forecastle or forepeak.

BOW — the front or forward end of a vessel.

BUCKET — a plank attached to the spokes of a paddle wheel which drives the vessel through the water.

BULKHEAD — a partition in a vessel.

BUNKER — a compartment in which fuel is stored.

BUOYANCY — a vessel's capacity for floating.

CABIN — the passenger spaces on a ferry vessel.

CAMSHAFT — the shaft of a steam engine which operates the valves.

CAPSTAN — a vertical drum, either steam or manually operated, to haul in a mooring line.

CHARLIE NOBLE — the galley smokestack and smokestack head.

CHOCK — a deck fitting for a mooring line to pass through.

CLEAT — a metal deck fitting used for belaying ropes.

COFFERDAM — a void or empty space separating two or more compartments for the purpose of preventing the contents of these compartments from becoming intermingled.

COLLISION BULKHEAD — a watertight bulkhead at the forepeak to prevent the entire vessel from flooding in the event of a collision.

COMPOUND ENGINE — a steam engine in which the steam is used in two stages, the first being the high-pressure or primary cylinder, and again in the low-pressure cylinder.

COPPER SHEATHING — copper sheets placed on the hull of a wooden vessel to protect the hull from deterioration.

DAVITS — a set of cranes or radial arms on the deck of a ship from which the lifeboats are suspended.

DEPTH — extreme depth of the ship from keel to main deck.

DISPLACEMENT — total weight of a ship while afloat measured in tons.

DOUBLE-ENDER — a ferry vessel either end of which may be the bow, which can travel equally well in either direction, and which is equipped with rudders at either end.

DOLPHIN — name given to a piling cluster to which a ferry is moored when not in use.

DRAFT — the vertical distance between the lowest point on the keel and the deepest line of flotation.

DRIFTBOLT — long, stout metallic fastening which penetrates all the timbers which it joins. Used to fasten main framing members of a ferry vessel.

ENGINE ORDER TELEGRAPH — device consisting of a dial, pointer and warning bell located in the pilothouse and engine room of a vessel to convey the deck officer's instructions to the engineers.

EYE SPLICE — rope splice, particularly in mooring lines, to create a closed loop for quick mooring.

FALL — the line used to lower and hoist a boat at the davits.

FATHOM — six feet; a marine unit for measuring depth.

FIDLEY — that sector of the upper decks of a vessel which houses the boiler uptakes, stack and escape pipes. (Sometimes spelled "fiddley.")

FORE — the forward part of a ship, the stem.

FORECASTLE — crew's quarters on the forward part of a vessel, generally below the main deck on ferry vessels.

FOREPEAK — that part of the hold which is farthest forward.

FRAMES — the ribs of a ship.

FREEBOARD — the distance from the line of flotation to the main deck.

FUNNEL — a ship's smokestack.

GALLEY — place on shipboard where food is prepared.

GANGPLANK — the hinged portion of the apron in a ferry slip which makes immediate contact with the ferry vessel's deck.

GIRDER — a heavy supporting beam.

GRIPE — a preventer sling to keep lifeboats from swaying while a vessel is under way.

GUARDRAIL — protective timber of hardwood, normally ironbark, which circumvents the main deck of a ferry vessel against which contact with the ferry slip piling is made.

GUDGEON — a metallic eye cast in the stern post of a vessel on which the rudder is hung.

GUYS — wires to support masts, funnels or davits and prevent them from excessive sway.

HAWSER — a mooring line.

HOG TRUSS — an above-deck framing used on river and ferry craft where the depth of hold is insufficient to form a suitable longitudinal girder.

HULL — the main body and form of a vessel, the floating portion.

INBOARD — from the shell or side of a ship to the center; inside the house.

JACK STAFF — flagpole.

JET CONDENSER — tank with jet spray of cold sea water used to condense steam to water and thus create a vacuum on the exhaust side of a steam engine. Although not economical, it was commonly used on ferry vessels.

KEEL — main timber and the backbone of a vessel to which the frames or ribs are attached.

KNEE — a wooden brace from a deck beam to a frame, made of stout hardwood timber of select right-angle grain.

KNOT — a nautical mile of 6,080.26 feet or 1.15156 statute miles.

LOAD WATER LINE — the deepest permissible draft of a ship.

LONGITUDINAL — any portion of the ship's structure, other than the keel, which runs fore and aft.

MARINE RAILWAY — a frame-like structure on wheels and rails used for hauling out small vessels such as ferryboats for drydocking.

MIDSHIPS — that portion of a ship midway between the stem and the stern, usually the widest portion of the hull.

MOORING — securing a vessel in a position by means of lines.

NAUTICAL MILE — a knot or 1.15156 statute miles.

OAKUM — a material made of tarred rope fibers, used for caulking seams in a wooden vessel.

OUTBOARD — from the center to the sides of a ship.

PADDLE BOX — housing on a ferry vessel for the paddle wheel.

PADDLE WHEEL — wheel with steel spokes and rims with flat buckets attached to the extremes of the spokes, used to propel a vessel through the water.

PILOTHOUSE — wheelhouse or steering station located at the forward end on the uppermost deck of a single-ended boat and at both ends of the uppermost deck of a double-ended ferry.

PINTLE — metal pin which fastens the rudder to the sternpost of a vessel.

PLANKING — material in wooden vessels of which the hull and decks are constructed.

PORT — the left-hand side of a ship, looking from stern to stem.

RIVET — a metal fastening used to join steelwork together.

RING BUOY — a round, doughnut-shaped piece of life-saving gear used to make buoyant a person who has fallen overboard.

RUDDER — a swinging vane at the stern of a vessel by which steering is accomplished. In double-end ferry vessels, a rudder is located at each end of the ship.

SHAFT — method of connecting the main engine to a propeller or paddle wheel in a vessel.

SIDE-WHEELER — a vessel with paddle wheels located approximately amidships on either side of the vessel.

SINGLE-ENDER — a vessel with a single bow and stern designed to travel in only one direction for any sustained length of time.

SLIP — a landing place at a ferry terminal made up of closely driven pilings shaped to contain a ferry vessel.

SPONSON — the overhang of the main deck of a ferry vessel beyond the beam of the main structure.

STARBOARD — the right-hand side of a vessel looking from aft forward.

STEM — the bow of a ship.

STERN — the after end of a vessel.

STERN-WHEELER — a vessel driven by a paddle wheel located at the stern of the vessel.

SURFACE CONDENSER — a shell-and-tube type of heat exchanger used to condense exhaust steam into feed water.

TONNAGE (GROSS) — the term used most frequently to describe the size of a ship. It is the total internal capacity of a vessel in cubic feet, certain spaces exempted, divided by 100.

TRIPLE EXPANSION ENGINE — a three- or four-cylinder steam engine in which the steam is used in two additional expansion stages beyond the primary cylinder.

TURBINE — a rotary type steam engine which uses bucket wheels and blading on a rotor shaft for converting steam into energy.

UPTAKE — that portion of the firebox outlet of a boiler which connects the firebox discharge with the smokestack or funnel.

VENTILATOR COWL — a device for furnishing fresh air to compartments below deck where forced mechanical ventilation is not used.

WAKE — the water pattern left by a moving ship.

WALKING BEAM — that portion of a vertical beam engine which connects the linkage bars from the piston rod of the main cylinder to the main rod which drives the main crank of the engine, reversing the direction of the motion in its accomplishment. On ferry vessels, beams were made of cast steel with a forged rim and were of great proportions.

WATER LINE — the line of flotation of a vessel or any other line parallel thereto.

WAYS — cradles and skids upon which ships are constructed.

Illustrated Roster

Vessels are listed alphabetically and, when names are identical, chronologically. Each is pictured here as it appeared at some time when it bore the name listed; elsewhere in this volume other pictures of the same boats may in some instances be very different, as the boats were subjected to much alteration. Alterations affect statistics as well as appearance and figures here, from American Bureau of Shipping records, may differ from other measurements on the same boats, taken at other times and by other agencies. The figures in this roster should serve as a reasonable basis for comparison between boats. Hull dimensions are length, breadth and depth respectively. On many boats, including all side-wheelers, the over-all width will be considerably greater than breadth of hull, for the decks were sponsoned far out on either side. Depth of hull is not to be confused with draft. Operators of the boats, as listed here, are to be understood as railroads, unless the company name specifies the ferry business.

Alameda   211868   Side Wheel
Prefabricated, 1913, N. Y. Shipbuilding Co.,
    Camden, N. J.
Operated by Southern Pacific
Steel hull, 273' x 42.3' x 15.3'   1320 tons
Two engines, 2 cyl. compound, 20" x 40" x 96"   1980 hp
Burned for scrap, 1947

Alvira   106687   Stern wheel
Built, 1889   Operated by Nickel Ferry
Wood hull, 144' x 33.6' x 6'   469 tons
Steam reciprocating engine   200 hp
Back to river, 1895

Alameda   1216   Side wheel
Built, 1866
Operated by San Francisco & Alameda, Central Pacific,
    Southern Pacific
Wood hull, 193' x 38' x 16.2'   813 tons
Vertical beam engine   350 hp
Broken up, 1898

Amador   1953   Side wheel
Built, 1869, Patrick Tiernan
Operated by Central Pacific, Southern Pacific
Wood hull, 199' x 39' x 14.5'   897 tons
Steam reciprocating engine   300 hp
Burned in fireboat demonstration, Panama-Pacific International Exposition, San Francisco, 1915

Amelia   1214   Side wheel
Built, 1863, Owens Shipyard
Operated by Central Pacific
Wood hull, 147' x 33.5' x 12'   386 tons
Vertical beam engine   300 hp
Sold, 1882

Asbury Park   107848   Twin screw
Built, 1903, William Cramp & Sons, Philadelphia
Operated by Monticello Steamship Co.
Steel hull, 297' x 50' x 15.5'   3016 tons
Two engines, 4-cylinder, triple expansion,
    23" x 37.5" x 43" x 43" x 30"   5900 hp
Renamed *City of Sacramento*, 1925

Antelope   1212   Side wheel
Built, 1847
Operated by San Francisco & North Pacific
Wood hull, 202.6' long   581 tons
Vertical beam engine   350 hp
Broken up, 1888

Aven J. Hanford   220972   Screw
Built, 1922, James Robertson, Benicia
Operated by Rodeo-Vallejo Ferry, Golden Gate Ferry
Wood hull, 176.8' x 30.5' x 12.7'   353 tons
Triple expansion engine,
    20" x 29" x 30" x 30" x 18"   900 hp
Renamed *Golden City*, re-engined Diesel, 1927
Sunk in collision, April 24, 1927

Arrow   107819   Screw
Built, 1903, Puget Sound
Operated by Monticello Steamship Co.
Wood hull, 147' x 22.5' x 9.25'   318 tons
Triple expansion engine
    14" x 21.5" x 35" x 30"   1000 hp
Retired, 1924; beached at Hunter's Point

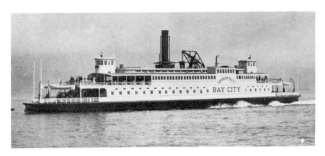

Bay City   3068   Side wheel
Built, 1878, William Collyer, San Francisco
Operated by South Pacific Coast, Southern Pacific
Wood hull, 247' x 66' x 15'   1283 tons
Vertical beam engine, 52" x 144"   860 hp
Dismantled, 1929

Benicia   3185   Side wheel
Built, 1881
Operated by O. C. Coffin (Martinez-Benicia Ferry)
Wood hull, 92.5′ x 24.7′ x 7.1′   144.77 tons
Vertical beam engine   165 hp
Sold to San Diego & Coronado Ferry, 1888,
    dismantled, 1904

Berkeley   3770   Screw
Built, 1898, Union Iron Works, San Francisco
Operated by Southern Pacific
Steel hull, 279′ x 40.2′ x 14.1′   1883 tons
Triple expansion engine, 22″ x 34″ x 56″ x 36″   1450 hp
Sold, 1958. Moored at Sausalito, used as store

Bridgit   211089   Screw
Built, 1913, Moore & Scott Iron Works, Oakland
Operated by Oakland, Antioch & Eastern
Wood hull, 173.4′ x 38.7′ x 14.7′   594 tons
Gasoline engine   300 hp
Destroyed by fire, May 17, 1914

Calistoga   204629   Screw
Built, 1907, as *Florida*, Maryland Steel Co.
Operated by Monticello Steamship Co., Golden Gate
    Ferry, Southern Pacific-Golden Gate Ferries, Ltd.
Steel hull, 298′ x 45′ x 16.1′   2680 tons
Triple expansion engine, 20″ x 40″ x 47″ x 42″   2600 hp
Scrapped, 1941

Capital   5181   Side wheel
Built, 1866, John G. North
Operated by California Pacific, Central Pacific, South-
    ern Pacific
Wood hull, 277′ long   1989 tons
Vertical beam engine   900 hp
Broken up, 1896

Carquinez   272604   Screw
Built, 1956, Pacific Coast Engineering Co., Alameda
Operated between Martinez and Benicia by State of
    California
Steel hull, 169′ x 52′ x 13.5′   537 tons
Diesel engine, 8 cylinders   1000 hp
Sold to Florida, 1962

Cazadero   127756   Side wheel
Built, 1903, John W. Dickie, Alameda
Operated by North Shore, Northwestern Pacific
Wood hull, 228.5′ x 38′ x 17′   1682 tons
Vertical beam engine, 56″ x 144″   1600 hp
Scrapped, 1942

Charles Van Damme   214165   Side wheel
Built, 1916, James Robertson, Benicia
Operated by Richmond-San Rafael Ferry, Martinez-
   Benicia Ferry
Wood hull, 152.8′ x 36.9′ x 11′   342 tons
Compound engine, 2 cylinders, 16″ x 20″ x 54″ 300 hp
Vacated, 1958. Became floating restaurant; beached
   north of Sausalito, used as night club

Chrysopolis   5178   Side wheel
Built, 1860, John G. North
Operated by Central Pacific
Wood hull, 245′ x 40′ x 14′   1050 tons
Vertical beam engine   700 hp
Rebuilt as ferry *Oakland*, 1875

City of Martinez   215138   Side wheel
Built, 1917, Pittsburg, California
Operated by Martinez-Benicia Ferry
Wood hull, 150.8′ x 35.6′ x 12.9′   819 tons
Steam reciprocating engine   250 hp
Condemned, 1936, burned by city fire department

City of Richmond   221318   Side wheel
Built, 1921, James Robertson, Alameda
Operated by Richmond-San Rafael Ferry
Wood hull, 168′ x 34.1′ x 11.8′   408 tons
Cross-compound engine, 2 cylinders,
   18″ x 36″ x 72″   500 hp
Sold to American Sardine Co., 1939

City of Sacramento   Formerly *Asbury Park*
Operated by Monticello Steamship Co., Golden Gate
   Ferry, Southern Pacific-Golden Gate Ferries, Ltd.
Sold to War Shipping Administration; to Puget Sound,
   1942, renamed *Kahloke*; to British Columbia Gov-
   ernment, 1961; renamed *Langdale Queen*, 1964.
Rebuilt 1952, Diesel engines. In service 1967, Horse-
   shoe Bay to Port Langdale on Sechelt Peninsula, in
British Columbia

City of San Rafael   223873   Side wheel
Built, 1924, James Robertson, Alameda
Operated by Richmond-San Rafael Ferry,
  Martinez-Benicia Ferry
Wood hull, 172′ x 36.8′ x 13.4′   484 tons
Compound engine, 2 cyl. 20″ x 44″ x 72″   650 hp
Retired, beached at Sausalito, used as residence

Clinton   5177   Side wheel
Built, 1853, John G. North, San Francisco
Operated by Contra Costa Steam Navigation Co.
Wood hull   194 tons
Vertical beam engine   125 hp
Sunk in collision, October 27, 1877

City of Seattle   126536   Side wheel
Built, 1888, Puget Sound
Operated by Martinez-Benicia Ferry, Mare Island
  Ferry
Wooden hull, 121.5′ x 38.3′ x 8.5′   196 tons
Single cylinder engine, 16″ x 60″   270 hp
Engine dismantled, 1948; beached north of Sausalito,
  used as residence

Claremont   203912   Screw
Built, 1907, John W. Dickie, Alameda
Operated by Key Route
Wood hull, 189′ x 38′ x 19.2′   672 tons
Two compound engines, 2 cylinders,
  20″ x 42″ x 28″   2000 hp
To Golden Gate Ferry, rebuilt as steamer *Golden
  Way*, 1924

Contra Costa   5180   Side wheel
Built, 1857, John G. North, San Francisco
Operated by Contra Costa Steam Navigation Co.
Wood hull, 170′ long   449 tons
Vertical beam engine   150 hp
Broken up, 1885

Contra Costa   212630   Side wheel
Built, 1914, Southern Pacific, Oakland
Operated by Southern Pacific, train ferry, Port Costa-
    Benicia
Steel hull, 433' x 67.2' x 18.5'   4483 tons
Two compound engines, 2 cylinders,
    60" x 96"   3000 hp
Vacated, 1930

Ellen   135740   Side wheel
Built, 1883, Vallejo
Operated by Mare Island Ferry, Richmond-
    San Rafael Ferry
Wood hull, 133' x 24.7' x 7.5'   328 tons
Steam reciprocating engine   120 hp
Broken up, 1919

Edward T. Jeffery   211506   Screw
Built, 1913, Moore & Scott Iron Works, Oakland
Operated by Western Pacific
Steel hull, 218' x 42' x 16.6'   1578 tons
Two compound engines, 2 cylinders,
    20" x 42" x 28"   2500 hp
Renamed *Feather River*, about 1930

El Paso   224327   Screw
Built, 1924, Bethlehem Steel Co. Union Yard,
    San Francisco
Operated by Southern Pacific; Southern Pacific-Golden
    Gate Ferries, Ltd., Richmond-San Rafael Ferry
Steel hull, 234' x 45' x 17'   1953 tons
Triple expansion engine,
    19" x 32" x 56" x 36"   1400 hp
Retired, 1956

El Capitan   8230   Side wheel
Built, 1868, Central Pacific, Oakland
Operated by Central Pacific, Southern Pacific
Wood hull, 194' x 38.5' x 14'   982 tons
Vertical beam engine, 36" x 144"   365 hp
Sold, November 1925

Encinal   135972   Side wheel
Built, 1888, Charles G. White, San Francisco
Operated by South Pacific Coast, Southern Pacific
Wood hull, 244' x 40' x 15.9'   2014 tons
Vertical beam engine, 52" x 144"   972 hp
Dismantled, December, 1930

Eureka   25279   Side wheel
Rebuilt 1923 from steamer *Ukiah*, Southern Pacific,
    Oakland
Operated by Northwestern Pacific, Southern Pacific
Wood hull, 277′ x 42.7′ x 15.7′   2420 tons
Vertical beam engine, 65″ x 144″   1500 hp
On exhibit, San Francisco Maritime State Historical
    Monument

Fresno   226344   Screw
Built, 1927, Bethlehem Steel Co., Union Yard,
    San Francisco
Operated by Southern Pacific, Southern Pacific-Golden
    Gate Ferries, Ltd.
Steel hull, 242.5′ x 46.2′ x 17.3′   2468 tons
Four Diesel engines, two electric motors   1250 hp
To Puget Sound, renamed *Willapa*, after 1937

Feather River   Formerly *Edward T. Jeffery*
Operated by Western Pacific
To Southern Pacific, renamed *Sierra Nevada*, 1933

Garden City   85592   Side wheel
Built, 1879, William Collyer, San Francisco
Operated by South Pacific Coast, Southern Pacific
Wood hull, 243′ x 40′ x 15.6′   1080 tons
Vertical beam engine, 46″ x 144″   933 hp
Retired, June, 1929; used as fishing resort, Carquinez
    Strait

Fernwood   204736   Screw
Built, 1908, John W. Dickie, Alameda
Operated by Key Route
Wood hull, 194.3′ x 38.1′ x 19.2′   789 tons
Two compound engines, 2 cylinders,
    20″ x 42″ x 28″   2000 hp
To Golden Gate Ferry, rebuilt as *Golden Era*, 1924

General Frisbie   86541   Screw
Built, 1900, G. R. Whidden & Co., New Whatcomb,
    Washington
Operated by Monticello Steamship Co.
Wood hull, 187′ x 29′ x 11.9′   670 tons
Triple expansion engine, 4 cylinders,
    16″ x 25″ x 30″ x 30″ x 24″   1000 hp
To Puget Sound, 1927, renamed *Commander* of Wash-
    ington Navigation Co., operated Seattle-Bremerton;
    converted to cannery, 1940. Hull now basis of barge
    used as residence on Lake Washington.

Golden Age　　227249　　　　　　　　　Screw
Built, 1928, General Engineering & Drydock Co.,
　　Alameda
Operated by Golden Gate Ferry, Southern Pacific-
　　Golden Gate Ferries, Ltd.
Wood hull, 226.8′ x 44′ x 15.9′　　　　　779 tons
Three Diesel engines, two electric motors　　950 hp
To Puget Sound, renamed *Klahanie,* after 1937

Golden Bear　　226605　　　　　　　　Screw
Built, 1927, General Engineering & Drydock Co.,
　　Alameda
Operated by Golden Gate Ferry, Southern Pacific-
　　Golden Gate Ferries, Ltd.
Wood hull, 226.8′ x 44′ x 15.9′　　　　　779 tons
Three Diesel engines, two electric motors　　950 hp
Wrecked off Empire, Oregon, while being towed to
　　Puget Sound, 1937

Golden Coast　　Formerly *Harry E. Speas*
Operated by Golden Gate Ferry, Southern Pacific-
　　Golden Gate Ferries, Ltd.
Retired, 1937

Golden Dawn　　Rebuilt from steamer *San Francisco*
Operated by Golden Gate Ferry, Southern Pacific-
　　Golden Gate Ferries, Ltd.
Retired, 1937

Golden Era　　　　　　　　　　　　789 tons
Rebuilt from steamer *Fernwood*
Operated by Golden Gate Ferry, Southern Pacific-
　　Golden Gate Ferries, Ltd.
Retired, 1937

Golden Gate　　222308　　　　　　　　Screw
Built 1923, James Robertson, Alameda
Operated by Golden Gate Ferry, Southern Pacific-
　　Golden Gate Ferries, Ltd.
Wood hull, 206.5′ x 37.3′ x 15.9′　　　　598 tons
Two Werkspor Diesel engines, electric drive　1050 hp
Broken up, 1938

Golden Poppy   226687   Screw
Built, 1927, General Engineering & Drydock Co.,
    Alameda
Operated by Golden Gate Ferry, Southern Pacific-
    Golden Gate Ferries, Ltd.
Wood hull, 226.8' x 40' x 15.9'   779 tons
Three Diesel engines, two electric motors   950 hp
To Puget Sound, renamed *Chetzemoka,* after 1937

Golden Way   Rebuilt from steamer *Claremont*
Operated by Golden Gate Ferry, Southern Pacific-
    Golden Gate Ferries, Ltd.
Retired, 1937

Golden Shore   226767   Screw
Built, 1927, General Engineering & Drydock Co.,
    Alameda
Operated by Golden Gate Ferry, Southern Pacific-
    Golden Gate Ferries, Ltd.
Wood hull, 226.8' x 40' x 15.9'   779 tons
Three Diesel engines, two electric motors   950 hp
To Puget Sound, renamed *Elwha* after 1937; to San
    Diego, renamed *Silver Strand,* 1944

Golden West   222833   Screw
Built, 1923, James Robertson, Alameda
Operated by Golden Gate Ferry, Southern Pacific-
    Golden Gate Ferries, Ltd.
Wood hull, 214.1' x 44.4' x 15.2'   594 tons
Two Werkspor Diesel engines,
    two electric motors   1300 hp
To San Diego, renamed *North Island,* 1939

Golden State   225772   Screw
Built, 1926, General Engineering & Drydock Co.,
    Alameda
Operated by Golden Gate Ferry, Southern Pacific-
    Golden Gate Ferries, Ltd.
Wood hull, 226.8' x 40' x 15.9'   780 tons
Three Diesel engines, two electric motors   950 hp
To Puget Sound, renamed *Kehloken,* after 1938

Harry E. Speas   200207
Rebuilt from steamer *Yerba Buena*
Operated by Golden Gate Ferry
Renamed *Golden Coast,* 1927

Hayward   222773   Screw
Built, 1923, Los Angeles Shipbuilding Co., Los Angeles
Operated by Key System
Steel hull, 225′ x 42.1′ x 17.1′   1653 tons
Turbo-electric engine   1325 hp
Burned, dismantled, 1947

Issaquah   211983   Screw
Built, 1914
Operated by Rodeo-Vallejo Ferry, Martinez-Benicia
   Ferry, Mare Island Ferry
Wood hull, 114.4′ x 38.3′ x 8.9′   288 tons
Steeple compound engine   250 hp
Vacated 1948, beached north of Sausalito

James M. Donahue   75761   Side Wheel
Built, 1875, William E. Collyer, San Francisco
Operated by San Francisco & North Pacific, California
   Northwestern, Northwestern Pacific
Wood hull, 208′ x 37.4′ x 9.6′   730 tons
Vertical beam engine, 48″ x 132″   950 hp
Dismantled, 1924

Julia   13570   Side wheel
Built, 1870
Operated by Central Pacific, Southern Pacific
Wood hull, 170′ x 38′ x 10′   520 tons
Steam reciprocating engine   200 hp
Destroyed in boiler explosion, February 27, 1888

Klamath   224461   Screw
Built 1925, Bethlehem Steel Co. Union Yard,
   San Francisco
Operated by Southern Pacific, Southern Pacific-Golden
   Gate Ferries, Ltd., Richmond-San Rafael Ferry
Steel hull, 234′ x 45′ x 17′   1952 tons
Triple expansion engine, 19″ x 32″ x 56″ x 36″   1400 hp
Retired, 1956; rebuilt, 1964, as floating office and
   studio. Moored at Embarcadero, San Francisco

Lagunitas   141853   Stern wheel
Built, 1903, John W. Dickie, Alameda
Operated by North Shore Railroad, Northwestern
   Pacific
Wood hull, 250′ x 36.6′ x 10.7′   767 tons
Poppet valve engine, 18″ x 72″   400 hp
Dismantled, 1917

Lake Tahoe   226588   Screw
Built, 1927, Moore Dry Dock Co., Oakland
Operated by Southern Pacific, Southern Pacific-Golden
   Gate Ferries, Ltd.
Steel hull, 251' x 46.3' x 19.1'   2468 tons
Four Diesel engines, two electric motors   1250 hp
To Puget Sound, renamed *Illahee*, after 1937

Las Plumas   274346   Screw
Built, 1957, Albina Engine & Machine Works,
   Portland, Oregon
Operated by Western Pacific Railroad
Steel hull, 360' x 59' x 16.1'   2255 tons
Three Diesel engines, 8 cylinders   2100 hp
Still in operation on San Francisco Bay, 1967

Marin   Built 1912 on hull of steamer *Requa*
Operated by Northwestern Pacific between Tiburon
   and Sausalito
Standard gasoline engine   130 hp
Excursion boat, Stockton, until 1956

Melrose   205918   Side wheel
Built 1908, Southern Pacific, Oakland
Operated by Southern Pacific
Wood hull, 274' x 43' x 17.8'   2662 tons
Two inclined compound engines,
   23.5" x 38.7" x 96"   1040 hp
Dismantled, 1931

Mendocino   226712   Screw
Built, 1927, Bethlehem Steel Co. Union Yard,
   San Francisco
Operated by Northwestern Pacific, Southern Pacific-
   Golden Gate Ferries, Ltd.
Steel hull, 251' x 46.3' x 19.1'   2467 tons
Four Diesel engines, two electric motors   1250 hp
To Puget Sound, renamed *Nisqually*, after 1937

Monticello   92443   Screw
Built 1892, E. Sorenson, Ballard, Washington
Operated by Monticello Steamship Co.
Wood hull, 126' x 22' x 8'   175 tons
Triple expansion engine, 12" x 18" x 28" x 14"   140 hp
Off company roster about 1909

Napa Valley   207420   Screw
Built 1910, Bethlehem Steel Co. Union Yard,
   San Francisco
Operated by Monticello Steamship Co., Golden Gate
   Ferry, Southern Pacific-Golden Gate Ferries, Ltd.
Steel hull, 231.2' x 48.7' x 15.5'   2189 tons
Triple expansion engine, 4 cylinders,
   25" x 41" x 48" x 48" x 24"   2600 hp
To Puget Sound, 1942, renamed *Malahat*, Puget Sound
   Navigation Co. Towed to Portland, Ore., 1956 and
   burned for scrap

Newark   130118   Side wheel
Built 1877, William Collyer, San Francisco
Operated by South Pacific Coast, Southern Pacific
Wood hull, 268′ x 42.5′ x 18.8′   1237 tons
Vertical beam engine, 65″ x 144″   1400 hp
Rebuilt 1923 as steamer *Sacramento*

Oakland   19149   Side wheel
Built, 1858
Operated by San Francisco & Oakland, Central Pacific
Wood hull   285 tons
Vertical beam engine   200 hp
Dismantled, 1874

New Orleans   224347   Screw
Built, 1924, Bethlehem Steel Co. Union Yard,
    San Francisco
Operated by Southern Pacific, Southern Pacific-Golden
    Gate Ferries, Ltd.
Steel hull, 234′ x 45′ x 17′   1952 tons
Triple expansion engine, 19″ x 32″ x 56″ x 36″   1400 hp
To Richmond-San Rafael Ferry, renamed *Russian
    River*, November, 1938

Oakland   19447   Side wheel
Rebuilt, 1875, from steamer *Chrysopolis*, Central Pa-
    cific, Oakland
Operated by Central Pacific, Southern Pacific
Wood hull, 265′ x 41.5′ x 16′   1672 tons
Vertical beam engine, 60″ x 144″   1225 hp
Destroyed by fire, 1941

New World   18351   Side wheel
Built, 1849, New York City
Operated by California Pacific   525 tons
Vertical beam engine   250 hp
Broken up, 1879

Ocean Wave   115207   Side wheel
Built, 1891   Operated by Santa Fe
Wood hull, 180′ x 29′ x 9′   724 tons
Steam reciprocating engine
Dismantled, 1917, used as training ship for U. S. Ship-
    ping Board cadets 1918, broken up 1919

Peralta   226224   Screw
Built, 1927, Moore Dry Dock Co., Oakland
Operated by Key System
Steel hull, 256' x 68' x 15.7'   2075 tons
Turbo-electric engine   2600 hp
Destroyed by fire May 6, 1933; to Puget Sound, rebuilt
    as motor vessel *Kalakala*

Piedmont   150313   Side wheel
Built, 1883, Central Pacific, Oakland
Operated by Central Pacific, Southern Pacific
Wood hull, 257.1' x 39.5' x 15.6'   1169 tons
Single cylinder horizontal engine, 57" x 166"   1385 hp
Dismantled, 1944

Princess   20104   Side wheel
Built, 1859
Operated by Sausalito Land & Ferry Co.
Wood hull, 114' x 21'   193 tons
Steam reciprocating engine   80 hp
Broken up, 1881

Ramon   212870   Screw
Built, 1914, Oakland, Antioch & Eastern, Pittsburg
Operated by Oakland, Antioch & Eastern and suc-
    cessors, Sacramento Northern
Steel hull, 202.7' x 39.8' x 8.3'   775 tons
Standard gasoline engine   500 hp
Vacated, 1953

Redwood Empire   226783   Screw
Built, 1927, Moore Dry Dock Co., Oakland
Operated by Northwestern Pacific, Southern Pacific-
    Golden Gate Ferries, Ltd.
Steel hull, 251' x 46.3' x 19'   2467 tons
Four Diesel engines, two electric motors   1250 hp
To Puget Sound, renamed *Quinault*, after 1937

Requa   206003   Screw
Built, 1909   Operated by Northwestern Pacific
Wood hull, 97' x 18.5' x 5.1'   101 tons
Triple expansion engine   150 hp
Burned 1911, rebuilt as motor vessel *Marin*

Sacramento   23221   Side wheel
Built, 1869   Operated by California Pacific
Wood hull   540 tons
Steam reciprocating engine   150 hp
No record after 1885

Rosalie   111022   Screw
Built, 1893, Hay & Wright, Alameda
Operated by Nickel Ferry
Wood hull, 136.5′ x 27′ x 10′   227 tons
Compound engine, 2 cylinders, 15″ x 34″ x 24″   320 hp
Sold to Alaska Steamship Co.

Sacramento   130118   Side wheel
Rebuilt, 1923, from steamer Newark, Southern Pacific,
   Oakland
Operated by Southern Pacific
Wood hull, 268′ x 42.5′ x 18.8′   2254 tons
Vertical beam engine, 65″ x 144″   1400 hp
To Redondo Beach, California, 1956; in use as
   fishing barge

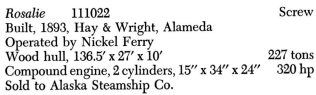

Russian River   Formerly New Orleans   Screw
Operated by Richmond-San Rafael Ferry
Retired, 1956

San Francisco   201830   Screw
Built 1905, John W. Dickie, Alameda
Operated by Key Route
Wood hull, 180′ x 38′ x 18.2′   612 tons
Two compound engines, 2 cylinders,
   20″ x 48″ x 28″   2000 hp
To Golden Gate Ferry, rebuilt, 1924, as Golden Dawn

San Jose   200206   Screw
Built 1903, John W. Dickie, Alameda
Operated by Key Route, Six Minute Ferry, Rodeo-
    Vallejo Ferry
Wood hull, 175.5′ x 38′ x 17′   630 tons
Triple expansion engine, 18″ x 27″ x 42″ x 48″   1200 hp
Extensively altered when transferred to Six Minute
    Ferry following 1919 fire; to Rodeo-Vallejo Ferry;
    to Richmond-San Rafael Ferry, rebuilt as *Sonoma
    Valley,* 1928

San Leandro   222781   Screw
Built, 1923, Los Angeles Shipbuilding Co., Los Angeles
Operated by Key System, Southern Pacific
Steel hull, 225′ x 42.1′ x 17.1′   1653 tons
Turbo-electric engine   1350 hp
Sold, 1958; maintained in serviceable condition

San Mateo   222386   Screw
Built, 1922, Bethlehem Steel Co. Union Yard,
    San Francisco
Operated by Southern Pacific, Southern Pacific-
    Golden Gate Ferries, Ltd.
Steel hull, 216.7′ x 42.1′ x 17.3′   1782 tons
Triple expansion engine, 19″ x 32″ x 54″ x 36″   1400 hp
To Puget Sound, 1940

San Pablo   117008   Side wheel
Built, 1900, Union Iron Works, San Francisco
Operated by Santa Fe
Steel hull, 209′ x 36′ x 16′   1584 tons
Compound engine,
    2 cylinders, 38″ x 77″ x 66″   2000 hp
Sold for scrap, 1937; hull used for fish reduction plant,
    San Pablo Bay

San Pedro   208653   Side wheel
Built, 1911, Bethlehem Steel Co. Union Yard,
    San Francisco
Operated by Santa Fe
Steel hull, 248.5′ x 36′ x 16.7′   1720 tons
Compound engine, 2 cylinders, 38″ x 77″ x 66″ 2000 hp
To Key System, 1938, renamed *Treasure Island*

San Rafael   115556   Side wheel
Built, 1877, John Englis, New York
Operated by North Pacific Coast
Wood hull, 205.5′ x 32′ x 9.7′   692 tons
Vertical beam engine   750 hp
Sunk in collision, November 30, 1901

Santa Clara   213389   Side wheel
Prefabricated, 1915, N. Y. Shipbuilding Co.,
    Camden, N. J.
Operated by Southern Pacific
Steel hull, 273' x 42.3' x 15.3'   2282 tons
Two compound engines, 2 cyl. 20" x 40" x 96"   1980 hp
Burned for scrap, 1947

Santa Rosa   226599   Screw
Built, 1927, General Engineering & Drydock Co.,
    Alameda
Operated by Northwestern Pacific, Southern Pacific-
    Golden Gate Ferries, Ltd.
Steel hull, 251' x 46.3' x 19.1'   2468 tons
Four Diesel engines, two electric motors   1250 hp
To Puget Sound, renamed *Enetai*, after 1937

Saucelito   115586   Side wheel
Built, 1877, John Englis, New York
Operated by North Pacific Coast
Wood hull, 205' x 32' x 9.7'   692 tons
Vertical beam engine   750 hp
Destroyed by fire, February 25, 1884

Sausalito   116635   Side wheel
Built, 1894, John W. Dickie, Alameda
Operated by North Pacific Coast, North Shore, North-
    western Pacific
Wood hull, 236' x 38' x 15'   1766 tons
Vertical beam engine, 56" x 144"   1400 hp
Vacated, 1934; used as rod and gun clubhouse near
    Antioch Bridge

Sehome   116940   Side wheel/Screw
Built, 1877, The Dalles, Oregon as stern-wheel *Moun-
    tain Queen*; rebuilt, 1889 as side-wheel steamer
    Sehome; rebuilt, 1914, for screw propulsion
Operated by Monticello Steamship Co.
Wood hull, 192' x 37.9' x 13.9'   692 tons
Triple expansion engine   900 hp
Sunk in collision, December 14, 1918

Shasta   222598   Screw
Built, 1922, Bethlehem Steel Co. Union Yard,
    San Francisco
Operated by Southern Pacific, Southern Pacific-Golden
    Gate Ferries, Ltd.
Steel hull, 216.7' x 42.1' x 17.3'   1782 tons
Triple expansion engine, 19" x 32" x 54" x 36" 1400 hp
To Puget Sound, 1940; now restaurant, Willamette
    River, Portland, Oregon

Sierra Nevada   Formerly *Edward T. Jeffery,*
    Feather River
Operated by Southern Pacific, Key System, Richmond-
    San Rafael Ferry
To San Pedro, now at waterfront shopping center,
    used for shops, restaurant

Solano   115694   Side wheel
Built, 1879, Central Pacific, Oakland
Operated by Central Pacific, Southern Pacific; train
    ferry, Port Costa-Benicia
Wood hull, 420.5′ x 65′ x 18.3′   3549 tons
Two vertical beam engines, 60″ x 132″   2500 hp
Vacated in 1930

Sonoma Valley   Formerly *San Jose*
Operated by Richmond-San Rafael Ferry
Scrapped, 1947

Stockton   226567   Screw
Built, 1927, Bethlehem Steel Co. Union Yard,
    San Francisco
Operated by Southern Pacific, Southern Pacific-Golden
    Gate Ferries, Ltd.
Steel hull, 251′ x 46.3′ x 19.1′   2468 tons
Four Diesel engines, two electric motors   1250 hp
To Puget Sound, renamed *Klickitat*, after 1937

Sunol   116371   Stern wheel
Built, 1890, operated by Aden Brothers Ferry Co.
Wood hull, 135′ x 27.5′ x 7.8′   294 tons
Steam reciprocating engine   250 hp
To Leslie Salt Co., 1924; renamed *Pyramid*, vacated,
    1946

Tamalpais   20105   Side wheel
Built, 1857, as *Petaluma;* renamed *Petaluma of Sauce-
    lito,* 1875
Operated by North Pacific Coast
Wood hull, 150′ x 31.6′ x 8.3′   365 tons
Two steam reciprocating engines   150 hp
Vacated, 1901

Tamalpais   145873   Side wheel
Built, 1901, Union Iron Works, San Francisco
Operated by North Pacific Coast, North Shore,
    Northwestern Pacific
Steel hull, 224' x 36' x 16'   1631 tons
Compound engine, two cylinders,
    36" x 73" x 62"   2100 hp
Burned for scrap, 1947

Telephone   200263   Stern wheel
Built, 1903, Portland, Oregon
Operated by Western Pacific
Wood hull, 201' x 31' x 8'   632 tons
Steam reciprocating engine
Broken up, 1918

Thoroughfare   24855   Side wheel
Built, 1871, Central Pacific, Oakland
Operated by Central Pacific, Southern Pacific
Wood hull, 248' x 38.4' x 12.7'   1012 tons
Steam reciprocating engine   400 hp
Dismantled, 1909

Thoroughfare   209734   Side wheel
Built, 1912, Southern Pacific, Oakland
Operated by Southern Pacific
Wood hull, 278' x 40' x 16.7'   2620 tons
Compound engine, 2 cylinders,
    22.5" x 38.7" x 96"   1300 hp
Sold, dismantled, 1935

Tiburon   145377   Side wheel
Built, 1884, San Francisco & North Pacific, Tiburon
Operated by San Francisco & North Pacific, California
    Northwestern, Northwestern Pacific
Wood hull, 215' x 38' x 13.5'   1284 tons
Vertical beam engine, 50" x 132"   1225 hp
Vacated, 1924

Treasure Island   Formerly San Pedro
Operated by Key System to Golden Gate International
    Exposition, 1939-1940
Bought by Martinez-Benicia Ferry, 1940, but never
    operated. Navy barracks, 1942; scrapped, 1946

Transit   145079   Side wheel
Built, 1876, Central Pacific, Oakland
Operated by Central Pacific, Southern Pacific
Wood hull, 310' x 52.5' x 17.5'   1566 tons
Vertical beam engine, 60" x 132"   1535 hp
Dismantled, February, 1934

Ukiah   25279   Side wheel
Built, 1890, San Francisco & North Pacific, Tiburon
Operated by San Francisco & North Pacific, California
   Northwestern, Northwestern Pacific
Wood hull, 271' x 42' x 15'   2564 tons
Vertical beam engine, 65" x 144"   2200 hp
Rebuilt as steamer *Eureka*, 1923

Vallejo   155011   Side wheel
Built, 1879, Portland, Oregon
Operated by Mare Island Ferry
Iron hull, 123.2' x 31.5' x 9.9'   414 tons
Inclined engine, one cylinder, 22" x 60"   455 hp
Vacated, 1948

Yerba Buena   200207   Screw
Built, 1903, John W. Dickie, Alameda
Operated by Key Route
Wood hull, 175.4' x 38' x 17'   616 tons
Triple expansion engine,
   12" x 25" x 42" x 27"   1200 hp
To Golden Gate Ferry, rebuilt as *Harry E. Speas*, 1924

Yosemite   27550   Side wheel
Built, 1862, operated by Central Pacific
Wood hull, 269' x 35.2' x 11.6'   1319 tons
Vertical beam engine, 57" x 122"   500 hp
To British Columbia, 1876, operated between Victoria
   and New Westminster; grounded and vacated, 1909,
   Bremerton, Washington

Yerba Buena   226360   Screw
Built, 1927, Moore Dry Dock Co., Oakland
Operated by Key System
Steel hull, 256′ x 68′ x 15.7′   2075 tons
Turbo-electric engine   2600 hp
To Army Transport Service, renamed *Ernie Pyle*;
    original name restored, 1946; scrapped in 1957

Yosemite   222722   Screw
Built, 1923, Bethlehem Steel Co. Union Yard,
    San Francisco
Operated by Southern Pacific, Southern Pacific-Golden
    Gate Ferries, Ltd.
Steel hull, 216.7′ x 42.1′ x 17.3′   1782 tons
Triple expansion engine, 18″ x 32″ x 54″ x 36″ 1400 hp
To Rio de la Plata, 1939, renamed *Argentina*

SOURCES OF PICTURES FOR ROSTER OF FERRIES

The completeness of the illustrations for the roster was only possible through the kindness and help of the persons and organizations listed below. To identify the 113 individual pictures, they have been numbered in the order they appear on pages 168-187.

1, 6, 8, 10, 19, 27, 28, 33, 38, 45, 49, 55, 78, 85, 96, 104, 111: Southern Pacific.

3, 13, 20, 22, 34: San Francisco Maritime Museum.

4, 11, 15, 18, 23, 26, 31, 43, 44, 66, 69, 70, 72, 73, 80, 99: Roy D. Graves collection.

5, 68, 74, 108: Society of California Pioneers.

7, 14, 39, 64, 93: C. Ferry Hatch collection.

9, 50, 51: Harry E. Speas collection.

21, 35, 41, 47, 97: B. H. Ward collection.

16: Raymond B. Giles photo courtesy Pacific Coast Engineering Co.

24, 53, 75: Robert W. Parkinson.

25, 30, 36, 61, 82, 83, 103, 107, 110; Robert McFarland.

29, 59: Western Pacific.

40, 48: Ralph Demoro.

42, 46, 76, 109: Marshall Silverthorn collection.

46: Zan Stark.

56: Walter Landor & Associates.

57: W. A. Silverthorn collection.

62: Northwestern Pacific.

60, 86, 92, 105: Mike Barnes.

87, 94, 113: Bethlehem Steel Co.

(James M. Morley)

Bibliography

Beebe, Lucius. *The Central Pacific and the Southern Pacific Railroads*. Howell-North Books, 1963.

Dickson, Samuel. *San Francisco Is Your Home*. Stanford University Press, 1947.

Gross, Charles F., and Green, Charles. *Some Considerations in the Design of Ferryboats*. Transactions of the Society of Naval Architects and Marine Engineers, 1926.

Harlan, George H., and Fisher, Clement, Jr. *Of Walking Beams and Paddle Wheels*. Bay Books, Ltd., 1951.

Heath, Earle. *Bay Memories*. Southern Pacific Co., 1940.

Heath, Earle. *Seventy-Five Years of Progress*. Southern Pacific Co., 1945.

Hoover, Mildred Brooke; Rensch, Hero Eugene; and Rensch, Ethel Grace, *Historic Spots in California*. Stanford University Press, 1958 Edition.

Kemble, John Haskell. *San Francisco Bay*. Cornell Maritime Press, 1957.

Kneiss, Gilbert H. *Redwood Railways*. Howell-North Books, 1956.

Lane, Carl D. *American Paddle Steamboats*. Coward-McCann, 1943.

Leale, Marion. *Captain John Leale: Recollections of a Tule Sailor*. George Fields, 1939.

Lewis, Oscar. *Sea Routes to the Gold Fields*. Alfred A. Knopf, 1949.

Lewis, Oscar. *The Big Four*. Alfred A. Knopf, 1938.

List of Merchant Vessels of the United States, 1868-1924. *Merchant Vessels of the United States*, 1925-1966. Annual list, U. S. Government Printing Office.

Lott, Arnold S. *A Long Line of Ships*. U. S. Naval Institute, 1955.

MacMullen, Jerry. *Paddle-Wheel Days in California*. Stanford University Press, 1944.

Marshall, James. *Santa Fe, the Railroad That Built an Empire*. Random House, 1945.

McNairn, Jack, and MacMullen, Jerry. *Ships of the Redwood Coast*. Stanford University Press, 1945.

Newell, Gordon, and Williamson, Joe. *Pacific Steamboats*. Bonanza Books, 1958.

Record of the American Bureau of Shipping. Annual publication, 1880-1966.

Riesenberg, Felix, Jr. *Golden Gate: The Story of San Francisco Harbor*. Tudor, 1940.

Sappers, Vernon (ed.). *From Shore to Shore: The Key Route*. Peralta Associates, 1948.

Shaw, Frederic; Fisher, Clement, Jr.; and Harlan, George H. *Oil Lamps and Iron Ponies: A Chronicle of the Narrow Gauges*. Bay Books, Ltd., 1949.

Stewart, Watt. *Henry Meiggs: Yankee Pizarro*. Duke University Press, 1946.

Stindt, Fred A., and Dunscomb, Guy L. *Locomotives of the Western Pacific*. Published by the authors, 1955.

Stindt, Fred A., and Dunscomb, Guy L. *The Northwestern Pacific Railroad*. Published by the authors, 1964.

Wilson, Neill C., and Taylor, Frank J. *Southern Pacific*. McGraw-Hill Book Co., 1952.

NEWSPAPERS AND PERIODICALS

San Francisco *Chronicle*. Various issues, 1885 to 1966.

Oakland *Tribune*. Oakland Centennial Edition, May 1, 1952.

Sausalito *News*. Issues from 1901 through 1903, also the Souvenir Edition of 1941 which contains "Saga of the Ferries," By George H. Harlan.

Westways. Issue of December, 1966.

PERSONAL RECOLLECTIONS

Bray, A. F., Justice, Appellate Court, Martinez, California.

Clarke, Raymond H., Captain, retired, Richmond-San Rafael Ferry & Transportation Co.

De Benedetti, Stephen, Benicia, California.

Graves, Roy D., former engineer, Key System, Rodeo-Vallejo Ferry.

Harlan, George H., Sr. (deceased), a dedicated fan of of the ferries from 1880 to 1960.

Hallin, Edward S., Captain, retired, Golden Gate Ferry.

Hatch, C. Ferry (deceased), counsel, Monticello Steamship Co.

Shipley, Roy W., retired engineer, Monticello Steamship Co.

Smith, Albert L. (deceased), engineer, Northwestern Pacific Railroad Co.

Thomas, William J. (deceased), master mechanic, North Pacific Coast Railroad.

Index of Vessels

~~~~~~~~~~~~~~~~~~~~~~~~~~~~

Vessels that had more than one name are indexed by the name appearing on the page indicated.

*Indicates illustration

— A —

Alameda (1886) — 87, 106*, 111, 115, 168*
Alameda (1913) — 25, 31*, 33*, 41*, 47*, 63, 68*, 71, 95, 115, 117, 168*
Alvira, 10*, 121, 168*
Amador, 71, 93, 115, 168*
Amelia, 71, 111, 113, 169*
Angel Island, 25
Antelope, 15, 19*, 135, 137, 169*
Aquilla, 61
Argentina, 153*, 187
Arrow, 103, 169*
Asbury Park, 68*, 104*, 105, 159, 169*, 171*
Aven J. Hanford, 72*, 73, 95, 145, 147, 148*, 149, 151, 169*

— B —

Bay City, 18*, 46*, 58*, 71, 112*, 114*, 115, 169*
Bear, 132*
Benicia, 97, 98*, 99, 170*
Berkeley, 33*, 42*, 63, 73, 83, 115, 116*, 117, 121, 161, 164*, 170*
Bridgit, 73, 105-107, 170*

— C —

C. A. Thayer, 165*
Calistoga, 105, 149, 170*
Capital, 15, 16*, 30*, 61, 71, 87, 101, 113, 115, 170*
Carquinez (1859) — 97
Carquinez (1956) — 73, 74*, 99, 170*
Cazadero, 20*, 37, 41*, 65, 71, 76*-78*, 80*, 85*, 135, 137, 138*, 141*, 171*
Charles Van Damme, 72*, 73, 93, 95, 99, 142*, 143, 161, 171*
Chetzemoka, 150*, 157, 176
Chrysopolis, 24, 61, 71, 110*, 111, 171*, 179

City of Martinez, 98*, 99, 171*
City of Pueblo, 86*
City of Richmond, 73, 143, 171*
City of Sacramento, 25, 104*, 105, 149, 150*, 152*, 153, 157-159, 162*, 169, 171*
City of San Rafael, 63, 73, 99, 143, 144*, 161, 172*
City of Seattle, 99, 101, 161, 172*
Claremont, 71, 73, 91, 125, 129, 172*, 176
Clinton, 71, 87, 107, 109, 133, 172*
Commander, 174
Confidence, 107
Contra Costa (1857) — 71, 87, 95, 107, 109, 172*
Contra Costa (1914) — 17, 71, 116*, 117, 173*
Coronado, 73
Crockett, 103
Crown City, 73

— D —

Delta King, 36*
Delta Queen, 119*
Diana, 131

— E —

Edward T. Jeffery, 63, 70*, 73, 117, 129, 163, 173*, 174, 184
El Aguador, 25, 146*
El Aquario, 25
El Capitan, 71, 87, 110*, 111, 114*, 115, 173*
El Paso, 73, 96*, 117, 145, 173*
Ellen, 100*, 101, 142, 143, 173*
Elwha, 159, 176
Encinal, 71, 115, 173*
Enetai, 157, 183
Erastus Corning, 15
Ernie Pyle, 128, 129, 187
Eureka, 20*, 32*, 49, 52*, 61, 63, 65*, 66*, 68, 71, 79*, 80*, 117, 120*, 139, 165*, 174*, 186

— F —

Farragut, 145
Feather River, 117, 129, 130*, 173, 174*, 184

Fernwood, 71, 73, 125, 129, 147, 174*, 175
Florida, 105, 170
Frank Silva, 121
Fresno, 73, 117, 153, 156*, 157, 174*

— G —

Garden City, 24*, 68*, 71, 113, 115, 116*, 164, 174*
General Frank M. Coxe, 25, 163
General Frisbie, 18*, 82*, 92*, 93, 102*, 103, 105, 174*
General Mifflin, 25, 82*
Golden Age, 73, 149, 153, 157, 175*
Golden Bear, 73, 149, 153, 175*
Golden City, 95, 149, 169
Golden Coast, 149, 151, 175*, 176
Golden Dawn, 147, 151, 175*, 181
Golden Era, 149, 151, 174, 175*
Golden Gate, 72*, 73, 84, 147, 148*, 175*
Golden Hind, 159
Golden Poppy, 73, 148, 153, 156*, 167, 176*
Golden Shore, 73, 148, 153, 158*, 159, 176*
Golden State, 73, 148, 153, 157, 176*
Golden Way, 148, 172, 176*
Golden West, 20*, 73, 146*, 147, 153, 158*, 159, 176*

— H —

H. J. Corcoran, 103
Harbor King, 155
Harbor Prince, 154*, 155
Harbor Princess, 154*, 157
Harbor Queen, 154*, 155
Harry E. Speas, 147, 148*, 149, 175, 176*, 186
Hayward, 25, 73, 125, 128*, 129, 177*
Holyoke, 123
Huron, 99

— I —

Illahee, 157, 178
Ion, 99
Ione, 97
Issaquah, 19, 99, 101, 145, 161, 177*

— J —

James M. Donahue, 19*, 60*, 71, 78*, 135, 136*, 137, 139, 157, 177*
Julia, 89, 111, 113, 115, 177*

— K —

Kahloke, 159, 171
Kalakala, 95, 125, 157, 158*, 180
Kangaroo, 12*-13, 23
Kate Hayes, 15, 107
Kehloken, 157, 176
Klahanie, 157, 175
Klamath, 70*, 73, 117, 142*, 144*, 145, 159, 160*, 161, 177*
Klickitat, 157, 184

— L —

Lagunitas, 20*, 61, 71, 135, 137, 140*, 177*
Lake Tahoe, 73, 117, 151, 153, 157, 178*
Langdale Queen, 157-159, 171
Las Plumas, 73, 131*, 132, 155, 178*
"Little Toot," the, 99
Lizzie, 99

— M —

Malahat, 178
Mare Island, 99, 100*
Marin, 20*, 93, 139, 140*, 178*, 180
Mary Garrett, 60*
Melrose, 68*, 71, 115, 119*, 143, 151, 178*
Mendocino, 26*, 36*, 73, 139, 141, 153, 157, 178*
Monticello, 103, 178*
Mountain Queen, 103, 183

— N —

Napa Valley, 18*, 73, 102*, 105, 149, 153, 178*
New Orleans, 73, 117, 145, 179*, 181
New World, 12*-13, 15, 101, 179*
Newark, 10*, 30*, 35, 51, 58*, 62*, 68*, 71, 77, 91, 93, 113, 115, 117, 163, 179*, 181
Newport, 95, 149
Nisqually, 157, 178
North Island, 159, 176

— O —

Oakland (1858) — 107, 109, 179*
Oakland (1875) — 24*, 51, 71, 92*, 93, 94*, 95, 106*, 110*, 111, 115, 129, 143, 171, 179*
Ocean Wave, 112*, 123, 179*

— P —

Peralta, 67, 73, 84, 94*, 95, 124*, 125, 128, 157, 158, 180*
Petaluma (of Saucelito), 60*, 87, 109, 133, 184
Phoenix, 120*
Piedmont, 10*, 31*, 71, 79*, 92*, 113, 115, 119*, 129, 180*
Princess, 131, 133, 139, 180*
Pueblo, 84
Pyramid, 103, 184

— Q —

Quinault, 157, 180

— R —

Ramon, 107, 180*
Redwood Empire, 73, 139, 140*
Redwood Empire, 73, 139, 140*, 153, 157, 180*
River Queen, 163
Rosalie, 71, 121, 181*
Russian River, 144*, 145, 179, 181*

— S —

Sacramento (1869) — 101, 181*
Sacramento (1923) — 2*, 38*, 43*, 57, 63, 71, 116*, 117, 162*, 163, 179, 181*
San Antonio, 107
San Carlos, 11
San Diego, 73
San Francisco, 71, 73, 125, 147, 175, 181*
San Jose, 69*, 71, 92*, 93, 124*, 125, 127, 142*, 145, 146*, 147, 182*, 184
San Leandro, 25, 50*, 54*, 64*, 73, 76*, 84*, 117, 120*, 121, 125, 129, 157, 182*
San Mateo, 73, 117, 153, 157, 182*
San Pablo, 69*, 73, 81, 122*, 123, 182*
San Pedro, 73, 123, 125, 182*, 185
San Rafael, 10*, 49, 53, 61, 73, 88*-90*, 91, 114*, 132*, 133, 135, 136, 182*
Santa Clara, 25, 26*, 34*, 41*, 63, 71, 95, 115, 117, 183*
Santa Rosa, 73, 139, 141, 153, 157, 183*
Saucelito, 73, 89, 133, 143, 183*
Sausalito, 20*, 30*, 53, 56*, 57, 69*, 71, 88, 91, 95, 132*, 133, 135, 137, 138*-140*, 164, 165, 183*

— S (cont.) —

Sehome, 93, 100*, 103-105, 183*
Selandia, 84
Senator, 12*
Shasta, 73, 116*, 117, 153, 156*, 157, 163, 183*
Sierra Nevada, 25, 117, 131, 144*, 145, 162*, 163, 173, 174, 184*
Silver Strand, 158*, 159, 176
Solano, 16*, 17, 71, 97, 99, 101, 113, 115, 116*, 117, 184*
Sonoma Valley, 142*, 145, 182, 184*
Sophie MacLane, 109, 111
"Squash," the, 145
Stockton, 73, 117, 153, 157, 184*
Sunol, 103, 184*

— T —

Tamalpais (1857) — 60*, 132, 133, 184*
Tamalpais (1901) — 20*, 30*, 31*, 38*, 59, 61, 62*, 64*, 65, 73, 81, 83, 89, 90, 95, 133, 134*, 135, 137, 139, 148*, 185*
Telephone, 128*, 185*
Thoroughfare (1871) — 71, 110*, 111, 115, 185*
Thoroughfare (1911) — 71, 115, 151, 185*
Tiburon, 10*, 46*, 61, 63, 71, 86*, 89, 136*, 137, 139, 157, 185*
Transit, 71, 111, 115, 186*
Treasure Island, 123, 129, 182, 185*

— U —

Ukiah, 68*, 71, 79*, 136, 137, 139, 157, 165, 174, 186*

— V —

Vallejo, 18*, 98*, 99, 101, 161, 186*

— W —

Wapama, 165*
Warden Johnston, 25
Washoe, 111
Willapa, 156*, 157, 174

— Y —

Yerba Buena (1903) — 25*, 69*, 71, 73, 125, 129, 147, 148*, 176, 186*
Yerba Buena (1926) — 25, 67, 73, 74*, 84, 95, 124*, 125, 127*, 128*, 187*
Yosemite (1862) — 111, 186*
Yosemite (1923) — 34*, 73, 117, 150*, 151*, 152*, 153*, 187

General Index

*Indicates illustration

— A —

Aden Brothers (Ferry Co.), 19, 103, 184
Alameda, 10, 23, 29, 30, 68, 71-74, 91, 109, 112-117, 163, 170-172, 175-177, 183, 186
Alameda County, 21
Alameda Pier, Point, Terminal, Wharf, 94*, 95, 109, 111, 112*, 113, 118*
Alaska, 99
Alaska Steamship Co., 121, 181
Albina Engine & Machine Works, 75, 178
Alcatraz Island, 25, 29-30*, 39, 59, 61, 91
Alta California, 11
Alviso, 23
American Bureau of Shipping, 168
American River, 11
American Sardine Co., 171
American Toll Bridge Co., 145
Anderson, Captain N. E., 23
Andes Mountains, 22
Angel Island, 25, 29, 32*, 163
Antioch, 99, 139
Antioch Bridge, 164, 183
Ark, The, 161
Arms, George, 73
Army Transport Service, 25, 187
Army, United States, 128, 129, 163
Arntzen, Captain Andrew, 64*, 65
Arques, C. L., 161
Atchison, Topeka & Santa Fe, 21, 68, 121-123, 125, 135, 137, 149, 179, 182
Atherton, F. D., 109
Atlantic & Pacific Railroad, 121
Austin Creek Canyon, 135
Ayala, Manuel de, 11
Azores Islands, 49

— B —

Babcock, A. H., 135
Ballard (Washington), 103, 178
Baltimore (Maryland), 105
Barnes & Tibbets shipyard, 68*, 71, 105
Bay Area Rapid Transit District, 155-157

Bay Bridge, San Francisco-Oakland, 19, 21, 23, 26*, 27*, 28*, 33, 96*, 117, 124, 125, 127*, 151, 157
Bay Point, 105
Belvedere (Island), 21, 63, 134*, 137, 138*, 139, 141
Benicia, 16*, 17, 72, 73, 97, 99, 101, 113, 115-117, 143, 145, 147, 169-172, 184
Berkeley, 21, 51, 99, 100, 110, 117, 149-151,
Berkeley Aquatic Park, 21
Berkeley Hills, 29, 125
Bethlehem Shipyard, San Pedro, 163
Bethlehem Steel Co. Union Yard, 70*, 99, 139, 147, 161, 173, 174, 177-179, 182-184, 187
"Big Four," the, 101, 113
"Big Game," the, 117
Big Trees, 61
Bissell, W. A., 121
Black Ball Line: See Puget Sound Navigation Co.
Black, Joseph, 109
Bonneville Salt Flat, 129
Boole & Webster, Shipwrights, Calkers & Sparmakers, 73
Boole, George W., 73
Boole, William A., 73
Bremerton (Washington), 156, 174, 186
British Columbia, 186
British Columbia Government Ferries, 157-159, 171
Broadway, foot of (Oakland), 23, 109, 113, 115, 116, 121, 143, 151, 161
Broadway Street Wharf, 23
Brooks, Captain James, 131
Brooks, James, 90*
Brown, Forbes H., 147
Buenos Aires (Argentina), 153
Bullock, Mrs. L. H., 74*
Bureau of Prisons, United States, 25

— C —

California Camera Club, 60*, 61, 63
California Northwestern Railway, 46, 136-137, 185, 186

California Pacific Railroad, 15-17, 101-103, 113, 170, 179, 181
California, State of, 13, 51, 99, 170
California Transportation Co., 17, 23-25
California, University of, 51, 117
Calistoga, 101, 103, 145
Caperton, John, 109
Capone, Al, 29
Carpentier, H. W., 107
Carquinez Bridge, 19, 99, 117, 145
Carquinez Ferry Co., 145
Carquinez Strait, 16*-19, 35, 97, 101, 103, 107, 113, 117, 145-147, 164, 174
"Caruso of the Ferries," 59
Castro Point, 21, 142*, 143
Cazadero, 133, 135
Central Pacific, 10, 16-17, 23, 24, 71, 87, 101, 103, 108, 110-113, 115, 161, 168-171, 173, 177, 179, 180, 184-186
Central Railroad of New Jersey, 104, 105
Central Valley, California, 129
Charleston (West Virginia), 163
Chicago (Illinois), 21
Chico, 107
Chile, 22
Chipps Island, 17, 105
Chronicle, San Francisco, 51
Cincinnati (Ohio), 119
Cisco Grove, 57
Clarke, Captain Raymond H., 53, 93, 95, 143
Classification Society, 75
Clinton, George A., 87
Cloverdale, 19, 135
Coast Guard, United States, 29
Coffin, Charles, 97
Coffin, Henry, 97
Coffin, Captain O. C., 97, 170
Cohen, Alfred A., 109
Cole, R. E., 109
Coleman, William T., 133
Colgate, Riggs, 135
Collyer, William E., 71, 169, 174, 179
Colonia (Uruguay), 153

Colorado River, 113
Colton, Judson, 99
Columbia River, 123
Commerce, United States Department of, 75, 82
Concord, 105
Conover, Luther W., 161
Contra Costa County, 19
Contra Costa Steam Navigation Co., 15, 87, 107-109, 172
Corinthian Island, 63
Corte Madera, 53
Costa, A., 62*
Cramp, William, & Sons, 159, 169
Creek Route, 13, 23, 91, 107, 109, 113, 115, 116, 121, 143, 163
Crocker, Charles, 113
Crockett, 17, 103, 147, 164
Cunningham Wharf, 12*
Custom House, United States, 137

— D —

Dalles, The (Oregon), 103
Davie, John L., 23, 121
Davis, 101
Davis Street Wharf, 106*, 109, 111
Delta, Sacramento-San Joaquin, 15, 17
Denver & Rio Grande Railroad, 129
DeSabla, Eugene J., 135
Diablo, Mount, 29
Dickie Brothers, 71
Dickie, John W. (shipyard), 69*, 91, 121, 125, 164-165, 170, 172, 174, 177, 181-183, 186
Diesel, Dr. Rudolph, 85
Disher, Andrew, 139
Donahue (Landing), 19*, 73, 135, 137
Donahue, James Mervyn, 137
Donahue, Peter, 135, 137
Drake (Sir Francis) Navigators Guild, 159
Drakes Bay, 159
Dumbarton Point, 13, 113
Dwinelle, John W., 109

— E —

Edwards, Captain L. B., 107
Eel River Canyon, 57
El Campo, 137
El Segundo, 163
Embarcadero, 111, 155, 177
Empire (Oregon), 153, 175
Empire Shipping Corp., 157
"Encinal Line," 109
Encinal Terminal, Alameda, 155
Englis, John, 73, 182, 183
Ennis, Earle, 51
Estuary, Oakland, 13, 23, 24*, 68*, 107, 109, 113, 121, 124*, 129, 151, 153, 161, 163
Eureka, 137, 139

— F —

Fair, James G., 113
Fairfax, 133
Farragut, David Glasgow, 17
Farwell, J. D., 109
Feather River Canyon, 129
Felton, 61
Felton, John B., 109
Fennema, Carl F., 151
Ferry Building (1874) — 10*, 19, 21, 23, 36*, 89, 108*, 111
Ferry Building (1898) Endpapers, 20*, 31*, 33*, 34*, 36*, 37, 44*, 45*, 46*, 52*, 55, 90-92, 116*, 123, 125, 128, 135, 137, 139, 149, 151, 155, 157, 159, 161
Ferry Point, Richmond, 122*
Fiedler, Arthur, 120*
Fireman's Fund Insurance Co., 107
Fisherman's Wharf, 155
Florida, 99
Fort Baker, 87
Fort Mason, 163
Fort McDowell, 29, 163
Foster, Arthur W., 137
Fouratt, Captain John B., 107
Franklin Machine Works, 157
Fulton Iron Works, 75

— G —

Gashouse Cove, 75
General Engineering & Drydock Co., 73, 139, 149, 175, 176
Gentry, 145, 147
Gibbons, Redmond, 109
Gibbons' Point, 109
Goat Island: See Yerba Buena Island
Gold Rush, 12-13
Golden Gate, 11, 13, 59, 131
Golden Gate Bridge, 21, 35, 37, 65*, 139, 151, 157
Golden Gate Ferry (Co.), 20-21, 55, 73, 84, 105, 125, 139, 141, 145-149, 151, 159, 169-172, 174-176, 178, 181, 186
Golden Gate International Exposition (1939-40) — 23, 31*, 117, 123, 125, 128*, 129, 185
Goss, George, 109
Grande, Second Officer, 41*
Graves, Roy, 129
Gray, Captain Thomas, 13, 23
Guernsey Island, 35
Gustafson, Anders J., 64*

— H —

Hallin, Captain Edward, 151*
Hanford, Aven J., 72, 145, 147
Harbor Tours, Inc., 155
Harriman, E. H., 90*
Hatch Brothers Steamship Co., 103

Hatch, C. Ferry, 53, 149
Hatch, Charles N., 103
Hatch, Tremaine, 105, 149
Hatch, Zepheniah Jefferson, 103
Havana (Cuba), 105
Hay & Wright yard, 71, 121, 181
Hayes, Rutherford B., 133
Haystack Landing, 109
Hayward, 109
Hearst, William Randolph, 61
Hillegass, William, 109
Hills, Austin, 71
Homburg, Captain M. J., 62*
Hopkins, Mark, 113
Horseshoe Bay (British Columbia), 159, 171
Howe Sound, 159
Hughes, "Baldy," 38
Humboldt Bay, 131
Hunter, Dick, 59
Hunter's Point, 71
Huntington, Collis P., 113
Hyde Street Terminal (San Francisco), 21, 57, 95, 105, 146*, 147, 149, 150*, 151, 165*

— I —

Ilwaco Railway & Transportation Co., 123
Immigration Service, United States, 25, 29
Interurban Electric Railway Co., 125

— J —

Jack London Square, 161, 163
Jacobi, Otto, 38*
Jaeckel, Captain, 65
Jersey City (N. J.), 105
Johnson, Mrs. Harold, 74*
Johnson, John, 62*
Jones, James, 89
Jones, Mrs. Tirzah, 74*

— K —

Kanawha River, 163
Keddie, 129
Kellogg, J. C., 109
Key Route, Key System, 23, 53, 59, 68, 73, 74, 83, 91-95, 117, 123-129, 147, 150, 155, 157, 172, 177, 180-182, 184-187
Key Route Mole, Key System Pier, 23, 25*, 93-95, 119*, 124*-126*, 127*
King Harbor, Redondo Beach, 163
Kircher, Charles A., 80*, 85
Kitsap County Transportation Co., 153, 157
Klatt, Oscar H., 72*, 145, 147
Knight, Governor & Mrs. Goodwin J., 74*
Knight, Captain Hiram, 143

— L —

La Rue, James B., 107, 109, 161
Lafayette, 105
Lagunitas Canyon, 61
Lake Washington, 174
Landor, Walter (& Associates), 161
Latham, Milton S., 101, 133, 135
Laughlin, 137
Lauritzen, Captain John, 123
Leale, Captain John, 35*, 58*, 59, 61, 62*, 77, 87, 113, 121-123
Leslie Salt Co., 103, 184
Lighthouse (Board) Service, United States, 25, 59
Lindstrom, Captain Axel, 64*, 65
"Loch Ness Monster," 53
London, Jack, 49, 88
Lorentzen, Captain John, 147
Los Angeles Harbor, 163
Los Angeles Shipbuilding & Drydock Co., 73, 177, 182
Los Gatos, 113

— M —

Mahoney, Andrew F., 143
Mahoney, Ed, 123
Mallard, 17, 105
Malone, "Babe," 38*
Manning, Chief Engineer, 87
Mare Island (Navy Yard), 17, 18*, 19, 53, 55, 93, 99-101, 103, 105, 133, 155
Mare Island Employees' Association, 93, 147
Mare Island Ferry, 18, 21, 99-101, 147, 155, 172, 173, 186
Mare Island Strait (Channel), 16*-18*, 19, 98-101, 105, 114, 155
Marin County, 15, 19-21, 29, 91, 95, 131-145, 147-153, 157, 159
Marinship yards, 161
Maritime Commission, United States, 25, 117, 129
Markham, Andrew, 137
Marshall, James, 11
Martignoni, J., 62*
Martin, John, 133-135
Martinez, 17, 97, 99, 101, 117, 145, 170
Martinez-Benicia Ferry, 17, 23, 97-99, 101, 145, 161, 170-172, 177, 185
Martinez-Benicia highway bridge, 17, 99
Martinez-Benicia railroad bridge, 117
Maryland Steel Co., 170
Marysville, 101
Mastick, E. B., 109
Mattheson, Captain John, 99
McClellan, James, 99
McCue, Jim, 53
McKenzie, Captain John Taylor, 89, 90*, 91
McNamara, J. H., 99

McRae, Gordon, 163
Meiggs, Henry, 22
Meiggs Wharf, 21-22*, 99, 100*, 131
Melrose, 109
Merrithew, Dr. Edwin, 99
Mexico, 11
Middlemas & Boole, 73
Millwood (private railroad car), 135
Minturn, Charles, 13, 21, 87, 107, 109, 133, 161
Mission Rock, 86*
Mission Street, foot of, 25, 121, 151
Mississippi River, 61, 119, 163
Molate, Point, 21
Monticello Steamship Co., 18, 19, 29, 53-55, 68, 82, 92, 93, 102-105, 149, 159, 169-171, 174, 178, 183
Moore & Scott Iron Works, 69*, 70*, 73, 105, 129, 163, 170, 173
Moore Dry Dock Co., 68*, 73, 74*, 84, 95, 139, 178, 180, 187
Morrow Cove, 17, 147
Mount Tamalpais & Muir Woods Railway, 29
Musshardt, August, 125

— N —

Napa River, 103
Napa Valley Line, 18, 102, 103
Natchez (Mississippi), 61
National Bank of Commerce, 103
National Service Co., 53
Navy, United States, 129, 185
Nelson, Captain A., 23
Nelsson, Nels, 62*
Nevada, 129
New Westminster (British Columbia), 123, 186
New Whatcomb (Washington), 174
New York City, 13, 73, 133, 179, 182, 183
New York Harbor, 105
New York State, 103
Nickel Ferry, 10*, 23, 71, 121, 161, 168, 181
Nielsen, Carl, 151*
Nielsen, Christian B., 48
"Nights in Venice," 63
Niles Canyon, 17, 101, 129
Nilsson, Adolph, 127
North, John G., 71, 107, 170-172
North Pacific Coast Railroad, 10, 19-21, 41, 61, 71, 73, 83, 87, 89, 91, 109, 131-135, 165, 182-185
North Shore Railroad, 21, 61, 133-135, 165, 170, 177, 183, 185
Northern Electric Railway, 15, 107
Northwestern Pacific, 20, 21, 36, 53, 56, 57, 59, 61, 64, 68, 71, 73, 78, 80, 93, 117, 129, 137-141, 143, 147, 148, 151, 155, 157, 161, 164, 165, 170, 174, 177, 178, 180, 183, 185, 186
Nova Albion, 159

— O —

Oakland, 10, 13, 17, 21, 23-27, 29, 30, 34, 37, 68, 70, 74, 91, 93, 101, 105-131, 151, 155, 157, 161, 163, 164, 170, 173, 178, 180, 183, 185
Oakland & Antioch Railroad, 15, 73, 105
Oakland, Antioch & Eastern Railway, 15, 105, 170, 180
Oakland Long Wharf, 22*-24*, 108*, 110*, 111, 115
Oakland Mole (Pier, S.P.), 10, 22*, 23, 33, 41*, 42*, 43*, 45, 46*, 87, 91, 103, 109, 110*, 111, 113, 115, 117, 118*, 120, 123, 129, 151, 157, 159, 161
Oakland Point, 71, 111, 113, 129
Ohio River, 119, 163
Old Bay Line, 105
"Old Dick," 49, 90*, 91
Olson & Mahoney Lumber Co., 143
Olson, Oliver, 143
Ortega, José de, 11
Our Native Land, 106, 108
Overland Route, 17
Owens Shipyard, 71, 169

— P —

Pacific Coast Engineering Co., 73, 74, 170
Pacific Mail Steamship Co., 103
Pacific Shipbreaking & Salvage Co., 163
Pacific Telephone & Telegraph Co., 55
"Paddle Wheel Masons," 51
Palace Hotel, 106*
Palmer, Captain August, 37, 65
Palo Alto, 117
Palos Verdes Peninsula, 163
Panama Canal, 104, 153, 159, 163
Panama City, 105
Panama Pacific International Exposition (1915) — 23, 93, 168
Paradise Cove, 137
Peninsula, the, (San Mateo County), 49
Petaluma, 19, 135
Petaluma & Haystack Railroad, 109
Petaluma Creek, 19*, 35, 107, 109, 135
Pettersen, Captain Randolph, 147
Philadelphia (Pennsylvania), 159
Piedmont Hills, 29
Pinole, Point, 13, 93
Pittsburg, 17, 105, 107, 128, 171
Pony Express, 15
Port Costa, 16-17, 97, 113, 115, 116*, 173, 184
Port Langdale (British Columbia), 159, 171
Portland, Oregon, 75, 99, 129, 131, 155, 157, 163, 178, 183, 185, 186

Portolá, Don Gaspar de, 11
Ports of Call Village, 162, 163
Portugal, 49
Potrero yard, 71
Princess Street landing, 21, 131
Prisons, United States Bureau of, 25
Prohibition, 53-55
Promontory Point (Utah), 111
Public Health Service, United States, 29
Puget Sound, 99, 103, 125, 145, 156-159, 163, 169, 171, 172, 174-176, 178, 180, 182-184
Puget Sound Navigation Co., 95, 125, 153, 157, 159, 162, 178

– Q –
Quartermaster Corps, 25

– R –
Raccoon Strait, 89
Railroad Administration, United States, 123, 139
Railroad Commission, California State, 147
Rancho Corte Madera del Presidio, 11
Rancho Saucelito, 11, 21, 131
Rank, W. M., 135
Rasmussen, Captain William A., 125
Rauhauge, Victor, 101
Ready, Mrs. Lester S., 74*
Recollections of a Tule Sailor, 35, 59
Red Rock, 29, 95
Redondo Beach, 162, 163, 181
Redondo Sportfishing, Inc., 163
Redondo Submarine Canyon, 163
Redwood Empire Route, 57
Reed, John, 11
Richardson Bay, 11, 29*, 134*, 138*, 161
Richardson, Captain William, 11, 21, 131
Richmond, 19-21, 25, 95, 121-123, 142-145, 151
Richmond, Point, 21, 121, 122*, 143, 149
Richmond-San Rafael Bridge, 21, 29, 53, 144, 145
Richmond-San Rafael Ferry (& Transportation Co.), 19-21, 93, 99, 101, 142-145, 159, 171-173, 177, 179, 181, 182, 184
Rio de la Plata, 153, 187
Risdon Iron Works, 75, 82*
Robertson, James (shipyard), 72*, 73, 143, 145, 147, 169, 171, 172, 175, 176
Rodeo, 17, 103, 145-147
Rodeo-Vallejo Ferry, 19, 72, 92, 99, 101, 145-147, 169, 177, 182
Rolph, James, Jr., 147
Russian River, 13

– S –
Sacramento, 15, 17, 101, 105, 110, 119
Sacramento Northern Railway, 15, 105-107, 125, 180
Sacramento River, 13, 101
Sacramento Short Line, 107
St. Patrick's Church, 106*
Salt Lake City (Utah), 23, 129
San Antonio Creek: See Estuary, Oakland
San Antonio Steam Navigation Co., 107
San Diego & Coronado Ferry Co., 73, 99, 153, 170
San Diego (Bay), 59, 73, 98, 99, 159, 176
San Diego Historical Society, 159
San Francisco & Alameda Railroad, 23, 109-111, 168
San Francisco & Humboldt Bay Railroad, 135
San Francisco & North Pacific Railway, 10, 15, 18-19, 61, 71, 73, 86, 135-137, 157, 165, 169, 185, 186
San Francisco & Oakland Railroad, 107-109, 111, 179
San Francisco & San Joaquin Railroad, 121
San Francisco Earthquake and Fire of 1906 – 90, 91
San Francisco Maritime Museum, 161, 165*
San Francisco Maritime State Historical Monument, 165*, 174
San Francisco Municipal Band, 121*
San Francisco, Oakland & San Jose (Consolidated) Railway, 23, 123
San Francisco-Oakland Bay Bridge: See Bay Bridge
San Francisco-Oakland Terminal Railways, 123
San Francisco Port of Embarcation, 128
San Francisco-Sacramento Railway, 107
San Francisco World Trade Center Authority, 155
San Joaquin River, 13, 121, 163, 164
San Jose, 17, 113
San Juan Islands, 156
San Leandro, 109
San Pablo Bay, 135, 182
San Pablo, Point, 13
San Pedro (California), 162, 163, 184
San Pedro, Point, 29
San Quentin, Point, 13, 19, 21, 89, 93, 107, 109, 133, 139, 142-144, 159
San Quentin Prison, 53, 93
San Rafael, 135, 137
San Rafael & San Quentin Railroad, 19, 109, 133
Sandy Hook, 104, 105

Santa Cruz, 115
Santa Cruz Mountains, 57, 61
Santa Fe: See Atchison, Topeka & Santa Fe
Santa Rosa, 135
Santa Rosa Auto Stage, 141
Sausalito, Saucelito, 11, 20, 21, 25, 32, 36, 37, 62, 87, 105, 131-141, 143, 147-151, 153, 157, 161, 164, 170-172, 177, 178
Sausalito Land & Ferry Co., 21, 131, 133, 139, 180
Sawdon, John, 62*
Scott, George, 62*
"Sea Wolf, The," 49, 88
Sears Point, 149
Seattle (Washington), 145, 156, 174
Sechelt Peninsula, 159, 171
Second Street Wharf, 23
Semple, Robert, 97
Shafter, James, 131
Sherwood, 137
Shipping Board, United States, 179
Shoobert, Fannie, 91
Showboat, the, 163
Sierra Nevada, 57, 129
Silva, M. V., 62*
Silviera, A., 62*
Silviera, Manuel, 38*
Simas, A., 62*
Simas, Tony, 38*
Six Minute Ferry, 17, 19, 92, 101, 117, 125, 145, 182
Smith, Albert Leslie, 62*, 84
Smith, Harry C., 38*
Smith, Sydney V., 137
Sneve, Hans A. B., 153
Solano Aquatic Club, 101
Sonoma County, 147
Sorensen, E., 178
Soulé, Mrs. Edward L., 74*
South America, 153
South Pacific Coast Railroad, 23, 35, 57, 61, 112-115, 121, 163, 164, 169, 173, 179
South Vallejo, 16-19, 89, 101-103, 113-115, 117, 145
Southern Pacific, 10, 17, 18, 22, 23, 34, 37, 38, 50, 53, 57, 59, 70, 83, 89, 90, 91, 97, 113-121, 123, 125, 129, 135, 137, 145, 147, 149, 151, 157, 159, 161, 168-170, 173, 177-187
Southern Pacific-Golden Gate Ferries, Ltd., 21, 23, 105, 139, 142, 145, 149-153, 159, 170, 171, 173-180, 182-184, 187
Southern Pacific shipyard, 68*, 69*, 71, 93, 139, 163, 165
Speas, Harry E., 72*, 147
Speas, Marileah, 72*
Stanford, Governor Leland, 113
Stanford University, 117

Stanley Electric & Manufacturing
  Co., 135
Steamboat Inspection Service, 75
Stetson, James B., 133
Stevens, Charles W., 109
Stewart, A. C., 149
Stewart, C. V., 147
Stockton, 17, 101, 113, 121, 163
Stoneman, Camp, 128
Suisun, 101
Suisun Bay, 17
Sutter, Mrs. Iva, 74°
Sutton, Samuel, 103, 105

— T —

Tamalpais, Mount, 29, 35, 131, 132,
  139, 141°
Taylor, Camp, 61
Tehachapi Pass, 123
Tellis, Alexis, 161
Temple Emanu-El, 106°
Thearle, Philip H., 73
Thomas, Captain Richard, 54°, 64°,
  76°
Thomas, William J., 83
Tiburon (Point), 10, 15, 19, 20°, 21,
  46°, 65, 71, 93, 135-137, 139, 141,
  154, 157, 165, 178, 185, 186
Tiernan, Patrick, 71, 168
Tillman & Bentle, 145
Tobias, W., 62°
Tomales, 133
Tracy, 17

"Trade Fair," 161, 164
Transport Building, 25, 117
Transportation Corps., United States,
  25, 129
Treasure Island, 23, 31°, 117, 123,
  125
Tribble, Captain John, 91
Twain, Mark, 61

— U —

Ukiah, 137
Union Iron Works, 73, 75, 105, 117,
  121, 123, 137, 170, 182, 185
Union Pacific, 90, 111
United States, 11
Uruguay, 153

— V —

Vallejo, 15, 17-19, 29, 53, 99-105,
  145, 147, 149, 151
Vallejo, Benicia & Napa Valley Rail-
  road: See Napa Valley Line
Vallejo Junction, 17, 18, 89, 103, 113-
  115, 117, 145
Vallejo, Mariano Guadalupe, 103
Van Damme, Charles, 143
Vancouver (British Columbia), 159
Verdellet, Captain Victor L., 65, 165
Victoria (British Columbia), 186

— W —

Wahrgren, Captain Alfred, 65, 76°
Wakeman, Captain Ned, 13

Walnut Creek, 105
War Shipping Administration, United
  States, 25, 117, 153, 159, 171
Washington Navigation Co., 174
Washington State Ferries, 95, 125,
  157
Western Pacific, 23, 70, 73, 107, 117,
  128-131, 155, 163, 173, 178, 185
Western Pacific Mole. 23-24°, 129,
  130°, 155, 174
Westinghouse, George, 135
Whidden, G. R., & Co., 174
Whitelaw, Captain, 132
Willamette River, 163, 183
Williams, Robert, 38°
Willits, 137
Winehaven, 21, 95
Wood, Samuel, 109
World War I — 19, 73, 93, 101, 105,
  123, 129, 139, 147, 165
World War II — 21, 101, 117, 120,
  161, 163
Wosser, Joseph, 78°
Wosser, Lawrence, 139
Wosser, Richard S., 62°, 139
Wosser, Thomas, 131, 139

— Y —

Yellow Bluff, 87, 109
Yerba Buena (Goat) Island, 22°, 23,
  29, 30°, 33°, 34°, 86°, 106, 122°
Yukon River, 99